Golan.

Golani Commando

*A Memoir of Special Operations
in the Israel Defense Forces*

ELON PERRY

McFarland & Company, Inc., Publishers
Jefferson, North Carolina

All photographs courtesy of IDF and Defense Establishment Archives.

ISBN (print) 978-1-4766-8528-1
ISBN (ebook) 978-1-4766-4454-7

LIBRARY OF CONGRESS AND BRITISH LIBRARY
CATALOGUING DATA ARE AVAILABLE

Front cover image: "Reluctant'" Golani commando heroes (courtesy of IDF
and Defense Establishment Archives); *inset* photograph of author
after completing 12-months training in 1976
Back cover image: the morning after returning from a dangerous patrol
on Mount Har Dov on the Lebanese border in 1976,
part of our defensive operational activity

Printed in the United States of America

*McFarland & Company, Inc., Publishers
Box 611, Jefferson, North Carolina 28640
www.mcfarlandpub.com*

Table of Contents

Preface:
Reluctant Heroes

This is the story of young men—myself and many others—who were reluctant to take part in an adult war. Because of their personal motivations, due to a war of sheer survival they were born to, these young heroes chose to perform their military service in a commando unit that became known for performing the impossible. This is an account of Israeli Jews who were forced to fight heroically in order to survive. A story about victory against all odds, the triumph of the few over the many, often compared to the biblical tale of David and Goliath. Of how a small army defeated the powerful armies of five neighboring Arab countries, who threatened to destroy the young and vulnerable Jewish state. A story of involuntary heroism performed in an extraordinary and unique way, utilizing various sophisticated techniques, and calling on extraordinary courage, and with the willingness to sacrifice their lives for the sake of their nation's tenuous survival. It is the story of a determined people, who succeeded in building from the ashes of the Holocaust one of the best armies in the world, producing sophisticated weaponry and intelligent combat techniques that became the envy of the fighting forces of other nations. It is a story of Israeli Jews who were forced to fight back in order to avoid a situation in which they could again find themselves scattered around the world, encountering anti-Semitism and persecution for being Jews.

In the following pages, I share some remarkable stories about the Golani commando unit in which I served, one of the most renowned in the Israeli army. I relate some of the methods used by the Israeli intelligence services with whom my unit participated in several raids and operations in Lebanon and Gaza, and in the West Bank. On occasion these operations involved face-to-face and short-range combat, where the individual's qualities and skills were the key to success. I reveal

1

the exhaustingly tough training regime, which has been described by many as "Mission Impossible." During these months, the selected fighters would be shedding gallons of sweat, breaking limbs, and passing out from the unbearable heat during the exhausting exercises, which were designed to bring the combatant to total physical and mental exhaustion in order to examine his level of endurance.

The enrollment into this commando unit starts while still in high school, when teachers were asked by the military authorities to pass on information about pupils who stood out from their classmates in their actions and reactions. Pupils who were seen to be flexible and improvisational, who would respond to situations with a creative mind, visualizing the whole picture ten steps ahead, and making speedy decisions, especially when under pressure. These characteristics were more highly regarded by the military than excellence in math or physics.

In this book, I candidly describe the moral dilemmas soldiers can face during battles, and share some that I personally experienced, such as shooting at children who were facing us with Russian RPG missiles, explosive belts or hand grenades, or with rifles or knives in their hands. We had to make split-second decisions about whether to shoot at them or run away.

Another dilemma we faced was whether to save the life of the enemy. During a hard-fought battle against hundreds of terrorists, I voluntarily carried a wounded terrorist on my back to get him medical treatment. This wounded terrorist was the very same enemy soldier who, just a few minutes earlier, had been trying to kill me. I will also reveal some of the operations I have participated in with the undercover "Mista'arvim" unit in the "Cat and mouse" war against terrorists.

Mista'arvim are trained commandos who operate undercover by posing as Arabs, both in their appearance and by speaking fluent Arabic. They assimilate among the local Arab population to capture wanted terrorists, gather information and help other combat units like us when fighting. While assimilating among the local Arab population, the Mista'arvim are commonly tasked with performing intelligence gathering, law enforcement, hostage rescue and counterterrorism, and to use disguise and surprise as their main weapons to accomplish their missions.

I analyze the history of terror and the Israeli/Palestinian conflict from the day the leaders of the Palestinian terrorist organizations adopted a militant approach against Israel in the wake of the surge of radical Islam that plagued the Middle East in the late 1970s and early 1980s. This process, which has been reflected in events such as the Islamic Revolution in Iran and the assassination of Egyptian President

Anwar Sadat by the fundamentalist Muslim organization known as the "Muslim Brotherhood," has also taken root within Palestinian society.

I describe my childhood experiences, living under the shadow of war from the day I was born. "Child under fire" is the story of thousands of Israeli children and millions of others around the world, including Palestinians, who live out their childhoods under the terrifying threat of war, and find themselves spending days and nights in shelters, living in constant anxiety, unable to play in the yard freely for fear of sirens and shells.

For many years I struggled with the debilitating effects of Post-Traumatic Stress Disorder, a result of an accumulation of the horrific scenes I witnessed. I saw massive explosions and burning corpses and have been in near-death situations. My PTSD would manifest itself in my aversion to eating meat grilled on a barbecue, as this reminded me of the sickening smell of burning bodies.

I will describe the process I went through to heal myself without any medication, in the hope this can help others who suffer from all kinds of anxiety to try to heal themselves, or at least reduce and minimize attacks and have the ability to control them.

My book differs from others on the subject because I infuse the story with real events and harrowing operations from the battlefield, as a commando fighter who took part in them. Some of these accounts have never before been published, and only today, 40 years after the events, has Israeli censorship allowed them to be shared. Some of them have gone on to inspire books and movies. I feel I am best placed to write this account, not only due to being a combatant for 28 years of mandatory and reserve military service, but also as a journalist, who for 25 years covered the wars in the Israeli national media, even at times risking my life to speak to the enemy, often traveling to Gaza and the West Bank to interview local Palestinians.

The readers will get a comprehensive picture about the bloody Israeli/Arab and Israeli/Palestinian conflict, and read from a primary source about the battles, events, bloody clashes and confrontations that are continuing to this day.

Prologue

In the spring of 1976, almost a year into my combat service in the Golani Brigade, my company was tasked to infiltrate a small village in Lebanon and blow up a two-story house that served as the headquarters and training base of the Palestinian Fatah terrorist organization. As we approached the target, the terrorists inside the house started firing at us from the windows. My entire company, with its three platoons, immediately split into three teams. One began attacking the house from its west side, the second flanked the back of the house from its east side, while my team fought in front of the house, targeting a nearby bunker and its trenches from where several other terrorists were also firing at us. Our intention was to get inside these trenches, clear them, and then take over the bunker situated behind them. Meanwhile, the two other platoons would take over the house. As we approached the trenches, the terrorists inside intensified their fire at us. The bullets whistled by and threatened anything in their path; they did not care what type of material they penetrated, whether it was a human body or a concrete wall. Grenades were flying through the air. We lay on the ground and waited for the terrorists to use up all their supply of grenades. When that did not happen, our commander shouted an order, and we all, around 14 fighters, jumped down into the trench, spraying it with our automatic rifles. Once inside, we moved between its narrow sides in one column, with only the fighter at the head of the column being able to shoot forward. If he ran out of ammunition or got hit, he would sit down and cling to the side of the trench to allow the next in line to move forward and continue the shooting, and so on, until the clearance and takeover of the trench was completed.

Despite the intense and stubborn battle that took place inside that trench, we managed to get to the bunker. When we entered it, we realized it was much larger than it had seemed to us from the outside. It appeared to contain several rooms, something that could complicate the purging and taking over of the entire bunker. We threw grenades into each room and started clearing them one by one. Even though their bare light bulbs were still switched on, there was a thick haze filling each room due to the dust caused by our grenades. This made it very hard to see what was going on around us. We had to find our way by patting the walls with our hands and making sure there were no surprise doors or exits from the room. However, within minutes, we had taken over the bunker and the trenches were totally cleared. The battle was over. After a final thorough search, we started making our way out of the bunker towards the helicopter waiting to take us back to our base. On the way, I paused for a moment at the point where the wounded were concentrated. I approached three stretchers on the ground. On the first two lay two of our wounded fighters, but on the third, lay a fighter whose face was covered by a blanket.

Myself an hour before the raid on the Fatah training base.

The house behind the bunkers which served as a headquarters for the terrorists.

This is the most frightening moment in any raid or operation, even more than the fear experienced inside a trench when being shot at and seeing your own certain death. This is the moment you are about to find out which of your friends has been killed, as the faces of those who have been injured are not obscured by a blanket. With a trembling hand, I lifted the blanket from the dead soldier's face, and immediately a shiver shot down my spine. My knees buckled. It was our revered force commander. A special commander, not only brave and charismatic, but a person with remarkable abilities, a superman who inspired us all. "How can this be?" I shouted. I did not have the strength to cry. I felt like I was choking. "How can such an experienced and brilliant professional fighter be killed?" I muttered to myself. I could not tear my eyes away from the motionless face of my beloved commander who had taught me how to overcome my fears, how to prevail in the most dangerous situations, and had planted the idea in my head that nothing is impossible to achieve.

One of the fighters came over and gently placed the blanket back over the face of our dead commander. He helped me to my feet and whispered that I must proceed to the helicopter as quickly as possible because we needed to vacate the area before more terrorists arrived. I headed towards the helicopter without looking back. I did not want to say goodbye to my commander. I wanted to cry but my eyes were dry. I could not even force myself to take a sip of water, much needed after our intense battle. I continued walking like a zombie. When I climbed on to the helicopter, I sat down on the floor, huddled in the corner, my rifle between my legs, my head bowed, not saying a word nor looking at anyone. As the helicopter lifted to the sky, the smell of burnt oil and gasoline rose in my nose. An hour later, at the post-battle debriefing, I finally awoke from my shock, as I was required to answer questions coherently and provide clear operational details.

It was only during this debriefing session, when everyone involved began to describe the course of the battle and its stages, did we learn that our dead commander had sacrificed his life to save ours in an unusual act of heroism. It happened when we were still dealing with the trenches. Due to the heavy billowing smoke that blurred and restricted our vision, we had not seen that at the top of one of the trenches, a terrorist was hiding behind a machine gun, waiting until we got closer. The only one of our force who had spotted the danger was our courageous dead commander, who immediately ran completely exposed towards the terrorist, firing at him and paralyzing his actions. By doing so, he not only saved some of us from certain death, but he also made it easier

IDF helicopters landing to pick us up.

for us to move on towards the bunker. This act of heroism greatly influenced me throughout my military combat service, which was replete with dangerous shooting incidents, where courage and heroism were much needed. However, when we hear or read about an act of heroism, our natural human tendency is to admire, cherish and appreciate it. But when digesting the heavy price paid, we may reconsider these values. This is the conundrum I went through with the heroic death of my revered commander.

I sometimes felt schizophrenic. One side of me concentrated on sharpening my fighting abilities, while the other side of me loathed the war, and did not want to hear about acts of heroism during battle. Both these conflicting sides of me were trapped. Neither of them could choose a getaway option because I was in the midst of my compulsory military service.

The foundation of heroism is not just courage. It is more the readiness to sacrifice oneself to save others, a willingness that is the definition of the protagonist. Heroism may be manifested in different contexts, both in unique situations and in everyday ones, and is witnessed in many different forms: physical and spiritual, military, civil, national or social heroism. At its core, heroism is a deep empathy with others. An act of heroism is a value choice, one in which the enactor overcomes his own immediate needs or interests and performs an action for the benefit of one other or the whole. It is a concept that can be traced back to the mythology and folklore of peoples since ancient times, notably in ancient Greece. In human society, the term usually defines a person who is considered altruistic in his actions, an extremely courageous, noble and resourceful person endowed with chivalrous qualities. But there is another kind of heroism; one which is performed in situations where we are forced into acting heroically.

When I shot a terrorist at such close range that I could see the nicotine stains on his teeth, in doing so, I was able to save two of my company soldiers, but I still do not think I acted heroically. Compared to my commander's act of heroism, during which he saved others, I did not feel I was carrying out this act to save others. I was actually saving myself first. I wanted to survive the situation that was forced on me. I was not happy to kill. Killing is wrong and inhuman. But there are situations where you are compelled to kill, or you will be killed. And sometimes such situations give rise to an act that in the eyes of others is considered heroism. Although there were several other such incidents during my combat service, I never thought of giving them the title of heroism. I considered them a necessity, something I had to perform in order to survive. Nonetheless I was reluctant to act in such a way.

The term "reluctant heroes" describes how we, the Israeli Jews, were forced to fight heroically in order to survive. We were grotesquely outnumbered, facing an enemy that was larger and more powerful, hence our fighting had to be extraordinary and unique. If we had fought this giant foe in the conventional way, we would not have prevailed. We would have been defeated and perished, or scattered around the world, encountering anti-Semitic persecution just because we were Jews, not to mention possibly having to endure another Holocaust.

I was part of the best army in the world and performed things that the average person does not get to do in his lifetime. I felt like a hero when I subdued the enemy in face-to-face combat in bunkers and trenches. I was fulfilling my ambition to avenge the enemy who had ruined my childhood—a childhood that was stolen from me because I had to spend so much of it in bomb shelters, in fear of sirens, and even of thunder, which to us as children sounded like shelling. However, it turns out that as you grow older the glory alternates with bitterness. Those sublime feelings of invulnerability from being in extremely dangerous situations, in some cases spanning a period of years, and the pride in accomplishing the impossible, slowly subside and become blurred by the bitterness lurking behind each story of battle. This is a rancor that never leaves me, sometimes making me lose my appetite before a meal, or not wanting to laugh, dance, or at least look at the world with optimistic eyes. A bitter taste that continues to swirl around my mouth, and slowly penetrates my heart with the true understanding of the consequences of war. This is an understanding that only appears once the time you were involved in dangerous, almost impossible, operations is well behind you. Only when you have reached the age of wisdom after the age of 40 do you realize that any war, except a purely defensive one, is the dumbest invention of mankind of all time.

War is an old-fashioned and primitive act. It is an act of violence and brute force, the opposite principle of social norms of the progressive enlightened world. It is a failure of the use of brainpower. War does not lead to any solution. No one has ever ultimately won any war.

In spite of the acknowledgment, appreciation, and the number of medals I received during my 28 years of combat service in an elite commando unit and having the privilege of spending those years among the best fighters, in the best army in the world, I hated war. Even with the exhilaration of participating in dangerous operations in the depths of hostile enemy territory, operations resembling those seen in gripping Hollywood movies, and some which included face-to-face fighting with my bare hands, I still hated war. I also hated its victories. "There are no winners in war," I once shouted at our Minister of Defense who had come to deliver a eulogy at the funeral of a soldier from my platoon, as he announced his promise to continue fighting the enemy until total victory was ours. Despite the numerous victories that the army I served in achieved, I never thought of winning a war as a victory. I saw only funerals, pain, tears, suffering, grief and sorrow.

It became more difficult over the years when I realized that the war was not against the millions of Arabs around us, something I was so sure about when I was younger. I came to realize that our war was against a limited minority of those Muslims and Arabs. I learned that most Muslims were decent people, not eager for war, and apart from their leaders and the extremists among them, they did not entertain the messianic idea of exterminating the Jews. On the contrary, many of them greatly valued the Jews and saw them as a model for success. Even their Prophet Muhammad preached about embracing the Jews and not harming them. This is written in the Qur'an. After all, Muhammad, while fleeing from his persecutors who sought to harm him, found refuge with Jewish tribes in Saudi Arabia. From them he learned some of the important principles about the Jewish religion, and drew on these for inspiration when drafting the first Qur'anic writings. This insight has caused me many dilemmas on the battlefield, or in the pursuit of wanted terrorists. Each time, the harsh images of those innocent civilians who were caught up in the fire against their will echoed in my mind. The last thing we wanted was to hurt these good Muslims, who made up the majority. Those we fought were the extremist groups of terrorists, and those who sent them on their deadly missions. These made up less than one percent of all Muslims in the Middle East.

After my military service I suffered from severe post-traumatic stress (PTSD). It would manifest itself in my aversion to eating meat grilled on a barbecue, as this reminded me of the sickening smell of burning bodies I had encountered on the battlefield. I did not report my trauma as I was too ashamed to get medical treatment and become categorized as mentally ill, when everything in my personal military file had been noted as excellent.

It was only after six years that I decided to expose my personal wound and agreed to take the medication prescribed by a caring physician at the local clinic. I still insisted on withholding my trauma from the military authorities, even though I could qualify for free treatment from them. But these drugs did not heal me, they only eased the symptoms of my illness, and there was a serious downside to the medication.

For many years, I refused any invitation to speak publicly, either individually or on a panel, or be interviewed about my experiences for any TV documentaries. I was also asked by a production company to act as a script advisor on a war movie but had to decline as I knew it would be too emotionally difficult for me and might trigger distressing memories that would return to haunt me. Finally, in 2010, after several sessions with an eminent psychotherapist who advised me to start speaking and writing about my combat experiences, I started to give lectures about the history of the Middle East conflicts, mainly the Israeli-Palestinian one, and shared with my audiences stories from my own experiences.

In 2017, I decided to stop using the drugs, which had been causing me anxiety and even some behavioral disorder. I researched about alternative therapies online and started applying them on myself. For the first year I had difficulties in persevering in this because I didn't see any noticeable results. Nonetheless, I refused to give up. Today, I can reveal that my tenacity and perseverance has paid off. For the past few years, I have not suffered from any of the frightening phenomena that accompanied my life for so many years. I realized I had healed myself from PTSD without the use of drugs.

It was only in 2020, with the encouragement of my wife Gillian, that I was able to get these stories on to paper for a book to share with you the reader, in the hope that the writing of it would prove to be the ultimate catharsis for me. Gillian had long been party to my anxiety, traumas and nightmares, sometimes involving hospital visits for high blood pressure and rapid heart rate. Relaying the many battles and life-threatening operations I took part in over so many years of compulsory military service and revealing combat incidents that were previously subject to censorship, has in fact proved a therapy.

Over the following chapters, I describe my personal combat experience and the many daring operations my unit undertook in enemy territory, including those carried out in cooperation with the Mossad and other Israeli intelligence services. These were complex operations during which we underwent great risk and fear of death. Many of these dangerous and awe-inspiring activities and operations were accomplished using sophisticated techniques, and by employing imagination, creativity and clever use of deception. Some of them have gone on to inspire books and movies.

I will describe operations and raids on well-fortified terrorist strongholds to which we were sent, despite their slim chances of succeeding, and where the intolerable conditions gave justifiable feelings of fear and uncertainty. Sometimes these involved face-to-face and short-range combat, where the individual's qualities and skills were the key to success.

The qualities you needed to draw on, and for which you were selected to serve in an elite unit, had been recognized long before the

"Reluctant" Golani commando heroes.

soldier put on his uniform for the first time. These were first noted while still in high school, when teachers were asked by the military authorities to pass on information about pupils who not only possessed a high IQ and signs of personal bravery but had also stood out from their classmates in their actions and reactions. These were pupils who were seen to be flexible and improvisational, who would respond to situations with a creative mind, visualizing the whole picture ten steps ahead, and making speedy decisions, especially when under pressure. These characteristics were more highly regarded by the military than excellence in math or physics.

In addition to explaining the background of the relentless war between Israel and the Palestinians, the civil war in Lebanon, and the history of Palestinian terrorism, I will describe the 1978 Operation Litani, which took place in response to a brutal terror attack in which terrorists from Lebanon murdered 38 Israeli bus passengers. This supposedly short and sharp response led to a further 18 years of war, including the Lebanon War of 1982, against the terrorist organizations who were operating mainly from south Lebanon.

During war, soldiers and commanders often encounter another battle, one that takes place inside the combatant's mind and which is often termed a moral dilemma. In telling my story, I will relay situations involving moral dilemmas that I have personally experienced, such as:

Shooting at children—During the 1982 Lebanon War, we
   encountered a disturbing phenomenon where Lebanese
   children were facing us with Russian RPG missiles (rocket
   propelled grenades) in their hands. To the world's media they
   became known as "the RPG children of south Lebanon." We had
   to make split-second decisions about whether to shoot at them
   or run away. Our dilemma was two-fold, firstly whether to shoot
   at children or turn and flee, and secondly, that commando units
   are trained to deal with danger, never to run from it.

Checkpoints—The decision for a soldier whether to allow a child
   or a pregnant woman to pass through an Israeli checkpoint
   for critical hospital treatment carries a high level of risk. The
   soldier assessing the individual situation is aware that there
   have been many deadly incidents previously in which an
   innocent looking woman or child had blown themselves up with
   explosives hidden on their body, taking along with them the
   lives of both soldiers and civilians.

Saving the life of the enemy—During a hard-fought battle against
   hundreds of terrorists, who were protected by hiding within
   densely packed terrain, I voluntarily carried a wounded terrorist
   on my back to get him medical treatment. He was the very same
   enemy soldier who, just a few minutes earlier, had been trying
   to kill me. It was not an easy thing to do. I remember pointing
   my gun at his head, wanting very much to end his life, but after a
   few seconds, I controlled myself and let my vengeance and fury
   subside. I chose to save his life.

I have tried as much as possible to give my writing an anti-heroic,
peace-promoting, and humane touch. I have also omitted some situations in battles and operations in which I know I acted courageously. My
intention here is to tell a story based on real events, while emphasizing
the events themselves and not their participants. I did not like the things
I was forced to do or experience in the many operations I took part in,
even though many of them brought with them great achievements, both
nationally and personally.

As I got older, I came to hate everything to do with politics and
war. I found myself going to talk to those in the enemy camp to see how
a solution could be found for coexistence. I risked my life traveling to
Gaza and the West Bank to spend time with Palestinians in order to hear
their views. This led me to a firm conclusion, and it is that Palestinians
want peace and need Israel, but the extremist terrorist organizations,
acting in the perpetuation of their own interests, will not allow it. From

these conversations, I discovered to my amazement that the Palestinian people for the most part no longer want to be living under war, but that they are locked inside the violent struggle imposed on them by the terrorist organizations who continue to brainwash them. Hence my sympathy towards the Palestinians, even though I fought against them for much of my life. They were my enemy, but over the years, I learned that their misery has increased only because they are constantly in fear of their Hamas leaders, not of the Israeli tanks. The majority of Palestinians wish to live alongside Israel, who throughout the years of occupation provided them with work and services such as electricity, water and free medical treatment. They see in Israel a solid democratic and free state, as well as a technologically and scientifically advanced country in which a profitable future could be planned and built.

Although I sought revenge and fought those whom I blamed for ruining my childhood, I avoided harming Palestinian civilians and even risked my life many times to do so. I also saved many of them from being harmed by the terrorists who showed no concern for their safety. To them, Palestinian civilians were just cannon fodder. To me, and I have no doubt to the army to which I belonged, these Palestinians were as human as all human beings, and they deserved the right to live. Something that unfortunately, as you will see over the following pages and in the stories I share, those from the terrorist organizations did not understand.

1

Child Under War

On a fiercely stormy night in the winter of 1960, with bursts of thunder and flashes of lightning getting ever closer in succession, my mother came to the room where my two brothers and I were sleeping in the large double bed shared by the three of us boys. My mother wished to make sure that the window in our room was tightly closed, and that none of us would be frightened by the deafening noise of the thunder. I was three years old, and my two brothers were five and seven. As she entered the room, my mother was horrified to discover that our bed was empty. She was overcome by panic, not knowing what to think. She woke up my father who was fast asleep. "The children are gone!" she screamed in panic. My dad jumped from the bed and searched the entire house, including the backyard, while reassuring my mom who continued to cry and whine. Only after many minutes of tension and panic, did they find out what had happened to their small children during that stormy night. It turned out that their usually disciplined children, who had been woken up by the thunder, had jumped out of their beds, and without waiting for instruction, raced down to the bomb shelter about 30 yards down the road, believing the thunderous noise was yet another bombardment from Gaza.

To us as children, our run down to the bomb shelter was no more than our daily routine, and we were sure our reaction was a necessary and normal act. However, to the adults around us, it was a disturbing incident that symbolized the horrific reality we were living in, the madness of growing up under the shadow of war.

According to my mother, the first time I entered a bunker was as a three-month-old baby. Since then, sitting in an underground ditch or shelter became part of our lives. As I became accustomed to spending so much time in shelters, a strange and illogical insight began to develop in my mind. Each time we ran towards the shelter, I found myself worrying more about the discomfort and the overcrowding of sitting for several

15

hours in the concrete bunker than about the shelling outside. It was not pleasant to inhale the breath of others, especially those who had been eating garlic that day, and to endure the strong odor of sweat from those who were forced to abandon their work in the field or in construction, and rush to the shelter. The only times I enjoyed sitting in a crowded shelter was if I was crammed next to a perfumed woman, or one of the prettiest girls in town.

I was born under fire and brought up under constant war. Much of my childhood was spent in fear and running in and out of shelters. I did not choose to be born into such a reality. I did not choose to be born at all. But from the moment I was born, almost every day I felt that this was the day I could die or be severely injured. I never remember experiencing a feeling of safety since my earliest days of memories. I was born and raised not far from the border of the Gaza Strip, which in those days was under Egyptian rule. The Egyptians, in coalition with other Arab states, had vowed to wage an eternal war on Israel until the day of its destruction. During the 1950s, '60s and '70s everyone who lived near Israel's southern border with Egypt suffered from incessant shelling and terror attacks, including those occasions when we were attacked by terrorists armed with large knives, insurgents from nearby Gaza. One incident I remember very well. I was only five years old but to this day, I recall all the details and even the face of the terrorist who tried to attack me and my family inside our own home. As a result, my entire childhood was swathed in fear and anxiety. The dread of the wailing of a siren, the long periods of sitting in a bomb shelter, the frightening noise of explosions, the panic I felt every time I heard a plane passing overhead, the fear of the violent infiltrators who used to come to us from Gaza with guns or deadly knives in their hands, all contributed to my difficulties in concentrating at school by day and my bedwetting by night. These fears and traumas eventually led me to avenge my destroyed childhood by joining a commando unit to fight my country's enemies as soon as I became an adult. However, even though I joined my country's war effort with great motivation, I was reluctant to take part in it as I detested the term "war."

For a helpless and inexperienced child, I probably witnessed death too many times and in too many situations. I did not get to experience a calm and normal childhood like children who were brought up say in America or the Netherlands, nor a fun-filled youth spent at parties with the enjoyment of my first kiss, like a happy go lucky Swiss boy would. I spent much of my childhood and teenage years inside a dark and oppressive bomb shelter, hiding from the incessant attacks of armed and brutal terrorists who infiltrated our homes and our souls on a nightly basis. Instead of playing football in the school yard or running and jumping around in the playground with other children, I was forced to spend the early years of my life enduring long stays in the cold and frightening shelter to seek refuge from the wars imposed on us by our Arab neighbors.

I felt disgusted with war and violence from the age of five, when I quarreled with children who would step on ants and kill them as a fun game. One time I was beaten for this, but I retaliated and would not give up until I called a teacher over who ordered the children back inside the school building so the ants could be left alone. While other children were playing with war toys and rifles, I would run to the ravine just outside our town, where I spent hours observing the natural phenomena and the different species of snakes, lizards and birds, plants and flowers. War and confrontation were to me violent, frightening and despicable concepts. Even as a child, I understood instinctively that war was wrong, a terrible act that only brought sorrow and pain.

As a result of spending long stays in shelters, I was plagued by fear and anxiety throughout my childhood. I became panicked every time I heard a plane passing overhead or the noise of a siren. Even today, as a mature man and former commando soldier, the wailing of a siren still unnerves me, even if it's an ambulance rushing a pregnant woman to hospital or a fire engine on its way to rescue people from a burning house.

I had nightmares about Arab insurgents coming from Gaza with guns or deadly knives in their hands and killing us all, terrifying dreams that led to my constant bed wetting, and difficulties in concentrating at school. To this day, I am still not comfortable watching war movies, or any form of bloodshed, even though I took part in daring and dangerous

Children under fire. Inside a bomb shelter in 1966.

operations and saw the whites of the enemy's eyes more than once. The trauma of being a child under constant war left me with an invisible, non-bleeding wound. There is a deep scar in my soul, a delicate soul, which belongs more to the world of nature, art and creativity, and less to the world of weapons and bloody battles. To overcome my childhood fears, I would venture into the caves and dark crevasses in the nearby ravine, hoping to encounter a poisonous snake or any other kind of dangerous animal. I would climb to the very top of a tree, while the other kids would look up at me and cry out to summon an adult to come and order me down before I fell. My fearlessness honed as a child came in handy when I grew up to become a commando fighter, particularly in an exercise designed to strengthen courage, where we had to jump from a plane at night in full combat gear, dropping in total darkness into a stormy sea.

During the tense period leading up to the 1967 Six Day War, we, mainly the children, had to spend more and more time in the shelters, due to the frequent movements of military vehicles and the fighter jets above. When it came to the 10th birthday of Rami, one of my classmates, the teacher suggested that the party being prepared by Rami's parents be postponed. But the boy, today a very successful lawyer, insisted it go ahead. He cried, complained, and refused to accept this. The adults eventually acceded and decorated the bomb shelter with the colorful decorations that we had all prepared for adorning our classroom, where the party was to have taken place. The drab concrete walls and ceiling of the shelter were transformed into a much more attractive sight after our teacher had hung the colorful balloons, while in the background, cheerful songs were blaring out of an old record player. An iced birthday cake stood invitingly in the center of the shelter, and I could swear there was not one pair of eyes of any of the children in that space that was not drooling at the sight of the cake. And so, while outside the shelter the echoes of falling shells and the wail of sirens were heard, we celebrated Rami's birthday. Life can win over war.

"Why don't we all go and live in America?" I once innocently asked our teacher.

"This is our home," my teacher replied. "Jews must have a safe home. Suffering from the frightening shelling and the long hours of sitting in a shelter is far better than being murdered in pogroms and massacres carried out by those who want to exterminate us Jews."

At that age, I did not understand the teacher's explanation. We were just children. War and politics were topics we could not comprehend. We wanted to play and laugh and get up to mischief. But the reality of endless war imposed on us a life of fear, tension and poverty. We, the children, paid a heavy price for the actions of the adults. We suffered from persistent deprivation that damaged our soft souls, and long oppressive days of hunger during which our parents found it difficult to feed all of us children. Apart from Rami, very few of us experienced the joy of celebrating a birthday with a party, and certainly not in our family. A birthday party was considered an unnecessary luxury in the eyes of our parents who were busy working long hours to feed us.

But not only children are, and forever will be, victims of war, even though they are the most vulnerable and are more likely to develop fears than adults. War causes extensive damage to all humans. It creates a perfect storm of death, agony, grief, serious injury and dysfunction. It raises the levels of psychological distress and the number of those affected by mental illnesses, including trauma, anxiety and depression. War is not only the rumble of the tank and the acrid fumes of thick black smoke, but it also inflicts trauma on those directly or indirectly exposed to it. A trauma that causes a fracture in a person's psyche, rending a deep tear in his or her mental tissue. It creates a terrifying situation in the mind that makes a person feel abandoned and helpless, while crying out for help. There has never been a quiet time in history when it comes to human conflict. The phenomenon of war has been known since the beginning of mankind and has been conducted from the moment humans chose to live in tribes and ethnic and religious groups, while marking and determining territories. Although war between armies and soldiers takes place on the battlefield, the impact on civilians back at home, away from the front, is inevitable. The conflict on the battlefield permeates the civilian population, who find themselves exposed and sometimes more vulnerable than the combat corps. I am not only referring to the economic damage, to the increase in the number of unemployed, the evacuation of the population, demographic changes and inability to maintain a semblance of normal life, but also to the psychological damage of traumatized children, who inarguably are the most susceptible in times of war. Children who had no hand in the decision to go to war. I was one of them. As a child who was born into an ongoing and terrifying war situation, I felt exposed and vulnerable. There were many situations where I stood helpless facing a mighty force that was stronger than me, an external threat that I did not have the power to deal with. This force was the war.

As a result of the ongoing war that began on the first day after the birth of the country in which I was destined to be born and grow up, my life was one of continual poverty, hunger and difficulties. What had led us to this "living by the sword" was an endless bloody conflict between two stubborn nations. The Arabs, who felt aggrieved by the loss of their land to the incoming people from Europe, the Jews, who had survived the horrors of the Holocaust and had a desperate need for shelter and a safe haven, where they could live their lives away from pogroms, persecution and the fear of another Holocaust. In a sense, both sides were right and both believed equally in the righteousness of their cause to the point of sustaining a never-ending violent reality. However, as a child, I did not understand this and neither did I care about it; all I wanted was to be able to lark around in the playground with other kids. All I really craved when I was 15 was to continue playing with the rock band my friends and I improvised, and to cover with sweet and innocent amateurishness the songs of legends like Deep Purple, Led Zeppelin and Black Sabbath. These wars tore me to pieces during my childhood and youth, the years when children and teenagers were supposed to learn, grow, develop, dance, party, dream and weave plans for the future. Instead, I was doomed to experience those critical years in a hard way.

I felt a helpless victim caught up in the maelstrom of wars fought over land and holy places, carried out in the name of religion and other issues that leaders and politicians took seriously and based their decisions on. Wars that are usually declared by men dressed in suits and ties, the politicians who speak eloquently on TV and are driven around in black armored limousines, surrounded by security guards and with their advisers trotting beside them, straightening their ties and whispering in their boss's ear with a serious look implying they were telling them something important, or reminding them of the name of the person whose hand they were about to shake.

I did not choose to be a part of this madness called war. I never dreamed of being a war hero. My dreams were about movies and theater and wild rock concerts. I pictured myself playing drums in a rock band in England, from where most of the music legends came from at that time. But my reality was far from what I dreamed. I was doomed to live under an ongoing war that was imposed on the tiny little piece of land that for some is considered holy, and for which they were willing to fight fanatically at any cost.

Most of my childhood was spent in severe poverty and deprivation. This was not because my father refused to work or was in any way lazy or an alcoholic; on the contrary, my father and mother were both very diligent and willing to work in any job that was available to them. My father sustained three different jobs simultaneously to support us. The problem was the incessant war which was sucking up all the money possessed by the young Jewish state, a country that has lived under war since its inception. I remember continuous days of hunger. There were days my parents were just not able to feed our many mouths. The uncomfortable sight of our parents eating only vegetables and bread, while they would ladle the pieces of meat onto their children's plates, will never leave me until the day I die. I was never asked what I fancied for breakfast, as I never had a choice between a hardboiled egg or an omelet. I ate anything and everything my mother put on the table. I certainly do not remember dessert options during those years, only a large tin of jelly from which we all sweetened our tongues. When I recently heard my granddaughter objecting to her mother at breakfast that the egg she had been served was not "runny" enough, I felt a sharp pang in my chest. In my childhood there were no complaints ever expressed about the egg put in front of us, whether it was soft, runny, or hard-boiled. In my childhood there was a problem in the presence of the egg. Consequently, I have never been fussy about what I eat, and have had no problem choosing what to eat when perusing a restaurant menu.

As a child my birthday was never celebrated with a party. The first birthday party of my life took place when I was 16, when I financed the party myself with money I had saved from working a few hours a week after school at the printing shop in town.

Throughout our childhood, none of us children received any pocket money from our parents. This was considered to be an unaffordable luxury. Their primary concern was to feed us, and pay for our school materials, including books. "All our money is going to the army for the war," my grandmother muttered when I asked her why she no longer brought the precious chocolate she used to bring us.

I did not know what a bathtub looked like, and our lavatorial needs were serviced by an improvised WC situated behind the house. Once a week, a truck with a large black container and suction pipes would arrive and pump out everything that had accumulated in the pit below the makeshift toilet. A weekly visit to a movie theater, or consumer culture in general, were nothing but a wishful illusion. I only got to know what the world looked like outside Israel through a small black and white TV in our main room. My father had bought it with the money he had saved by supplementing his income from doing small repairs in the homes of the local people.

While the adults understood that the shortages were the result of constant war, we, the children, could not understand the link between the war and the lack of food, toys and chocolate. All we knew about war was the obligation to run to the shelter.

The shortages worsened further during 1965 and 1966, the years in which Israel needed to purchase weapons to deal with the threats from all the neighboring Arab countries who were vowing to wipe our country off the map. This was a hopeless situation, forcing my father to swallow his pride and stand in the long line outside the town hall, where they would occasionally hand out secondhand clothing, footwear and toys donated by supportive Jews in the U.S.

I grew up in the 1950s, in a large family of nine children crowded together in a modest two-bedroom house. I was born and raised in a small town called Netivot, located only a few miles away from the enemy town of Gaza City. To strangers entering its perimeter, our town had the appearance of a temporary military camp, a kind of wretched and wilting human orchard. A car, or any type of vehicle, was seen in town about once a week. The residential streets, extending out like octopus tentacles on either side of the main streets, were narrow, dimly lit alleys with no house names or numbers. The small houses were built in pairs, of uniform shape and size, and in straight measured rows that stretched the length and breadth of the town. Outside every house was a taut gray metal wire that was used as a laundry line, most of the time densely packed with drying laundry due to the large number of babies and children in each household. Each house contained no more than two small rooms and a kitchenette. We, the children, would sleep crammed together under thick blankets in a big double bed, while our parents would sleep on mattresses laid out on the floor of the other room.

From a bird's eye view, my small town of Netivot was surrounded by wheat fields to the south and also from the west, near the border with Gaza. These produced a handsome yield each season.

My small town of Netivot in 1962.

A wide ravine, which was full of mysteries, surprises, and even challenging dangers, stretched for several miles between the agricultural fields near Gaza and my town. As children, we loved to use it for games, hiding places and exploring. The ravine was in fact my "school" where I developed a love of the natural world and its living creatures. Snakes and lizards in a variety of sizes and colors were seen skipping between crevices, and from days spent at the ravine, I discovered that I had no fear of snakes, but instead, a great fascination for them. I would peer down into a hole in the ground and admire the coiled snakes close up, whispering to them as if they were my confidantes, until my protective older brother would drag me away shouting "You're crazy!"

One day I was playing a game of hide and seek at the ravine with my peers, and found an ideal spot to hide beneath a protruding rock. Whilst hiding, I glanced up at the rock above me and there, basking in the sunshine about a foot above my head, was a snake. I heard my friends calling me but I could not bring myself to leave, not from fear of the snake reacting to my sudden movement, but because I was mesmerized by this beautiful creature. I found myself having an imaginary two-way conversation with it. When the round of hiding was over and I had not appeared, my friends, with my big brother among them, came to look for me as they were concerned something untoward had happened. When they found me sitting motionless staring into the eyes of a snake, my brother grabbed me fiercely and pulled me away, throwing me to the ground.

"Your stupid curiosity will kill you one day," he shouted at me.

"The snake will only attack a human if it feels under threat and that you are about to step on it," I tried to explain. "Stop your philosophical nonsense, get up and go home," was my protective brother's response. I guess an understandable response as I was only eight years old at the time.

When I was a teenager, I became interested in current affairs and politics, and listened to the news at least five times a day. All this coincided with continuing to play music with the amateur band we had formed, music that was the love of my life back then. The more I studied the events of history, the more I realized that the ongoing bloody conflict between us the Jews and the Arabs was against terrorists, groups of extremist Muslims banded together under institutionalized terrorist organizations, who were not bound by any of the conventions of war. This was a cruel enemy who would not hesitate to kill babies, and it was this discovery that became the prime motivation for me to enlist in the army, and fight the terrorism that had one goal, and that was to destroy Israel. Thus, in May 1975, when I reached the age of 18, the age of enlisting in the Israeli army, I became part of that ongoing bloody conflict.

I did not enlist in the military only because it was mandatory, nor due the urgent need for a shelter for the persecuted Jews. As a teenager, I did not truly understand the concept of a safe haven for the oppressed Jewish people. I enlisted in the army only because I was looking for revenge and to confront those who had ruined my childhood by their acts of terror and had forced me to spend my best years cowering in shelters. But I did not wish to be a pawn on a chessboard. I wanted to be right at the vanguard and have the chance to encounter the enemy at close range. The enemy who not only took away what should have been my happy childhood years, but was also continuing to threaten me, my family and the entire Israeli nation with terrorism. I felt this was the only legitimate opportunity to find revenge, as well as a degree of compensation. I wanted to kill them with my own hands.

I was mentally and physically ready. The question now remained as to which corps to join. After all, it was going to be three years of continuous service. Should I join the armored corps or the navy? The tank corps or maybe the air force? But then, when I was 17, just a year before my enlistment, a letter arrived and spared me from the dilemma I was going through. I was being summoned for tests and examinations to determine if I was suitable material for a commando unit. Unknown to me at the time, the army had been checking the records of teenagers in every Israeli high school to identify suitable candidates to serve in elite commando units, based on their personal skills and IQ. I had a high IQ, perfect physical and mental health, no known allergies to anything, sharpened senses and excellent vision, and most importantly, tons of motivation. It looked like my choice had been made for me.

The recruitment process for the commando units in the Israel Defense Forces (the IDF) begins long before the candidate first puts on an army uniform. In all Israeli high schools, teachers are asked to provide the IDF with information about the character traits and skills of any students they find distinctive, particularly those who showed a colorful streak and "out of the box" thinking. After the first selection, and only after ensuring they were in excellent health, the commando units' recruitment team would invite the chosen boys to come for a one-day assessment in which the candidate would demonstrate their character and skills through various tests. Emphasis on perfect health is so high that even wearing glasses, or suffering from a minor allergy, can invalidate a candidate. The assessment day, which for some of the boys is a welcome opportunity to have a day off from school, was held at one of the army bases, where we would be taken by bus from Tel Aviv.

At the beginning of the day, the tests presented to us are relatively easy and non-threatening, but gradually they become more difficult and challenging. The recruitment team at this stage are not interested in the candidate's courage or his military knowledge, and not even in his level of achievement in the school curriculum, even if he was considered a genius in math and physics. What they want to know is about his character. Does he have analytical skills and how does he react in different situations? Is he a fixated person or is he flexible and open to other ways of thinking and doing? The recruiters would be looking for those pupils who have creative, imaginative minds, with the ability to improvise and utilize what is available in order to solve a seemingly intractable problem. The candidates are also asked to calculate speeds and distances correctly in a split second, and to find the fastest route out of a labyrinth puzzle. During the second half of the day, we would be assessed for our physical as well as mental abilities. A physical fitness instructor would ask us to follow the strenuous exercises he demonstrated to us. We all thought, quite naturally, that the purpose of these exercises was to test our bodily fitness and ability. But it was only after more than a year, when we had already been admitted to the commando unit and started our service, that we were told that the real purpose of those physical exercises was to test our ability to withstand pressure, our determination and our perseverance.

A month later, after going through that long day of rigorous initial assessments, I was informed that I was among those who had passed all the tests and examinations, and had demonstrated the uncommon, required skills (this is usually only about 50 percent of the applicants). I was also informed that I was suitable material for an infantry commando unit. But which one would I be headed for? This I would only learn on the day of my enlistment.

The difficulties I experienced in my childhood have followed me throughout the rest of my life and taught me how to make do with little, to appreciate everything, and live modestly. I learned that I could survive any bleak times and any conditions. This was severely put to the test during my army service, and notably on one occasion during the arduous survival course in the early stages of my service in the commando unit. We were tasked to live for three days in the Sinai Desert on water only. We were left to feed ourselves on what could be found in the area, including any indigenous moving entity. I survived that unpleasant experience not because I was stronger than the others. I survived only because I had previously endured the experience of being desperately hungry.

My miserable and worrisome childhood did not end when I became a teenager. It only ended when I enlisted in the Israeli army at the age of 18. The special military service I was privileged to take part in resulted in changes to my perspective on life. Significant changes that would accompany me for the rest of my independent adult life. Most importantly, I was not scared anymore. I became a fearless commando soldier performing things I had previously only seen in movies. I became part of a dangerous but interesting, exciting and challenging world. Furthermore, it was only during my military service that I discovered traits about myself that I did not even know existed within me. Characteristics and attributes I had not recognized, simply because I had not had the opportunity to apply them during my childhood and youth. Suddenly I found out that I had extraordinary courage. I learnt that I possessed the ability to rapidly solve problems and complicated issues, to improvise, to think outside the box, and to see ten steps ahead, sometimes ahead of most of those around me. It was a comforting feeling, and for a time helped me to erase my harsh childhood phase from my memory.

2

My Enrollment into
a Commando Unit

Throughout my youth and my years of growing up under the situation of war, I soaked up exciting stories and articles about the Israel Defense Forces' commando units and the way they operated. I had heard stories of intrepid warriors and inspiring acts of heroism by soldiers from most of the Israeli commando units. Through these stories, I realized that as a commando fighter, I could get closer to the enemy and more frequently. I was so much in awe that I was determined to enlist in one of these units. I just needed more detailed information to be able to choose the one that would be suitable for me. From the hundreds of articles and news items I read, one of the commando units particularly caught my eye. This was the commando unit attached to the Golani Brigade. I learned that not only had this unit participated in thousands of daring operations, and had been involved in many acts of heroism, it was expert in combating terror, especially in the Gaza Strip. I, as someone who was looking to avenge the terrorism that had come mostly from Gaza, felt pleased about this.

The event that sealed my decision was an operation I read about when I was 17, which the amazing Golani fighters took part in. It took place in 1974, when Israel was busy fighting the ongoing terror attacks carried out by terrorist organizations based in southern Lebanon. One of these organizations was the Democratic Front for the Liberation of Palestine (DFLP). This group based itself along Lebanon's border with Israel, from where they carried out many brutal and deadly attacks on Israel. The Israeli army decided to strike back hard in an operation involving the forces of intelligence personnel, the navy, the air force, undercover fighters, plus commando fighters from the Golani Brigade. The objectives of the operation were threefold:

1. To destroy the DFLP's houses and bunkers that served as their
   headquarters in the Lebanese coastal city of Damour, 12 miles
   south of Beirut, and eliminate as many terrorists as possible. This
   objective was assigned to a Golani force.
2. To seize important documents and capture two wanted leaders
   of the DFLP, bringing them back to Israel for interrogation in
   the hope of extracting valuable information from them about the
   organization's activities.
3. Following the completion of the infantry operation, and once
   the forces were back safely on the naval ship, air force jets would
   bomb and destroy other targets in the area that housed the DFLP.

Late at night in the summer of 1974, the operation began.

An elite force of 36 Golani fighters, together with nine fighters
from their undercover unit dressed in civilian clothes, were taken
to the waters off Damour by an Israeli navy ship. This was equipped
with spare ammunition and medical staff, plus an improvised operating theater. Above them, a helicopter, with a rescue force on board
ready to act if needed, was hovering and monitoring their movements.
The entire assault force was collected from the ship by six commando
boats and brought to shore. Arriving on Damour's beach, they split
into two teams. One, the Golani force, swiftly boarded a truck displaying local identity plates which had been prearranged for them by a
Mossad intelligence agent. They were immediately transported to the
area where the bunkers and houses they had been sent to destroy were
located.

The other force, the undercover unit, quietly got into the three civilian cars that were waiting for them, also hired locally by another Mossad
agent. The drivers, who happened to be Mossad agents too, drove them
to the address of the house where they would find the wanted terrorists
and the documents they needed to seize. When they reached the area
of the house, the undercover fighters calmly got out, making sure their
weapons were well hidden under the civilian clothes they were dressed
in, and slowly walked towards the target property. The drivers kept the
engines running, waiting for them as if they were simply local taxi drivers. Mission completed, and along with the captured terrorists and documents, the fighters climbed back into the waiting cars and were driven
away inconspicuously at a normal speed towards the sea and to the ship
waiting for them. Ten minutes after the forces had left the area, including the Mossad agents who disappeared back to their rented apartments
somewhere in Beirut, Israeli Air Force planes bombed the offices and
training bases of both the DFLP and PFLP terror groups, eliminating

at least 27 terrorists, and destroying bunkers and houses that served as their headquarters. The operation was crowned a success. All the forces involved had met the mission goals faultlessly, with no mishaps and no casualties.

To me, as a teenager who was passionate about challenges and actions that involved tension and risk, it symbolized a perfect commando operation. This was just the kind of activity I wanted to take part in. Thus, on May 5, 1975, I joined the Golani commando unit.

During those years of the 1970s, terrorism struck not only in Israel and around it, but also in remote locations around the world. The IDF was called on to react in many operations. The most famous was Operation Entebbe in 1976, in which combined forces, including the Golani unit, were required to fly more than 2,000 miles from Israel to rescue Israeli hostages being held in Uganda in central Africa. It was an operation that stunned the world with its boldness.

Such events and operations would accompany me for all the three years of my compulsory service between 1975 and 1978, the years during which not only did the terrorist organizations continue to act against Israel, but also more organizations were springing up like mushrooms after the rain. They all had the same goal—the destruction of Israel. This increased my motivation to excel in the unit I joined, so I could fight these organizations with the hope of gradually eliminating them, bringing a degree of relative peace to the lives of the citizens of Israel, and to rescue them from this horrible reality in which I had grown up.

My enrollment into a commando unit began.

After completing the requirements of the Absorption Sorting Base, which is the starting point of every IDF recruit, including the Chief of Staff himself, we boarded a truck to be transported to a remote base, close to the city of Jenin in the West Bank. The surroundings we were met with lacked any spectacular views or green fields. The base was in a rocky area, encircled by hills. The inhabitants' living quarters were tents, huts, and anything else that did not resemble a normal residential structure. My 12 months' period of arduous training to qualify to serve as a member of the hallowed Golani unit had begun.

It started with the three-month basic training period, during which we learned how to use weapons that are commonly used by infantry fighters, such as M16 automatic rifles, hand grenades, bazookas and shoulder missiles such as RPGs. But mostly the training involved lots of strenuous and harrowing physical exercises. During these initial training sessions, fighters are given the chance to experiment with a variety of simulators for combat in built up and complex terrain; use special means of camouflage; and many other types of combat tools and

equipment that contribute to enhancing the unit's capability. Throughout this period, in addition to the tasks and training to test the fighter's
personal skills, not a single day goes by without tough physical exercises to test the physical and mental strength of the combatant. We had
to walk tens of miles a day over harsh ground conditions, through cloy-
ing mud in winter and in stifling temperatures of extreme desert heat in
the summer. The aim of these training exercises was to bring the future
combatant to total physical and mental exhaustion so that his level of
endurance can be assessed, and to determine whether he is able to continue his service in the unit.

At the end of the three months of basic training, we would all
be granted a very welcome three days' rest to spend with family and
friends and enjoy the comforts of home again. While we were away,
a screening process would be going on to remove those who failed to
pass the basic training. Those who didn't meet the required standard
for a commando unit would then be transferred to serve in other corps,
or as part of the Golani Brigade's maintenance teams. Those who did
manage to survive the grueling three months successfully would move
on to the next step, a further period of three months during in which
they will be shedding gallons of sweat, breaking limbs, and passing
out from the unbearable heat during the exhausting exercises. Three
months sounds like a short period of time, but those 13 weeks can still
be unbearably difficult. The training was hard and sometimes inhuman, the hours of sleep were few, no more than three hours each night,
but the motivation among us was immense. We were trained how to
navigate by using the stars and the moon while walking long distances
at night with combat gear on our backs, sometimes weighing nearly
80 percent of our body weight. We also learned how to use bombs and
explosives for blasting through walls and doors and were trained in
how to operate effectively under pressure. We were put in situations
where we had to develop our ability to quickly analyze data and make
life-saving decisions instantaneously.

After successfully completing these six months of rigorous training, we were then sent to carry out a three-month defensive operational
activity. This was mainly spent on the borders with Syria and Lebanon to combat terrorists who would constantly infiltrate into northern Israel to carry out attacks. These terrorists were particularly cruel
as they directed their murderous activities against civilians, including
children. They refrained from encountering us soldiers so they could
inflict harm on the soft underbelly of society, the elderly and helpless
children.

During this period, our commanders would closely monitor the

Completion of the six-month training course to determine continuation in the Golani Brigade, 1975.

soldier's behavior, his attitude, discipline, and other qualities that indicate his ability to command and lead.

Immediately upon completion of this defensive operational activity, some of us would be sent for a three-month commander course to conclude the one-year training period. Those who have completed the entire year successfully would be scattered among the three battalions of the Golani Brigade to continue their combat service.

My personal experience of this obligatory defensive operational activity took place on the blazing northern border of Israel. We were based on a lookout post called

After completion of the six-month training course in 1975.

"Motzav Har-Dov," situated on Mount Dov, close to the Golan Heights and Mount Hermon. The outpost comprised a main bunker connected to trenches, in which we would have to sleep. Above the outpost were three further observation posts. These were considered the eyes of the outpost, through which we could overlook and observe the whole span of southern Lebanon, and act if necessary on almost every movement coming from it. Each morning we were sent on a four-mile foot patrol along the Lebanese border. As we walked ahead, an armored vehicle would follow close behind us, manned by fighters with their fingers gripped tightly to the triggers of their heavy machine guns, ready to paralyze any terrorists we might encounter.

Our tasks were divided each day as such: some would be sent to man the lookouts, observing and examining every inch of southern Lebanon through large binoculars. Others would be assigned to the patrols along the border fence. Around midnight, some of us, normally a group of 10 men, would be sent to the northern side of the border, inside Lebanese territory, to lay in ambush awaiting any terrorists who would try to sneak into Israel during the night or early morning. After midday, we would rotate our duties. Those who were on patrol in the morning would be sent to one of the lookout posts for a four-hour shift, and those who had spent the morning in the observation lookouts would join the patrol. Those who spent all night in ambush would be privileged to go and get some sleep and be relieved of duty until the evening.

The patrol that took place each morning was not a regular patrol. It was referred to as the "fire patrol," as we would be firing our rifles into the bushes and rocks behind the fence every few yards of progress along the four-mile route. This was to root out any terrorists who might have been lurking in the bushes and rocks waiting for an opportune moment to penetrate Israel. Above us hovered our army helicopter that would report to us any suspicious movements they picked up. In the event of a report of any terrorists in the field, we would be asked to give chase, sometimes entering a cave or ravine and tackling them head on. There were some who had to be eliminated in the field at very close range, often in face-to-face battle, and there were others who surrendered. This type of dangerous patrol was banned after the introduction of electronic means, by which the presence of any terrorists could be picked up by the team stationed inside the protection of the bunker.

One of those later-banned patrols still sticks in my mind. It was in December 1975, when a phosphorus grenade was thrown at us by one of the two terrorists we had encountered along the fence, hitting the paramedic who was walking right next to me. When he fell to the ground, I leaned over him and quickly stripped him of his clothes and combat vest

The four-mile "fire patrol" on foot along the Lebanese border.

that were starting to burn, while the rest of our fighters stormed the two terrorists and eliminated them.

Compared to a regular hand grenade whose shrapnel hits the body, a phosphorus grenade is designed so that when it explodes, fire engulfs the body of the attacked soldier and begins to burn the flesh while it gnaws at the muscle and consumes it. The immediate treatment in such a case is to strip the victim of all his clothes and spray water over his body. According to the Geneva Convention, this type of grenade is prohibited for use. The terrorist organizations apparently had not heard of war conventions.

At the end of this challenging year, I was delighted to be promoted to the rank of sergeant, and was assigned to the 12th Battalion of the Golani Brigade, where I was proud to be given the chance to take a modest part in commanding platoon 2, in Company C, under the direction of Lieutenant Ron Shechner, who became my inspiration and role model.

However, I did not have time to celebrate this due to a series of terrorist incidents that were being orchestrated by terrorist organizations based in south Lebanon.

Immediately after we had completed the full year's training period (in which to my mother's delight I had not been killed or severely injured), we were sent to a small Israeli village called Edmit, on the Lebanese border, after a squad of terrorists had entered Israel through that village's border fence. For three consecutive days, we scoured the area until we located the three terrorists. In a short sharp battle, we eliminated them.

As from that point, my combat journey in the ranks of the army began. An intense, challenging and dangerous journey in which I did what I had dreamed of doing, that is to confront the enemy that terrorized my country and sabotaged my childhood.

I was ready for my first baptism of fire.

3

My First Baptism of Fire

The target for my first combat experience was to be a well-fortified compound of bunkers in southern Lebanon being used by the terrorist organization the PFLP-GC, the Popular Front for the Liberation of Palestine-General Command, led by the notorious mega terrorist Ahmed Jibril.

Everything I had learned and realized during that almost inhumanly tough 12-month training period was now to be applied in the battlefield. I am neither ashamed nor embarrassed to admit that I was scared as hell of what was to come. I remember a crippling fear that shot through my body from the top of my head to my toes as we approached the target. To this day, I can still remember the dryness on the lips, and the sweat forming into beads on my forehead, even though the temperature outside was cold. This was a genuine fear caused by the knowledge that fighting inside trenches, or any type of fortified target, is fraught with unparalleled dangers. This form of combat is characterized by an element that does not favor the attacking force, and this element is the position. When attacking a fortified target, the attackers' position is critical, and sometimes more so than the quantity and quality of the weapons in the attackers' possession. For the attacking force, taking on a fortified target is immensely challenging, as the soldiers must perform their onslaught from an inferior and lower position. They are totally exposed to the enemy, who is firing from above while being well dug into, and thus protected, by a concrete bunker. Even a massive bombardment of skilled and sophisticated fighter jets would not be able to destroy the bunkers, nor an accurate artillery barrage. Battles of this kind are in the hands of the infantry fighters only, hence the genuine fear that gnaws at every infantryman on his way to a fortified target. In addition, there will inevitably be some unexpected discoveries that had not been brought to our attention by the intelligence provided to us while preparing for the operation. But despite all these factors, soldiers such

35

as myself still experience an adrenaline rush at the outset of battle, and this did not diminish in the future onslaughts I took part in. And now as a new combat soldier, I felt I was ready. This would be the kind of combat that I had trained for and was awaiting. Although I was to almost lose my life in it, it was exciting and gave me a chance to put into use my acquired combatant skills.

During our preparation, we had learned that there could be face-to-face battles against the PFLP-GC terrorists fortified in underground bunkers on the rocky slopes surrounding the coastal city of Damour, the same town of the Golani Brigade operation of 1974 which had so fired my fascination. Although I had already experienced face-to-face combat during my operational activity period on Mount Dov, this one would be different. Compared to the incident on Mount Dov, which was pretty straightforward as it was against only two or three individuals, this was to be a long and complex battle in trenches and bunkers, where there would be a genuine feeling of danger.

I was relieved when I heard this raid on the PLFP-GC compound was to be only against terrorists and was not going to be happening in an urban area populated by civilians. It would be in an isolated area, far from the civilian population, markedly different from operations and raids I subsequently took part in in refugee camps populated by civilians. These were intensely crowded, something that left us no

A long and complex battle in trenches and bunkers.

freedom of maneuver in the pursuit of wanted terrorists, not to mention the moral dilemmas we repeatedly faced in whether to shoot at a house where the terrorist we were chasing was hiding and from where the screams of women and children were clearly heard. I have always feared encountering a civilian population during any of the battles and operations in which I participated. It was my recurring nightmare over 28 years of combat activity against terrorists who were operating from urban areas populated by civilians, and mainly by children, since a Palestinian family can have a large number of children. My apprehension further increased after we the soldiers, and subsequently the whole world, discovered how the terrorists were exploiting civilians as human shields, in the full knowledge that Israeli soldiers will refrain from firing on children or civilians.

I was so concerned about encountering conflict areas populated by civilians that I found myself risking my own life. Situations arose where I deliberately did not shoot at the enemy, or I took on a terrorist with my bare hands who was armed with a knife, simply to avoid firing my gun inside a house where there were children and adult civilians. I can still picture the fear in their eyes, and the heart-breaking cries of a little girl who was cringing in the corner of a room of the house we had entered. She was weeping bitterly and her whole body was shaking in fear. My friends and I swiftly carried out the task we were assigned and eliminated the wanted terrorist who was armed with a knife, as well as his comrade armed with a Kalashnikov rifle. Once this was done, I swung my weapon behind my back and gently approached the crying girl. I leaned over her, stroked her head, and was able to calm her.

In another incident, this time taking place inside the Beit Hanoun refugee camp in Gaza, I remember there were tears in my eyes when I saw a woman with two small children sobbing over the ruins of her humble house. Her home had been destroyed as a result of a shoulder missile fired by one of the Palestinian terrorists, who was grossly incompetent at firing. His missile had whistled past the armored vehicle in which we were patrolling and landed directly on the poor woman's home. After eliminating the amateur terrorist, we collected the woman and her children and brought them to the Red Cross administration building in Gaza so that they could find an alternative home for them. On the way, we stopped at a kiosk and bought the kids drinks and candies.

I loved my military service, which gave me an opportunity to build my character and the self-confidence that continues to accompany me to this day, but I hated witnessing the shocking scenarios of wounded innocent civilians, and especially children. I was so sensitive to the suffering of Palestinian children that I was sometimes ridiculed or laughed at among my platoon. One of these incidents was in the town of Hebron in the West Bank. During a search for terrorists, we encountered a crowd of civilians throwing stones at us. Three of our commandos and I found ourselves inside a house. After searching and questioning the occupants of the house, we decided to get out of there. On the way back to rejoin our force, I saw a young boy sitting hunched over on the side of the road. He looked very sad. I walked over and sat down next to him and started talking to him in Arabic. I asked what he liked to watch on TV and what his favorite games were. "TV? We have no TV and I don't have toys," he said despondently. I pulled a bar of chocolate out of the pouch in my combat vest and offered it to him. I remained there for a while chatting to him, and also making him laugh with a few of the terrible jokes in Arabic that I had been told by a local kiosk owner where I used to buy candies and soft drinks for myself and for Palestinian children. I had a regular habit of carrying candies and chocolate in my combat vest, not only to keep my energy levels up due to the lack of sleep we experienced, but also to comfort Palestinian children who found themselves caught up in the madness of war. During the time I was sitting with that sorrowful little boy, I did not feel like I was in enemy territory. It was an irresponsible thing to do as there were dozens of stone-throwers still around who could easily harm me, but something in my heart was broken at the sight of this miserable child who did not choose to be born into the reality in which he was doomed to live. In this boy, I saw myself when I was a child.

Miraculously no one had tried to kill me, but I knew it was time to leave. I stood up and stroked the boy's head. I then delved again into my "chocolate pouch" and gave the boy another bar. When I arrived back at the base, my commander rebuked me for not only being late but also risking my safety for what was considered an unnecessary act. The soldiers made a joke out of it and one of them, an individual with far-right leanings, called me a "soft-hearted Palestinian fan."

There was no point in arguing with the far right on any issue. It sapped my energy to try to explain to him that not all Palestinians were terrorists, and not all Muslims had blood on their hands. Although the ones who had terrorized my childhood were Muslims, I have never thought that all Muslims are bad. In fact, 95 percent of the Muslims in the world are peacemakers, decent people, but there sadly exist those five percent of war-mongering extremists who besmirch the name of the good Muslims.

Knowing the Palestinians with whom I came into contact for many years, both as a soldier and as a journalist, I can say with complete confidence that most of them do not want an endless war with Israel. On the contrary, they wish for coexistence and a fertile, prosperous region. They view Israel as the only democracy in the Middle East, a country where its citizens are not afraid of its leaders, as the Palestinians in the Gaza Strip are of Hamas who govern them. To them, Israel is an advanced country from which neighboring Palestinians could only benefit if their hands were not tied by Hamas, which controls them by using threats and instilling fear in its population.

I remember as a journalist having conversations with Palestinians in Gaza in the mid–1980s, and it was from them that I had learned this. Prominent among them was Saeed Anwar, a 70-year-old local man who told me tearfully how much he missed the years of 1968–1970 in which the economy flourished in Gaza because of Israelis doing business with Palestinians there. He described how thousands of Gazan workers found jobs in Israel and were able to support their families, until the Fatah terrorist organization was born and set about demolishing the idyll. He banged his fist hard on the table as he told me that Fatah had destroyed the future of the Palestinians when they dismantled the progressive infrastructure that had been built by the Gazans with their Israeli neighbors.

My entry into real combat was now about to take place.

The well-fortified compound of bunkers we were tasked to raid had already been attacked by our airborne forces several times in the past weeks, but nonetheless, the Israeli Air Force attacks had been unsuccessful, and the compound was still standing. The bombs dropped by the pilots were accurate but non-effective as they could only scratch the surface. The only solution was to send a commando force that would reach the target from close range, to conduct accurate and individual fire contact with the terrorists inside the bunkers.

A force from the Golani Brigade had been selected to carry out the mission. I felt lucky to be one of the chosen ones. However, I knew that I had not been chosen because I was considered an outstanding soldier, on the contrary, I was a young and inexperienced warrior and was only 19 years old. I assumed then, and I still hold the same assumption today, that I was chosen to allow me my first opportunity to take part in real combat, in this case a dangerous and challenging battle that involved attacking a fortified target. This would prepare me as a commando fighter for the next 25 years, during which I would continually fight the endless terror as a mature and experienced combatant in the reserve service, the twice-yearly mandatory service in the Israeli army after the soldier has completed his three years of compulsory service.

All operational preparations for the raid on the PLFP-GC compound near Damour had been completed and each fighter had memorized all the details and the structure of the entire compound. According to the plan, our force would split into two separate teams of fighters upon arriving at the compound. One was tasked to attack the main bunker, which was on the right-hand side of the compound and served as the main headquarters. This bunker was marked on the fighters' map as the highest placed and largest of the bunkers. The second force, which I was in, was tasked to attack the three other bunkers on the left. During our exercises leading up to the operation, and from the intelligence information we had received about the structure of the bunkers, we understood that the task of capturing the main bunker on the right would be more difficult and complex than the other three bunkers. The bunkers we were assigned to take over were smaller and not so high up and could certainly be climbed very easily. In contrast, the "top bunker," as we called the main bunker, was not only higher than anything in that area, but was also booby-trapped by explosives that endangered anyone who approached it. The team whose task was to attack this bunker was also joined by three fighters from the Engineering Corps, whose job was to defuse the explosives in order to prepare a safe access for the fighters to break into the bunker. Their other function was to carry on their backs explosives which would be used to blow up and destroy the bunkers just moments before we retreated.

Damour, the nearest town to our target, came to be regarded as a perfect place for terrorist organizations who began building bunkers on the city's surrounding slopes, training its terrorist fighters and sending them to strike at Israel, a fact that caused Israel to respond.

The condition of the terrain in the Damour area was, and still is, ideal for conducting a guerrilla war. The steep and rocky ridges, caves, and the large amount of perennial vegetation, made it easy for the terrorists to assimilate into the field. In all respects, it was a perfect space where they could train and establish themselves without being discovered, so they could successfully infiltrate Israel to carry out terrorist attacks, which were not only against the civilian population but also against IDF patrol soldiers. They would lay ambushes from where they would fire shoulder missiles at the Israeli patrols, then, like frisky rabbits, quickly disappear back into their bunkers leaving no trace behind them.

Over the years there were other terror organizations who also saw the value of establishing bases in this territory, and successfully embedded themselves there as their sights of aggression were firmly fixed on Israel. They would regularly send armed terrorists to carry out attacks or dispatch a suicide bomber to major cities in Israel, and in between, fire rockets on the towns and villages of northern Israel. Gradually, they managed to take control of all of southern Lebanon, as they were being financially supported by Syria, and later on also by Iran. To eradicate the threat posed by these organizations, mainly by the Palestine Liberation Organization and Popular Front for the Liberation of Palestine-General Command, Israel first tried diplomatic means by asking the Lebanese Government to restrain them. This did not dissuade these organizations from continuing to cause harm to Israel, leaving her with no other option but to launch military operations against them.

The raid began.

The element of surprise matters, and so late one night in the winter of 1976, we reached our destination from the northwest, after an arduous trek over very difficult rocky terrain. As we arrived at the perimeter of the compound, we replaced our magazine of red tracer bullets with regular ones. This was so that in the event of a shooting encounter before entering the trenches and bunkers, we could disguise our position as much as possible. Red tracer bullets help to direct nighttime shooting as the shooter is able to see the bullets coming out of his rifle and thus improve his aiming according to whether they are finding the target. But on the other hand, if you are the shooter, then the enemy is able to identify the source of the shooting and thus your own position. In this case, we were aiming to be the shooters.

Final preparations before entering Damour. Defense Minister Ariel Sharon (seated in white shirt) instructing Army Chief of Staff Raphael Eitan on the right.

We cut a narrow opening approximately 20 inches wide in the fence that surrounded the compound, and continued to move towards the bunkers, about 200 yards away. We were proceeding quietly, in single file, and holding on to the shoulder of the person in front. This type of connection as we walked towards the target helped us ensure we were proceeding in the right direction in total darkness, as we couldn't use any means to light our way, not even a tiny flashlight. This way, we could also be sure that the entire team remained together and would be following our commander who was leading us and navigating the way towards the compound. During the walk, orders and instructions would be relayed from our commander at the front, by way of each fighter whispering them to the fighter immediately behind him.

We were approaching the objective.

Usually, when we enter an enemy area, the feeling is of fear, anticipation, tension, of walking into the unknown. However, this time, for some reason, a strangely calm feeling flooded us. We felt everything was going smoothly without any glitches. If the terrorists had not discovered us up to this point, then the chances were high that they would not be able to do so at all. That way we could catch them completely unawares. One of us whispered, "This is too good to be true."

I was also a little concerned. I was afraid the terrorists were waiting for us in a deadly ambush where they would slaughter us all. But our force commander who was leading us did not seem at all worried. This offered us a sense of comfort. We had always put our trust in our commanders. They were more experienced, they were bold and brave, and they were able to observe the battlefield in a wider and more comprehensive way than us.

But then, just as our force arrived at the point we were planning to split into two teams, we found out that the intelligence information about the area that we had in our hands (and our memory) was wrong. The distance between the three bunkers and the main upper bunker was different from what we had been told, and the upper bunker was not in fact connected to the other three bunkers by a trench, a wise decision by the bunker's builders I would say. In addition, the area leading towards the three lower bunkers was covered in dense thicket bushes, and the bunkers themselves were surrounded by tangled vegetation of dried out branches and thorns that looked very much like rusty metal barbed wire. This meant we would have great difficulty in being able to see the target with a clear line of vision. Worst of all, the route leading up to the main "top bunker" was blocked by large boulders that had probably been deliberately brought there from a quarry in the Lebanon Valley. This meant a change of approach to the bunkers was drastically and swiftly needed and that the plan to split into two forces was now impossible.

"How can this be?" I muttered to myself. During the practice stages, when we had been going through the aerial photographs taken by our Air Force over the area a few days before the operation, no-one had spotted any rocks or tall vegetation near or around the bunkers. The aerial photographs we received in preparation for operations were always accurate. The only plausible explanation was that the terrorists had laid these rocks earlier that same day. The feeling was of terrible frustration mixed with momentary confusion. I, as a young rookie warrior, began to comprehend one of the basics of war; this is that the plans you make prior to the operation are not necessarily the actions that will take place on the battlefield. In war, you know how you get in, but you never know how you will get out. Commanders and planners of an operation or battle can only speculate and evaluate the outcome of the battle, but there has never been accuracy in predicting the final results of a battle or war. However, to me, this momentary confusion was actually challenging and exciting. As a child, I had quickly become bored with games or situations whose outcome was assured, or that I found too easy. This trait accompanied me when I was a soldier, and I have to admit, still remains with me to this day.

Although our confusion did not last long, we were still feeling that we had made a mistake in navigating to this destination and had perhaps been brought to a different destination altogether. The mystery was solved only after the end of the operation, when we returned to the base for the post battle investigation. This is a procedure commonly carried out after our return from each battle or operation, in order to learn from mistakes and to improve the fighting abilities of the soldiers for future engagements. During that particular post battle investigation, it was revealed that the rocks and vegetation had indeed been brought to the compound on that morning, the very day of the operation, and that this was in fact a pure coincidence and not because the terrorists had known we were on our way.

Whether it was an error in navigating or incorrect intelligence, the changes in the topography of the target did not lead our force commander to even consider the possibility of canceling or postponing the operation and returning to base. He did not even report these unexpected changes to the commanders of the Front Command Squad back at our base. He understood in that moment that he had to make a crucial decision, one that was typical for generations of Golani fighters. This was to continue the mission, to perform the task with dedication and determination, while adhering to it despite any difficulties, obstacles or surprises. We in the Golani unit simply did not know how to say "impossible" or "there has been a problem with intelligence." We were trained to act in situations using a different perception and visualization. We were born with certain character traits that led us to be recruited into a commando unit. Those character traits, such as a colorful streak, "out of the box" thinking, a creative and imaginative mind, and the ability to adapt and utilize what is available and on hand in order to solve a problem, gave us the confidence needed to continue the mission in spite of unforeseen obstacles. In this particular operation, our perseverance and determination were highly charged due to the characteristics of the target. It was a terrorists' nest, from where they were constantly terrorizing Israel and inflicting harm on innocent civilians.

The mission continued.

Our commander noticed that just to the side of the left-most bunker of the three, almost hidden among the vegetation and rocks, was a small path leading upwards behind the bunkers. It had probably been cleared when the bunkers were being built and used by the occupants to bring supplies, as well as for any emergency escape needed. It was decided to use this path to carry out the attack instead of the original plan to take over the bunkers through access trenches. The experienced force commander estimated that the terrorists would not expect an attack on them from a path that they used in their daily routine.

Tricks and deception in battle are necessary to deceive the enemy in such situations where you feel trapped and unable to press ahead with your task due to changes or surprises in the field. These techniques were not invented in recent times, nor even during the extensive battles of the Roman Empire or the Mongol Empire of Genghis Khan. They have been ingrained in man since the dawn of history, in times when hunting animals was the only way for man "to put bread on the table." It can still be seen in nature when watching a beast pursuing its prey. If Charles Darwin's theory is correct, then it is clear from where we humans have inherited this trait. The Israeli army managed to achieve victory in all its wars, in spite of being greatly outnumbered, only because of its lateral way of thinking. Throughout my training period, and after each operation in the post-battle debriefing process, I learned a lot about methods of deception and tricks, even though they have been used in much more dangerous and life-threatening situations than I witnessed. The necessity of using tricks and deception during combat can even outweigh the greater risk to the safety of the fighters.

When our commander silently gave us the hand signal, we understood that our strike was about to happen. We quietly made our way towards our designated left-hand bunker. We were so close that we could clearly see the trenches connecting the three bunkers. Our aim was to surprise the occupants of the bunkers from the path behind. The force commander, along with eight of his fighters, began to creep quietly, hunched over, towards the path. My team was ordered to remain in front of the bunkers, as we were to attack the bunkers from the front in perfect coordination with the attacking team from the path behind. We were also serving as a blocking force in case the bunkers' occupants would try to find refuge in the trenches.

But just as we were about to begin our assigned tasks came another unexpected incident. On his team's way to the path, our commander noticed one of the terrorists standing by the side of the vegetation and urinating (this amusing fact became known to me only during the post battle debrief, and I really wish I had seen it for myself). The terrorist spotted the force moving towards him, immediately aimed his Kalashnikov rifle and started firing on the force while shouting in Arabic to warn his comrades in the bunkers.

The battle had begun.

The terrorists inside the three bunkers did not only spot the force moving down the path above them, but were also able to see us, as we were literally positioned in front of their eyes opposite the bunkers. In addition to firing from their Kalashnikov rifles, the terrorists began throwing grenades and shooting shoulder missiles at us. We threw ourselves down behind rocks for cover. I tried to lift my head above a rock but could not see anything. My greatest concern, and I assumed of all of us, was that some of the terrorists' missiles and grenades would hit our three fighters who were carrying the explosives to be used for blowing up the bunkers. If this were to happen, our disintegrated bodies would be unrecognizable.

The force commander acted fast. He shouted his commands and instructions to us, but those of us who were not close to him could not hear them clearly due to the cacophony of the gunfire and grenade blasts. His orders were being shouted and received intermittently, in the pauses between a grenade or a missile explosion, hence we were able to hear only fragmented instructions. As we were under heavy fire, we had to bring our combatants' instincts into play, needing to analyze the situation logically and calmly and weigh up the possibilities for a shrewd and effective attack. I felt an urgent need to initiate a move without waiting for an order or guidance. I assumed the tangled shrubby area, which made it difficult for us to see clearly, would have the same impact on the bunkers' occupants who may not be able to easily identify where our firing was emanating from. Also, our helmets were covered in shreds of

gray-green colored cloth for camouflage, so we could assimilate successfully into the tangle of vegetation.

I decided to get up on my feet to create a strong burst of fire that
would silence, even if just for a few seconds, the occupants of the first of
the three bunkers on the left, behind which, by the path, were my force
commander with his fighters, waiting for a suitable moment to break
into the other bunkers. I had a MAG machine gun that fired bullets of
0.3 inches in diameter, so I was sure that a massive round of fire from
such a gun could definitely do the job.

Shooting from such a heavy machine gun is carried out with the
assistance of one of the other fighters. He is known as a "MAG 2," and
his job is to load the bullets into the machine gun while the combatant
is shooting.

The MAG machine gun, or FN MAG 58 to give its full name, is a
medium-sized machine gun manufactured in Belgium, which is used as
a "Squad Automatic Weapon." The advantages of this MAG are its reli-
ability and great firepower. When used by infantries, the MAG would
play two roles during battle. One role is for "suppressive fire" and the
other is "covering fire." "Suppressive fire" is when you are firing at the
enemy to stop them from firing back at your force. The enemy is paralyzed by the fire and this facilitates the assault of the attacking forces.
"Covering fire" is when you are firing at the enemy to allow your own
troops to advance towards the enemy targets.

The MAG machinegun.

I got to my feet, holding the machine gun in my left hand. With my right hand I squeezed the trigger to the maximum, while maintaining the gun's stability and precise height as I aimed towards the bunker. I could not see clearly but used my senses to direct my shooting towards the left-hand bunker to paralyze its occupants. My shooting was strong, continuous and ferocious, and my machine gun was becoming red hot, as if the metal was about to melt from the heat generated by the massive volume of fire. Luckily, the bipod with which I was gripping the gun was designed and shaped for this situation, so I did not feel any burning of my left hand throughout the shooting. My intention was only to paralyze the bunker's occupants, as I was well aware of the fact that my shooting alone would not destroy the bunker. This would be done later on by our three fighters carrying the explosives.

The rest of my team noticed what I was doing and used my covering fire to advance towards the three bunkers simultaneously, coordinating with our commander's team. I kept up the firing with my MAG, while my No. 2 was slowly and carefully pulling the chain of bullets out of its bag, placing them into my machine gun's chamber at precisely the right pace for my shooting. I was amazed to see he was doing this as calmly as if he was back at an exercise training at our base. For my part though, I was becoming crazily high and my adrenalin was spiking to superhuman level. It felt like I was in the middle of a hallucinogenic dream. This was the first time I had fired at such a pace from a machine gun, or in fact from any automatic rifle, as in all my training exercises I had never experienced this speed of shooting. I would never have believed I could keep up such a pace. In a matter of seconds, the terrorists, who were probably stunned and not expecting such a fierce battle, began to ease the rate of their firing to the point that was nowhere near as strong as when it had started. I was trying to figure out why, and assumed they were by now running out of ammunition. MAG 2 and I raced to join the rest of the team who were busy storming the three bunkers, facing the firing coming at them head on.

To storm head on into fire is contrary to every natural impulse—the instinctive fear of every human being. Therefore, during our training, we were taught how to overcome and control our fear and anxiety, in order to be sharply focused on the target, while calling on our own self-confidence and belief in victory. This vital training for a much-feared combat situation was given steadily and incrementally over an extended period of time. The process was based on tough and demanding training methods developed in all the commando units of the IDF as the norms of basic combat values. These demanding training methods prepared the combatants to perform with excellence in all their operations. Our force commander, who had also noticed the lessening of the enemy fire, shouted an order, and all of us jumped into the trenches that were connecting the three bunkers and began inching towards our target. Our progress was made slowly and cautiously, but all the while we were keeping up our massive fire. Around the bunkers we found several more trenches, so we divided into small groups and dispersed ourselves throughout them as much as possible.

For some incomprehensible reason there was no response of fire coming from the main upper bunker. "The silence of the upper bunker" as we described it when we returned to our base after the battle. We were worried about the ominous lack of response from the bunker which we were most wary of. My fear was that its occupants would suddenly overwhelm us with a massive round of firepower, and that they were just waiting for the moment we would all be in their range of fire to pick us off one by one. Our commander was also wondering about "the silence of the upper bunker," as the bunker in question was not connected to the trenches we were currently moving along. He got up out of the trench and started climbing towards one of the lower bunkers, calling for his team to follow him. The rest of us continued edging our way inside the trenches. These were extremely narrow, barely 20 inches wide, which meant that while we moved along them, only the fighter at the head of the line could fire. The trench was disconcertingly small and gave me a feeling of being trapped and confined.

Being limited in what I was able to do was something that had always been contrary to my nature since my early days as a rebellious child. Here in the restricted and crowded trench, despite being young and inexperienced in such battles, I instinctively felt that this form of fighting, where only one fighter could shoot forward, was dangerous for the situation we were in. Every second counted, and we were all perilously exposed to an enemy shooting at us. I felt I had to do something radical. I jumped up out of the trench and quickly crawled along parallel to it towards a nearby rock. When I reached the rock, I hid down behind it, raised my head slowly and aimed my MAG directly at the center of the bunker's opening. This time I was firing my MAG and loading the chain of bullets completely on my own, as my No. 2 had suddenly disappeared. He was no doubt busy helping the rest of the fighters by shooting with his personal rifle and using the grenades he had with him in a bag on his back. Meanwhile, I swung from my own back my spare bag containing a long chain of bullets and put it on the ground beside me. After placing the top end of the chain of bullets into the feeder box in my MAG, I straightened my body, shouted the words "Covering fire" and started shooting towards the bunker. At that moment, some of our fighters emerged from the narrow trenches and started running towards the bunkers while firing. One of the fighters knelt down, aimed a shoulder-fired missile directly at the middle bunker and hit it directly.

During such a fierce battle, the last thing you want is any unwanted surprise or unexpected obstacle. However, those who were still inside the trenches and advancing towards the bunkers, discovered that the network of trenches was more complicated than we had thought. It turned out that the already narrow trenches split into even smaller ones, in which the fighters came across some of the enemy lying in wait for them. Inside these constricting trenches, fighters fought face-to-face battles, like those we had only seen before in the movies. One of the men from my team literally wrestled body to body with a terrorist he encountered in a small gulley leading off the trench.

My spontaneous covering fire action was indeed helping the onslaught on the bunkers, however, like everything else that has a limit, so too did my MAG machine gun. Relying on my senses, as I could not see the contents of the ammunition bag, I estimated that my bullets were about to run out. What was more worrying was that more terrorists had begun to appear. As they started adding to the firing raining down on us, I realized that my huge shooting machine was no longer of use due to my lack of ammunition. Although the rest of the fighters were successfully advancing towards the bunkers, the battle had become even more intense and was by now at very close range. Two of our fighters whose mission was to storm the upper bunker had been wounded, but even so continued firing at the bunker as they advanced with the fighters inside the trenches. One of the fighters from our other team crawled towards me carrying a green sack. When he reached me, he quickly opened it and pulled out a chain of bullets, placing the tip of the chain into my hand. "You must continue what you're doing. Stay here and just keep shooting." I nodded, loaded the chain into the machine gun and continued firing.

Suddenly there was a loud explosion, and immediately following that a huge blast that almost blew us off our feet. From experience I could tell it was not the sound of a grenade, nor a missile. From the intensity of its blast, I could assume this was a booby-trapped explosive device, probably placed just in front of the bunker's entrance. I saw two of our fighters drop to the ground, but I could not tell if they had been hit or were just taking cover, I was too busy firing towards the bunkers from behind the rock. After a few moments, I felt a stream of warm liquid trickling down from my head to my neck, but I could continue to function and shoot with my machine gun. I was sure it was blood, but I did not feel any pain. I did not have the time or opportunity to touch it and check, as I was so madly engaged in my powerful firing which required both hands and huge concentration. If the injury is in my head I thought, then it's better that I continue my covering fire shooting until I fall and lose consciousness. Because of the colossal amount of enemy fire, the machine gun I was holding could be essential to the success of the battle, so I was determined to continue as long as I was able to function. I must admit though, I was literary counting the seconds until I would collapse.

Two of our fighters who were near to the bunkers were already lying on the ground. I couldn't tell if they had been killed or injured. But when I looked more closely, I saw that one of them was my No 2. He had been hit in the head. The other was one of the squad whose job was to break into the upper bunker. I tried to get closer to them to pull them out of the fire zone and back into one of the trenches, but the commander shouted at me as he threw two fresh sacks of bullets towards me. "Don't stop. Keep on firing!" I returned to my position behind the rock and continued to shoot towards the bunkers, facilitating the way as much as I could for my fellow fighters.

"Good thing the three are not here," I mumbled to myself as I continued to shoot. I was referring to the three fighters carrying the explosives on their backs which would destroy the bunkers. The force commander did the right thing when he had ordered them to stay behind and lie down on the path until the bunkers had been captured and the trenches cleansed. Only then could they approach the bunkers and lay the explosives as planned. It did not take much imagination to guess what would have happened if they had been in the vicinity of the huge explosion close to us.

The battle was heating up as the seconds passed, with the unremitting shooting by us and from the terrorists' direction getting ever stronger. Our shooting was accurate and incessant as we were determined to reach the bunkers, but despite this, the terrorists showed no sign of surrendering. We felt we were literally fighting for our lives. It was no longer the conquest of the bunkers and the elimination of terrorism from southern Lebanon, it was in all regards a battle for life or death. The fire coming at us was becoming more accurate and threatening. Even our paramedics were participating in the firing and were ordered not to attend to anyone who got hit until the battle was over.

The noise was deafening. Thick clouds of smoke and dust were billowing up. There was a feeling of being involved in a world war, and that all the armies of the world were taking part in this one fierce battle. "These are the scenes of real war," I told myself. I was starting to feel that my first baptism of fire would also be my last. I was extremely scared.

Thoughts of parting forever from my family were going through my mind. I even pictured my military funeral. The fear passed through me as if it had cut my flesh with a knife. My heart was beating so fast that I could hear its loud pulse. I was sure the pressure in my chest would tear my heart and lungs apart. Suddenly I felt I was suffocating and couldn't inhale any air. "Is this a heart attack? Could I be dying now from heart failure instead of enemy fire? How embarrassing!" I shouted to myself. I was willing to reconcile with the fact that my death was just around the corner and would come at any second, but I could not come to terms with the fact that it would be the result of the physical failure of my own body, when I was in the midst of a shootout with the enemy I despised so much. I decided I would try to deceive my mind. Despite the fact that the terrible experience of being in a real war was causing me severe physiological reactions, somehow the decision to overcome these surged up in me. I would control my fears by imagining and convincing myself that all this was all just an exercise. Soon everything would be over.

My stream of thought was suddenly cut short. I saw a smoke grenade being thrown, although it was unclear where from. The purpose of a smoke grenade is to create camouflage. Who the hell among us would want camouflage now, when we were all in the fateful seconds before storming the bunker? But then the mystery was solved. We noticed two terrorists emerging from one of the bunkers and running towards the

Advancing towards the trenches and bunkers.

bush by the access path used by the terrorists. One of our snipers opened fire on the fleeing terrorists, killed one and injured the other, who vanished into the bush. Our three fighters carrying the deadly explosives, who were still obeying the order to remain by the path, spotted the fugitive terrorist and, without waiting for any order, began chasing him, following the trail of blood he left behind. Within a few minutes they had reached and eliminated him. However, they were not content with eliminating just this lone terrorist. The three experienced fighters felt that there could be something else hiding in the bush the terrorist had fled to. They assumed he may have been trying to reach a well-disguised ditch where there were other terrorists or perhaps additional weapons. Despite the heavy fire in the background, they decided to deal with this unexpected development. Forming a semicircle, the three began to approach what seemed to them to show signs of the ground having been dug, even though it was covered with dense vegetation.

As they could not see anything through the bush, they decided to stop where they were and listen. They sat themselves down quietly on the ground. During our training exercises, we had been taught the value of listening for any noises from a potentially protective bush or area of woodland when pursuing an enemy. The principle was that once the enemy has disappeared out of your sight, you have to be completely silent in order to identify any slight noise or murmuring coming from the vegetation, as a hidden enemy could be lurking there. Indeed, the three soon heard a murmur. They immediately opened fire in its direction and sprayed the bush with a massive round of fire while advancing into its depths. When they came upon a fortified position that was well camouflaged among the bushes, they threw grenades at it from close range. Hiding inside were three men, the fleeing wounded one and two others who had been asleep when the raid on the compound began.

After eliminating the three terrorists, the three fighters discovered that this excavated hideout, which initially seemed to have been used by terrorists for resting between shifts in guarding the bunker, led to a trench that stretched 50 yards west to a cleverly disguised munitions depot containing a massive stockpile of weapons. A brief search revealed many explosive devices, mortars, shoulder-fired missiles, bazookas and a large pile of Kalashnikov rifle ammunition. The three commandos realized that this was the objective hinted at by the intelligence information they had received before they departed on the raid. This fortified ditch, covered with a tangle of thorny branches, was from where the terrorists had been firing mortars and bazookas at Israeli citizens living near the northern border with Lebanon.

I have expanded on this marginal incident because of the act of heroism that was inherent in it. The three fighters were aware of the great risk they had taken by chasing and eliminating those terrorists. The explosives they carried on their backs could have been set off by just a single shot emanating from the men they were chasing, or from a terrorist in one of the bunkers. There was also the possibility that, as the three commandos were in a semi-circular formation, the explosives could have been set off by one of them shooting accidentally at each other. After all, they were within a battle zone. Secondly, they had actually violated the order to remain near the path. They had been ordered not to take part in the assault due to the amount of explosive material on their backs, which could endanger the entire force. But these fighters were Golani commandos. Crazy fighters. God only knows and counted how much crazy stuff we did during those "mission impossible" actions, training regimes, and treacherous operations.

Our assault on the bunkers continued to intensify.

A colossal amount of fire was coming from both sides. I was squeezing the trigger of my machine gun to provide cover for my comrades, but without any warning my gun suddenly went silent. I had run out of ammunition. In a matter of less than 60 seconds I had gone through a sack of 500 bullets. Thankfully, my comrades were not that far from the bunkers they stormed, so I felt I had done a good job with my heavy machine gun. I left my cumbersome, and now redundant, MAG machine gun on the ground by the rock that had been shielding me, to make it easier for me to continue my part in the onslaught. I grabbed and loaded my automatic rifle and joined the other fighters who were heading towards the three bunkers. I ran fast and within seconds had reached the bunker on the left. Since I found myself the first to reach one of the bunkers, I decided to use my grenades to try to paralyze the terrorists inside before I sprayed it with my rifle. Neutralizing this bunker, and then the other two beside it, would be a significant step in making our way to the important upper bunker and ending the battle. I pulled out the two grenades from the pouch in my vest and removed their safety pins, one with my hand and the other with my teeth. Then I got myself as close as possible to the bunker's opening. With the two unpinned grenades in my hand, I counted to three and shouted "Grenade!" as I slid the grenades into the bunker. When using a hand grenade, there are four and half seconds from the moment the safety pin is removed until the grenade explodes, so even though it was a high-risk strategy, I made sure I dropped them into the bunker at the last possible second before they exploded so the terrorists would not have a chance to pick them up and throw them straight back at me.

Under normal circumstances, according to practice, as soon as the shout of "Grenade!" is heard from one of our soldiers, the rest of us must lie flat on the ground for a few seconds until we hear the explosion, then allow another five seconds until the shrapnel from the grenade has landed on the ground, and only after that could we get up and continue our assault. However, I realized that in this particular battle this procedure was not valid, due to the fact that we were all throwing large numbers of grenades at the bunkers, so none of the fighters bothered to flatten themselves on the ground.

It was a feeling of satisfaction when I managed to slide both my grenades into the bunker, however, later, as we approached the bunker's entrance, we discovered that the door was wide open and inside it was completely empty. I felt like an idiot. I thought I had performed a daring move when I risked myself to hold on to the grenades until the last second and get as close as possible to the bunker's opening, but in fact, there was not a single soul to be eliminated in that bunker. Only as we were coming to the end of the raid, when we reached the upper bunker, had it become clear to us that there had been no firing coming from the bunker into which I had thrown the grenades. My embarrassment was profound.

After a further strenuous and stubborn battle, we managed to get close to the other two bunkers. However, the upper bunker still seemed to be unexpectedly quiet. Not one bullet was being fired from there. This was a relief as we were already suffering from exhaustion. When we were almost at the two bunkers, we split spontaneously into three teams, one to take the bunker on the left, the second team to take the one on the right, and the third team to climb up to take the top bunker even though there was no sign of fire coming from it. I was among the second team. As soon as our teams had divided, my team and I raced to get as close as possible to the right-hand bunker.

This time and to my delight, there was no need to throw grenades, we simply stormed into the bunker through its half-open door and sprayed it with massive fire. The second squad did the same thing with the one on the left, and it took only a few seconds for the two bunkers to be under our control. Having checked if there were any useful documents we should take, we only found writing utensils and a few decks of cards.

As we started heading up to the upper bunker to help the other fighters to purge it, we heard a shout of "All cleared." We looked up and saw five of our fighters waving at us. It turned out that there was not a single terrorist in the dreaded top bunker, and neither were there any explosive devices around it. During the post battle debriefing, we learned that most of the terrorists had apparently fled through a disguised trench which led up to a parking area where a truck was waiting for them. They jumped on board and were driven north, deep into the heart of Lebanon. These were the "heroes" who did not possess the courage to fight us, the soldiers, and preferred to wield their power over unarmed, helpless children and civilians. To me, as a young combatant, this was a valuable lesson from which I learned more about this vicious enemy that I would have to fight for the next three decades.

The battle was over. Mission completed.

We were ordered to start preparing for our retreat back to base. The three fighters who carried the explosives began the demolition of all the bunkers, placing the explosives carefully around them, while we all made our way down towards the path. On the way down, I stopped by the rock and collected the machine gun I had left there. Only after the explosives had been placed, and we had scanned the entire compound to make sure there was no living terrorist left, was the final order given to head back towards our base.

As we retreated, I could not bear to miss the opportunity to watch the demolition of the bunkers. I asked one of the men who had placed the explosives how long he had timed them to detonate. He smiled at me as he walked quickly and told me, as if revealing a secret, "Three minutes." I estimated the distance and realized I could be safe from harm at about 50 yards. I ran those yards like a child involved in an exciting new game. I wanted to be sure to make it in case it exploded before the planned time. When I arrived at my well calculated safe vantage point, I stopped and stood up tall, despite panting from the weight of the equipment on my body. I looked back at the rest of the fighters, who were indifferent to what was about to happen and could not understand what I was so excited about. It turned out later that none of them had been aware that this operation was my first "baptism of fire," and the first time I had been able to watch an explosion of such magnitude and intensity. Most of them were lying on the ground waiting patiently for the explosion and only I, an enthusiastic child, continued to stand upright watching the flames and tall mushroom of dense smoke that reminded me of photos of Hiroshima.

The explosion was stunning, illuminating the sky with flashes of red-orange-yellow, followed by a cloud of black smoke that rose up and billowed over the ruins. As I stood upright, admiring the amazing sight, I said to myself, "So this is what real war looks like, these are the sights and sounds of a real battle." I felt like everything that had just happened was a thrilling dream. I did not believe it was real, it seemed to me more like I was in the midst of a terrifying nightmare, or I had stepped into a scene from a Hollywood movie. The fact that I was not hurt added to my joy and satisfaction. Except for a minor injury caused by shrapnel that had hit my forehead during the assault on the bunkers.

A few months later, the Israeli censor granted permission for a journalist to interview some of the soldiers from our unit. This was after a group of senior military officials decided that some positive public relations would not hurt, but would in fact contribute to strengthening the image of the Israeli army within Israel and around the world. It could also encourage young men about to enlist to choose to serve in the Golani commando unit.

"We do in reality what you see in the James Bond movies," I replied to the journalist who asked us what makes our unit special. The next day, this journalist repeated my very words to serve as the headline for his article.

The operation was crowned a success. Ahmad Jibril's terrorist network realized that we could reach them anywhere and in any way they tried to hide. It had been vital for us to destroy these bunkers and their occupants as, according to intelligence, the PFLP-GC organization were planning a special deployment to north Israel through southern Lebanon with only one goal in mind—harassing Israel by terrorist attacks.

Ahmad Jibril was a Palestinian terrorist who, together with George Habash, founded the PFLP, the Popular Front for the Liberation of Palestine, in 1967. It was an organization with a Marxist ideology that opposed Yasser Arafat's nationalist Fatah movement, which later on reformed as the PLO. Later on, with the rise of Hamas' power and control, Jibril's organization became less influential and slowly its power as a terrorist organization weakened until it was finally disbanded. In 2014, Ahmad Jibril died from natural causes.

Before he died, Jibril managed to blackmail Israel into agreeing to a deal known as the "Jibril Deal," which was signed in May 1985. Israel agreed to release 1,150 Palestinian terrorists from Israeli prisons in exchange for the release of only three Israeli soldiers. In the eyes of Israel, the release of one of its soldiers is worth a thousand prisoners of the enemy. The same principle was repeated in 2011, during which Israel agreed to the release of more than a thousand Palestinian prisoners in exchange for one soldier named Gilad Shalit, who had been abducted in 2006 by the Hamas terror organization and kept in captivity in Gaza for five years.

Among those released in the "Jibril Deal" were two notorious terrorists. One was Kōzō Okamoto, a Japanese terrorist who headed the suicide bombing squad that carried out the brutal massacre at Israel's Lod airport on 30 May 1972, during which he and his comrades murdered 24 people and wounded 78. Okamoto was arraigned in Israel and given three life sentences but was released through the Jibril Deal after only serving 13 years. The other released terrorist with blood on his hands, and whom Israel had promised never to release, was Sheikh Ahmed Yassin.

In 1987, Yassin established the Hamas organization. As the leader of Hamas, Yassin maintained a firm line against Israel, calling for its complete destruction and its replacement by a Palestinian state. He called on the Palestinians to "fight the Zionist enemy in all possible ways, down to the last drop of their blood," and encouraged Fatah to carry out suicide bombings to expel Jews from all areas of Israel. He supported the abduction of soldiers, the killing of children, and even trained and encouraged Palestinian women to carry out terrorist attacks, including suicide bombings.

4

Methods of Training
and Operating

The base where I spent my army training period, close to the city of Jenin in the West Bank, was extensive. It was surrounded by hills and dirt tracks that were used by the local villagers for their transportation, which was inevitably by donkey. These paths also served us on our arduous training expeditions, during which we not only learned how to walk long distances with combat gear on our backs, but also how to navigate accurately both by day and night. The training ground at the base contained most of the natural obstacles that fighters would be likely to encounter on a battlefield, including tangled bushes, rocks, dense woods, steep sided pits, winter mud, steep hills, and exposed open areas. Also, within the training base was a compound I had not seen during the first three months of my basic training. Perhaps during that initial period, I was not yet prepared for what using this compound entailed, or maybe it had only recently been built, either way, the compound contained several elements that simulated the various combat modes to be used within a built-up area. Some of it was designed to replicate a house or simply one room, some to replicate a row of small houses, and one structure that towered above all the rest replicated a three-story building, which was mainly used for practicing an operation to rescue hostages. In addition, a modular house was built with two rooms, three windows and a front and rear entrance. This modular structure could cleverly be adapted to reflect information obtained about a particular terrorist situation and location. Within a few minutes, a house with two rooms and three windows could be transformed into a house with three rooms and five windows. This well-designed training ground allowed commandos to prepare for dangerous and difficult combat, taking into consideration any type of terrain or weather conditions, any hour of the day or night, at any distance and against all odds. Because of this excellent training facility, we were able to practice and become expert in close range combat, especially for those operations that would take place in complicated locations, as well as in short-range combat where the individual's qualities and skills are the key to success. We were also instructed in the sometimes crucial use of camouflage.

Apart from being taught skills such as navigation, climbing hills and mountains and administering first aid under fire, our physical training exercises included a daunting 118-mile trek on foot over dusty and rocky roads, facing steep slopes and areas of ground thick with mud. Just two days after this was completed, we were ordered on a further 68-mile trek carrying a stretcher with a "wounded" soldier on it. Other training exercises involved carrying weapons, ammunition and personal equipment weighing nearly 80 percent of our body weight, while climbing an eight-mile uphill mountain path, scaling the mountain while at the same time shooting at marked targets. We also had to learn to parachute in the darkness towards an unlit and unmarked destination, while maintaining constant and accurate gunfire.

During our navigation course, our commanders demanded that we should learn the art of navigation at night in enemy territory and in real time, exposing us to the dangers of a surprise encounter with the enemy. As with parachuting, this was an extreme method of testing courage and giving the soldiers an authentic experience. Although most of us

A 68-mile trek carrying a stretcher with a "wounded" soldier.

loved the sheer excitement of such a crazy practice, some of the senior military officials considered this unprecedented method of training as unnecessary, and it was actually abolished in 1968 due to its high risks.

Another "highlight" was a week spent enduring hunger, living in a field where we had to forage for our own food each day. This involved eating grass, rhizomes, insects and reptiles, items that you would not find at the supermarket in your daily life. This survival course was aimed at hardening us to face the harshest of conditions, including persistent hunger, long hours of thirst, very high temperatures in summer and, in winter, unbearable cold. These exercises bring the combatant to total physical and mental exhaustion in order to examine his level of endurance.

Rescue Under Fire

This is an exercise that involves fighters in the field and a helicopter, tasked to rescue a soldier who could be wounded, dead, or unharmed, but exposed to the risk of falling into enemy hands. Firstly, we learn how to master our moves and coordinate with the helicopter's pilot during a rescue operation, while having to work against factors such as the wind, the speed and movement of the craft, and the physical condition

A rescue and evacuation operation, carried out under constant enemy fire.

of those being rescued. Then, we would simulate a dangerous helicopter rescue under real fire, with our commanders shooting around us and above our heads to intensify our fear and create the feeling of real combat. The entire exercise of being suspended by rope from a helicopter is normally synchronized between the rescue helicopter pilot and us the fighters, who glide down ropes from the helicopter towards the helpless soldier on the ground. To do this, the helicopter will hover over the rescue area, a highly difficult and dangerous operation for the helicopter pilot who needs great skill and extraordinary courage, to allow the fighters to slide down the ropes as speedily as possible to reach the target, place and secure the rescued combatant on a stretcher (if wounded or dead) and be winched safely back up to the helicopter.

Planning and Memorizing

This exercise, which I personally found very helpful during combat, entails being involved in the planning of a raid or an operation. Studying and memorizing all its details in order to understand what was happening throughout the entire operation, increased our operational capability for a perfect and successful execution. The logic behind this was simple. If the fighter has been involved in the planning, he will be exposed to more details and intelligence that would become embedded in his memory. He could then call on this knowledge during the heat of the battle. This principle, after being proven logical and practical, was immediately implemented and included in the training programs of other IDF units.

Rescuing Civilians Being Held Hostage

There are two techniques we learnt to use within a built-up area for storming and taking over a house, or any structure that had civilians inside. These are known as the "cold entry" and "hot entry."

For a "cold entry," we were trained in handling situations using as weapons a large commando knife, tear gas, or lethal suffocation techniques, and when necessary, neutralizing a terrorist with our bare hands. These techniques were all performed without firing a single bullet so as to minimize casualties among the hostages. To execute this kind of operation, the element of surprise is the key. We were trained to silently head towards the target and take it over by surprise in the blink of an eye. When necessary, tricks and deceptions would come into play.

The decision as to the type of action in this situation would depend on the information at our disposal regarding the type of weapon the terrorist possesses. However, if the "cold entry" failed, then we would have no choice but to use a highly skilled sniper to eliminate the terrorist. This sniper would have the ability to shoot with great precision to minimize any casualties among the hostages.

A "hot entry" involves a noisy assault on a house or a building where terrorists are firing from, using our guns and grenades to fend them off. However, the method of our assault would be totally different if an armed terrorist had barricaded himself inside the property along with vulnerable hostages. In such a case, any shooting from our side would only aggravate the situation and cause the terrorist to panic. These are the cases where psychological warfare is required, along with the ability to maneuver and deceive. While we assess the situation and plan the right way to paralyze the terrorist, we would send an Arabic speaking specially trained soldier to try to negotiate with him. While this is happening, one of us would count the number of bullets already used by the terrorist and would pay attention to the sound of his magazine replacement and gun loading, so we could estimate when he would run out of ammunition. We would then call on our "Monkey Team" to break into the premises by climbing up the walls, or abseiling down from the roof, breaking through a window and paralyzing the terrorist with short bursts of highly accurate shooting.

The "Monkey Team," is one of the four specialist squads each company consists of. These are nimble fighters, who are trained in how to surprise the enemy, using unexpected means and ways of storming places using their own body's agility, whether breaking into a house, scaling sheer-faced walls, or abseiling down from rooftops.

You may not believe it, but as part of the training of the Monkey Team, visits to the zoo were mandatory and these were on an almost daily basis. On their visits, each fighter would study the virtuoso movements of the monkeys' feet and hands. Afterwards, during training, he would discover time and time again the resemblance between his agile moves and that of the monkey.

The second squad is the "Sniper Team." These are fighters with an innate skill to hit a target accurately. Their task is to neutralize the enemy by being positioned away from the danger area of their own fighters. While the other fighters are running, jumping, shouting orders or screaming in pain from having been hit, the sniper will calmly focus all his attention on his target, disengaging himself from the hustle and bustle of the battle, even at the cost of not attending a wounded warrior from his own force.

The "Monkey Team" in action.

The third is the "Burglary Team." These fighters learn how to crack all types of locks, iron and steel doors, heavy metal gates, and break into a building through reinforced concrete walls, sometimes at the same time shooting with accuracy. This can often be the first force to encounter the enemy fortified inside a building, in some cases holding hostages. Nowadays each of these fighters uses a sophisticated rifle equipped with a tiny telescope, plus other advanced features that Golani fighters of the 1950s and 60s, and even fighters of the 1970s like myself, could only dream of.

The fourth squad is the "Sabotage Team." These are fighters who are expert in the use of explosives for blasting walls and doors, as well as placing explosives in complex situations around enemy targets. This team can destroy infrastructures in a matter of seconds. They are also expert fighters, trained to use all kinds of weapons that are in use among infantry commando units, and undergo all the combat training exercises within the unit. Their role is critical in certain situations, and necessary in any operation or battle, even the shortest. They not only help demolish buildings or bunkers where the enemy is hiding, but also help advancing soldiers to clear a field of mines or roadside explosives.

Parachuting with Full Combat Gear

In order to increase and strengthen our courage, the brigade's commander decided that each fighter would take a course in parachuting. The act of parachuting during a battle has not been used by armies since 1956. This was as a result of a catastrophe in which thousands of paratroopers were killed as they were dropped over enemy territory to prepare for a surprise attack, but many were in fact jumping to their deaths, as they were shot while in the air by the enemy on the ground. However,

Seconds after parachuting in full combat gear.

for an army under constant war, we had to prepare for every possibility, including parachuting over enemy heads.

Those who have experienced jumping out of an airplane will understand the paralyzing fear that shoots down your spine as you stand at the open doorway of the plane, waiting for that dreaded signal to jump, watching from a terrifying height the tiny houses and cars beneath your feet that look just like children's toys. Personally, I quite enjoyed these jumps and learned one thing I could pass on to others. This is that it would be reasonable to think that one's first jump would be the most terrifying, but I learned that in fact it is the least scary, and that the jumps that follow are far scarier, simply because on your first jump you do not know what to expect. But from the second jump onwards, you find yourself preparing for the alarming things you become aware of only after taking the first. Matters like the harsh blast of wind in your face, the distance and force in which you are shot sideways away from the plane, and the underlying fear that you will find yourself enmeshed in a tangle of ropes and strings.

Modus Operandi

The Golani Brigade operates only on the ground, as operations at sea are the responsibility of the naval commando, and likewise air operations of the Air Force. The Golani specialize in most of the dangerous and complex operations carried out in houses, bunkers, underground tunnels and enemy ambushes. Even though we had one of the best air forces in the world, fighting deep inside enemy territory became the remit of fighters and unit commanders, who were convinced that it achieved better results with fewer casualties, and also changed the battle outcome morally and psychologically. Raids that are carried out in towns, bunkers and against enemy ambushes are in most cases dangerous and bold, but on the other hand are very effective. These are combat situations in which the attacking force can choose whether to penetrate the enemy territory either quickly or slowly, and can then sneak into the target location and surprise the enemy.

Golani fighters are trained to extend anywhere, including deep into enemy territory. We operate at all times, in every arena and can be sent on complex missions, even if the chances of succeeding are thin. Each one of us needs to be well-versed in counterterrorism techniques, and specialize in close range combat, problematic locations, and using camouflage successfully, as well as close-range combat where the individual's qualities and skills are the key to success. We took part in hundreds of top-secret operations, many of which were in close cooperation with the covert Israeli intelligence organizations, the Mossad and Shin Bet. This is perhaps not surprising as one of Israel's most admired generals, and former Prime Minister, Ariel Sharon, was one of the Golani Brigade's first commanders.

In addition, in working with the Mossad and with other intelligence forces, we had the opportunity of working closely with a covert unit of the "Mista'arvim." These are the counter-terrorism units of the Israel Defense Forces which operate undercover. Their operatives are specifically trained to assimilate with the local Arab population. They are commonly tasked with performing intelligence gathering, law enforcement, hostage rescue and counterterrorism, and to use disguise and surprise as their principal weapons. They dress like local Arabs and familiarize themselves with Muslim customs, prayers and clothing. They have learnt to speak the Arabic language with the appropriate accent for each posting so they can pick up the local gossip in each village. Refining the accent may sound a minor detail but is crucial because the Arabic language has many varying accents and dialects that change from one Arab country to another, or from the different Palestinian areas of Gaza and the West Bank. The unit is involved in various operations to thwart terrorist attacks and capture or eliminate wanted and terrorists, so they must learn to camouflage themselves well inside a crowd of Palestinians. They have extraordinary courage and can tackle an armed terrorist with their bare hands.

In one training collaboration with this undercover unit, we were

Sneaking into the target location and surprising the enemy.

sent to a genuinely hostile location, and were shown how each of us as an individual fighter could find their way out if trapped in an enemy civilian crowd or left alone in the field surrounded by enemy soldiers. The principle was to show us how to use our intellect and character skills, more so than the weapons in our hands. We were trained to memorize all the details of the targeted location, the look of the shops, the names of the streets, shortcuts, alleys, the color and shapes of street signs, and be fully aware of any unexpected movement in the area, however insignificant seeming, to minimize any chance of being spotted. In the event of being spotted and attacked, a back-up unit would arrive quickly on the scene and storm the area, but this would escalate the mission into a larger-scale combat situation, something that commando fighters strive to avoid.

5

My Best Friend's Death
on the Battlefield

He was a member of my company with whom I shared the tent we slept in during training sessions, and to whom I expressed my fears before and after every operation, battle or dangerous raid. Zvi was the best friend I have ever had throughout my entire life, to whom I could divulge my deepest secrets, as well as enjoying laughs and gossip. Not only did we find we had similar character traits in common, even our dates of birth were remarkably close. He was born on May 16, 1957, and I was born on May 18, 1957.

Although we were punished many times for mischievous and impudent behavior, we continued these brazen activities simply because we knew that our commanders saw us as excellent, talented, brave, and most of all, extremely disciplined soldiers on the battlefield. Neither of us cared for conventions. We laughed at those who performed each everyday task according to the rules, as we considered that rules and societal norms should be viewed simply as recommendations. However, at the same time, in an emergency, during battle, in the moment of truth, we both proved great combat ability and extraordinary discipline.

Zvi was only 20 when he was hit in the head by a single bullet fired by a terrorist during a raid in southern Lebanon and died after 23 days fighting for his life.

In 1977, as terrorism towards Israeli civilians inflicted by the Palestine Liberation Organization (PLO) terror organization from southern Lebanon intensified, the Israeli Cabinet decided to permanently eradicate the terrorist cells throughout Lebanon. My unit of the Golani Brigade were sent to carry out one of the missions, in this instance the destruction of three bunkers in which terrorists were hiding, as well as a large ammunition depot, situated 200 yards away from the bunkers.

The target: a town called Bint Jbeil, located about three miles north of the Israeli border. The town was chosen for this attack because it was a significant firing base of the PLO, and according to intelligence reports, several PLO command centers were concentrated there due to the "Wild West" atmosphere in southern Lebanon at that time. The outbreak of the civil war in Lebanon in 1975 had created chaos in most parts of the country and allowed the establishment of Palestinian terrorist organizations in southern Lebanon. The PLO was the most powerful and well-equipped force, numbering thousands of terrorists. Many of the recruits who joined it were not only from among the Palestinians themselves but also from other countries and were handsomely paid by the PLO for their service. The PLO enjoyed unlimited support from Syria and Iran and this instilled in them a sense of superiority not only in their war against Israel, but also against the Lebanese Christians who, with regard to the conflict with Israel, were considered by the PLO leaders as too ambivalent by not showing any interest in joining their own jihadi war against the Jews.

Our force was divided into two teams: one would attack the three bunkers from the southern ridges of Bint Jbeil, and the other would destroy the nearby weapons depot. We all believed this was going to be a short-lasting action, the type of which we had performed many times before, and that we would soon be back at base enjoying a game of cards. Nevertheless, we prepared for the mission seriously, and even tutored eight young Golani fighters in how to fight more effectively in a built-up area in enemy territory while minimizing casualties. For these eight, this was going to be their first baptism of fire, so we imparted the principles that we had learned from previous operations about fighting in trenches and bunkers, methods that are not taught during the training period. But the supposedly "short-lasting action" threw up a nasty surprise.

We entered Lebanon from its southern border and made our way across agricultural fields divided by long weathered dry-stone walls. When we were only half a mile away from the target, we ran into a sophisticated ambush that was well camouflaged behind a dry-stone wall. We found ourselves facing massive fire from machine guns, rifles, and hand grenades. The battle was ferocious. We fought like lions under fire, using reserves of both bravery and composure, determined to eliminate the terrorists in the ambush no matter what the cost in lives would be, so we could quickly reach the target in Bint Jbeil and accomplish the mission we had been sent for. Our reconnaissance squad, which included Zvi, saw an opportunity to set an example for the eight rookie warriors who were with us and soaking up each new experience.

We got to our feet and started advancing forward, discharging massive fire towards the stone wall. We stormed towards it completely exposed to the frenzy of the terrorists' shooting. Our commander who was leading the onslaught found himself face to face with one of the PLO terrorists who suddenly came out from behind the wall and was shooting as he ran towards us.

Fortunately, our commander was able to eliminate him with a short round of fire. We then divided into several squads and surrounded the dry-stone wall, purging all who were hiding behind it. Remarkably, we managed to eliminate all the terrorists in the ambush without any casualties among our forces. However, during our march onwards to Bint Jbeil to carry out the destruction of three bunkers and the ammunition depot, we had to face yet another nasty surprise. It turned out that there was another ambush lying in wait, as the PLO plan had been to mislead us into feeling confident that we only had one surprise attack to deal with. Even though we were very experienced and trained for the possibility of encountering an ambush and eliminating it quickly and successfully, this time we were caught completely off guard. This was a highly unusual situation, as for every operation we went on, we would always receive the most accurate and reliable intelligence, but this time the intelligence we had in our hands did not indicate the presence of any ambushes, let alone two. Only after the post-battle debriefing would it become clear that the two ambushes had been set up just minutes before our force arrived.

The second ambush proved to be more problematic. The size of the terrorists' forces was twice that of the previous attack, and this time they were hiding behind two different stone walls. Instinctively, we split up into two squads, and fired as fiercely as we could within our limits of vision. We progressed slowly, crouching down and walking towards the dry-stone walls with our backs hunched and firing continuously. Within a few minutes we had managed to eliminate a few of the terrorists, whom we could spot as they raised their heads over the stones of the walls to improve their firing. Others of their group decided to call it a day and ran off northwards, heading towards Bint Jbeil.

But in fact, the battle was not coming to an end. Although we had managed to eliminate some of the terrorists, and forced others to flee, our impression was that there were still many more terrorists hidden behind those stone walls, as they were firing heavily firing and throwing hand grenades at us.

Without any warning, they suddenly changed tactics and added to our vulnerability by firing shoulder missiles at us. In addition to these shoulder missiles, the gunfire from their Kalashnikovs was spraying the entire area and there was not a single inch of ground for us to take cover in. There was by now a feeling of suffocation and loss of hope amongst

A dry-stone wall used to camouflage terrorists.

us. Five of our fighters had already fallen to the ground covered in blood, and we could not determine if they were killed or wounded. They made no sound or cries of pain. Knowing the nature of Golani warriors as one of them, I knew that if they had been wounded, they would not let out any cries of pain, or call out to a medic to come and assist them. They would remain quiet and suffer their pain as they lay bleeding, until we had completed the onslaught. This is a worrying situation because you cannot know for sure what their condition is. The paramedics who had dashed over to them immediately they fell would be the only ones to know if they had been killed or injured. We the warriors would continue the onslaught and would be told only at the end of the battle.

One of them lying there was my best friend Zvi. I had a hard time watching him bleeding profusely. But there was no time to express my feelings or make room in my heart for any emotion. All I had to focus on at that moment was keeping up the firing on this nasty ambush that had disrupted our entire operation plan for the Bint Jbeil bunkers. And the situation was getting even worse for us. As we continued firing at the terrorists, we saw additional forces of terrorists flocking to the battlefield and positioning themselves behind the dry-stone walls.

Then, against all our principles of combat, we heard a sudden and surprising order to retreat.

The chief commander of the operation, who was monitoring the operation from the front command squad base on Mount Dov, instructed our commander in the field to retreat to the Israeli border. Our field commander ordered us to lie on the ground and find any shelter we could among the rocks, while he radioed back to the chief commander, asking his permission to remain in the field until we had eliminated the terrorists and gathered up the five soldiers who were lying on the ground dead or wounded. Meanwhile, we raced over to our wounded comrades and dragged them as far away from the fire zone as we could, finding shelter for them in a small cave. Once this was done, our commander then reported to the chief commander that the retreat was about to begin, and that we would be carrying the five wounded and bleeding soldiers with us on our backs. But the commander-in-chief firmly ordered the retreat to start immediately and to leave the wounded soldiers behind. In the army, especially on the battlefield, you do not express any disagreement with your superior. The order to retreat had to be immediately obeyed.

A strange feeling swept over us. It was one of confusion and inability to digest the order to retreat and abandon our wounded soldiers in this blazing enemy territory and at the mercy of the terrorists. We felt we were being asked to betray the iron principle which we had grown up on of never abandoning a wounded soldier on the battlefield. "Do those in the front command squad know something that we fighters don't?" we asked ourselves, but we couldn't think of any possible answer to this question. The order had been given to start the retreat and we all saw the anger on our commander's face as he passed it on to us. His hands were tied, and his fury was twofold: we had not completed the mission and we were also abandoning our wounded friends in the battlefield. It was only when we were running back towards the Israeli border, that the commander told us that a special unit was already on its way to rescue our friends. Indeed, within minutes, we heard the noise of a helicopter above us. The pilot, directed by our commander, found the cave where we had hidden our comrades, and the special unit in the helicopter mounted a dangerous rescue and evacuation operation, carried out under constant enemy fire.

When we arrived back at our base, none of us wanted to talk. We were all feeling low, bitter and frustrated. Aside from the obligation to speak up during the debriefing, we were all enveloped in silence throughout the rest of that day. We were hungry, but we had no appetite for food. Two of our friends were dead, and another three were injured, one of them very badly. My friend Zvi.

While in a coma, Zvi fought with the same intensity as he had shown in dozens of daring and dangerous operations. He was bold and courageous, and I had no doubt that inside him, he was determined to defeat the slow death that was gnawing at him on that hospital bed. He was a young lion who did not expect to die on a bed enveloped in crisp

Returning to base an hour after the battle (myself on the left).

white cotton sheets. He had envisaged his death would come in front of nests of guns or tanks, on the burning earth, with his body sweating and tense, not loose, motionless, sterile and dependent on all the instruments that were connected to him. I spent 45 hours sitting beside his hospital bed, refusing to lose hope and whispering words of encouragement into his ear, totally believing that he could hear me. And despite being a confirmed atheist, I read a few verses of prayer from the little book his mother had placed by his head. I prayed to Moses, to Mohammed, to Jesus, to the Buddha, and to anyone who could possibly help. My combatant's instinct was to save him, to storm, to shoot forward at those who had fired at him, but I felt helpless and unable to do anything to bring him to life again.

One night, I suggested to Zvi's family that they go home, have some much-needed rest and let me stay the night by his side. Throughout the night I held onto his hand, squeezing it with a short, steady pressure in the hope of a response from him, a sign of awareness that he was feeling my touch. But no sign was given by any part of his motionless body. After more than six hours of trying, my eyes were no longer functioning. They drooped downwards as if by themselves and I fell asleep on the hard armchair. When I woke up after about an hour from hearing the voices of the medical staff, I realized Zvi was dead. He had died while I was asleep, as if he wanted to save me pain. As if he did not want me to witness the moments he took his last breaths. There followed a frantic few minutes of resuscitation efforts, but these could not bring him back. The faces of the medical staff who tried with such devotion to bring him back did not express any hope, knowing that his chances of recovering, or at least of opening his eyes, were slim.

I scanned Zvi's face one last time before they covered it with the white sheet. He was so peaceful. Still so handsome, the same good-looking wild young man who never hesitated to storm and lead. The same daring warrior, who always ran fearlessly into danger, was now lying before me motionless. The tough, but yet at the same time hilariously funny, young fighter who was always the first to volunteer for any dangerous mission to save lives, was unable to save his own now. A patriotic soldier, who saw the task of eliminating terrorism as the most supreme and sacred one during his time of combat service, and strove to kill as many terrorists as possible in order to save the Israeli civilians who were being constantly terrorized. He therefore found himself participating in a large number of the operations, including those he did not have to.

He never hesitated to kill terrorists. However, at the same time, he was cautious of shooting if we encountered civilians, even risking his own life more than once when he chose not to shoot. I, on the other hand, must admit that there were situations in which I hesitated before killing, even though the target in front of me was a terrorist. I killed but hated the killing. I saw in it something animalistic and inhuman. I recall a situation where I was hesitating to shoot at close range at a terrorist we had captured. I wanted to back away from him a little and only then shoot at him, but Zvi did not hesitate, he shot him right away. I was so close to his face that the blood bursting from his head splashed onto my face. Nevertheless, despite his zeal and his almost uncompromising professional fighting ability, Zvi had always mocked and condemned wars, and leaders of countries that go into any war which was not a purely defensive one. The irony of my friend Zvi was that he hated war but loved to take part in it.

I cried all that morning and did not want to leave the hospital. I felt a need to stay and look after my dead friend even though there was no need. I could not come to terms with his death. I wanted to believe that he was just playing a joke on me like he used to do often. Soon he would open his eyes, wink his left one, burst into his infectious laugh and say, "Hey! It worked on you." He had done this so many times during difficult exercises, when he flopped to the ground, pretending to have been accidentally shot by one of us. And it was not only during exercises. Zvi would wind us up even during a real battle. He did this once while we were pursuing a wanted terrorist through the streets of Gaza towards the Jabaliya refugee camp. The fugitive terrorist was shooting at us, and some young Palestinians were throwing stones at us from the roof above a shop.

We received an order not to shoot back at the terrorist and certainly at the stone throwers. Then, while we were focused on not losing sight of the wanted terrorist, Zvi keeled over on the ground, groaning and clutching his chest. When the paramedic approached him, he jumped to his feet and burst out laughing, saying "I got you," and immediately started running to join us in the chase to eliminate the pursued terrorist.

Although he was punished for this episode by the company commander, it did not stop Zvi from continuing to do it. When I tackled him about it, hinting that we might not help him if one day he would really be injured, he gave me a mischievous smile and said, "This is my way of dealing with the fear." And indeed, in every chase we have carried out throughout the refugee camps of the Gaza Strip and in the West Bank, there has always been an inexplicable latent fear, one that was even greater than the fear experienced on the battlefield with its tanks, planes and missiles. After all, by any logic, the fear experienced on the battlefield should be greater and more intense than the fear when pursuing a wanted person in a civilian locality. But on the battlefield, you are able to clearly identify the enemy in front of you, whereas during a chase through a populated town, where most people are innocent and do not constitute a fighting force, you can be attacked by a large number of the enemy dressed in civilian clothes and who spontaneously become a fighting force armed with stones and rocks or with knives and iron bars. Fighting within a civilian population presents great difficulties both tactically and morally. It has happened to us more than once that we would come across an elderly woman sitting quietly on a sofa inside a house where the terrorists we were pursuing had fled to. If you are inexperienced, you would assume this woman to be an innocent old lady sitting in her home and not posing any kind of threat, but those with experience would ask her to get up from the couch and would then conduct a search underneath and behind it. I have chosen this example deliberately, as it was a real incident that happened to me.

Compared to fighting in a traditional arena of battle, including in bunkers and trenches, armed combat in a civilian-populated built-up area is intrinsically more complicated. When storming a bunker, although I am exposed and unprotected, unlike the soldier inside his armored tank or the pilot in his fighter jet, at least I understand who I'm shooting at. I know for sure that I am shooting at terrorists. Conversely, when I fire back at terrorists who shoot at me in a street full of civilians, I'm not always sure I'm only shooting at the terrorists, simply because everyone is dressed in civilian clothes. Terrorists do not wear military uniforms like we do. These kinds of complex scenarios are the main cause of the accidental shooting of civilians that the world sees on TV afterwards.

Another difficulty in fighting within a civilian population is the difficulty in preparing and defending against an attack on us, due to the limitations on being able to shoot indiscriminately, as we are allowed to do when assaulting a bunker. When we patrol the streets of Gaza or Hebron during an anti-terrorist operational activity, we never know from where a hand grenade or a rock will be thrown at us. The overcrowded houses, their rooftops and alleyways, make it very difficult for a safe and smooth operation. On many such occasions, I would be cursing profusely that I would rather be in the killing fields of Vietnam or Cambodia than here in the dark alleys of the refugee camps of Gaza or the West Bank. Zvi understood all this and summed it all up so succinctly when he had told me that his anarchic behavior was simply his way of dealing with the fear.

Whoever fights within a civilian population, or indeed in trenches, and yet claims he is not terrified during a battle, is lying. The dryness in the mouth, the sweat all over the body even in very cold winter weather, the white haze over the eyes, the accelerated heartbeat, and above all, those last words you used when parting from your loved ones which keep running through your head. We were all scared, but the practice was not to show it outwardly. We were wrapped in an invisible shell of armor that embedded in our being the feeling that we were tough commando fighters, and that showing weakness or fear was not in our character. Zvi had found his own solution, and it was one that was not written in the textbooks from which we had learned the fighting methods of the best army in the world. My dead friend realized this long before any of us.

My dead friend had been special in many ways. A young man with rare character traits that the adults had not understood when he was a child, and the commanders did not understand when he was a soldier. That was why he and I bonded. We found ourselves very similar in our character and qualities, with so many traits in common. Some of these were embedded in us since childhood, when we had both often been punished by our teachers and our parents. Traits that even enlightened adults did not understand in their fixed minds. We each felt we had found our soul mate, and I once joked that it was a shame he was not a girl so I could marry him. Surprisingly, he answered me the same way.

The love between us was immense. I once even gave up a 24-hour vacation I was planning to spend with my girlfriend Talia, just to be with Zvi at one of his family events. His parents always welcomed and hosted me in their home as if I were their second son.

Zvi was dead but in my head he would always be alive. He and I had been party to so many shared experiences during our days of training together. As well as wild evenings, Zvi and I had shared the contents of our food parcels received from home, and even our supply of ammunition when we had been on exercise together and one of us was running low. We were peas from the same pod; wild and rebellious, radical thinkers and willing to break the rules, which we did on many Friday evenings. These were the times we would "avail ourselves" of (in actual fact steal) a military jeep and crazily take off towards the city of Tiberius and its lively beachside night life, conveniently located not far from our base on the Golan Heights. There we would hit the most popular nightclub and would swagger around proudly wearing our combat uniforms. As we sped towards Tiberius with our hormones raging, we felt invincible, but at the same time, we could not help feeling a little fearful of the trouble that could await us if we had been caught stealing a military jeep, leaving the base without permission, and above all, abandoning our rifles, which we had left behind in our barracks carefully hidden under our mattresses. For this last matter alone, we could face a severe term of imprisonment, as a combat soldier must never let his weapon out of his sight. The phrase instilled into us was, "You can leave your wife and your mother, but you must never leave your weapon."

The Golani cedar tree emblem on our sleeve would not only guarantee free entry to the night club and a handsome discount on drinks, but that Zvi and I, who also happened to be two rather good-looking and confident young men, would quickly be surrounded by a bevy of admiring girls. Neither of us had any problem in getting a gorgeous girl to spend the night

The Golani cedar tree insignia.

with. I recall that on one of those hot summer nights, as we entered the club, Abba's song "Ring Ring" was playing, and we headed straight to the dance floor. Even the DJ left his booth to dance wildly around the floor with us, and we were soon surrounded by local girls, a couple of whom went to the bar and got us cold beers. It was a heady atmosphere, with the mingled smells of beer, sweat and cheap perfume, and the taste of lipstick as the two girls threw themselves upon us all through the night.

My best friend Zvi, who was funny, naughty, extremely brave, smart and wild, was dead, but in my heart he would always be alive.

6

The Development
of Terrorism Against Israel

Terrorism against the Jews in Palestine began long before the 1948 declaration and establishment of a Jewish state within Palestine's territory, which was in accordance with the United Nations decision to divide Palestine between the Arabs and the Jews.

For nearly 700 years there was harmonious and amicable coexistence between Arabs and Jews living alongside each other in Palestine as good neighbors. They traded between each other, ate together, danced at each other's weddings. What destroyed this idyll occurred in 1917 as the Ottoman Empire, which had ruled Palestine for 400 years, was breaking up, and Britain was taking over its administration. This was sanctioned by the League of Nations and became known as the British Mandate for Palestine. On 2 November 1917, the British Foreign Secretary Arthur Balfour had written to Lord Lionel Rothschild, a leader of the British Jewish community, expressing the British government's support for a Jewish homeland in Palestine. This landmark document, which became known as the Balfour Declaration, offered hope of a sanctuary for Jews, particularly those who had suffered European anti-Semitism and pogroms.

Even under the British Mandate for Palestine, the leaders of the neighboring Arab countries, who vehemently opposed the new reality in which they would have to share Palestinian land with Jews, declared what would become a stubborn and long-lasting bloody war against the Jews. Thus began a long series of massacres of Jews, involving violent incursions into the homes of Jewish immigrants and the murdering of their occupants, ambushes and shootings at vehicles on the roads, and the destruction by arson of orchards and fields.

In August 1929, a massacre was carried out in the city of Hebron, in which 67 Jews were brutally murdered. In this astonishingly ferocious attack, children were slaughtered in front of their parents, they were mutilated or burned alive, women and little girls were raped, and more than 300 Jewish homes looted. As the brutal massacre was taking place, the British officer in charge of the Hebron police, Raymond Capriati, did not lift a finger to stop the killing. Simultaneously, Arab rioters broke into Jewish homes in the cities of Safed, Haifa, Tel Aviv and Jerusalem, killing the residents and set their houses on fire. The total number of Jews murdered during the 1929 massacres was 133.

These vicious attacks, which were directed not only against the Jews, but also against soldiers of the British Mandate, were orchestrated in order to send a clear message to Jews from Europe not to dare to immigrate to Palestine. Amin al-Husseini, who led the "Great Arab Revolt" between 1936 and 1939, not only wished to wipe out the Jews in Palestine, but also wanted to expel the British and put an end to their Mandate. About 200 British soldiers were killed during this uprising. After the establishment of the Jewish state in Palestine in 1948, the terrorist struggle against Israel did not die down, but instead greatly intensified. Without exception, all Arab states opposed the dividing up of Palestine between Jews and Arabs, a division that was implemented legally by the United Nations in November 1947, through a vote taken by most nations of the world. However, Egypt, at that time the leading nation of the Arab world, mobilized Jordan, Syria, Lebanon and Iraq for a jihadist war against the "occupier Jew." Egyptian fighter jets continually bombed Tel Aviv, and artillery from Jordan shelled the citizens of the new country, targeting civilian women and children. War was inevitable. A war that continues to this day, even though Egypt and Jordan have signed peace agreements with Israel.

The leaders of the Palestinian terrorist organizations adopted a militant approach against Israel in the wake of the surge of radical Islam that began to plague the Middle East in the late 1970s and early 1980s. This process, which was reflected in events such as the Islamic Revolution in Iran, and the assassination of Egyptian President Anwar Sadat by the Islamic fundamentalist organization known as the "Muslim Brotherhood," has also taken root within Palestinian extremists.

For many years, terrorism against Israel was mostly carried out by Hamas and the Palestine Liberation Organization. The PLO was established in Jordan in 1964 and led by Yasser Arafat, who was personally involved in planning many of its attacks against Israel. Although in 1993 Arafat had signed a peace agreement with Israel, documents later found in his office in the West Bank city of Ramallah suggested that he had continued to use Palestinian Authority funds to finance terrorist activities. Arafat was able to deceive the European Union and United States, who were contributing millions of dollars each year for improving infrastructure, such as by building schools and paving a path of hope for the younger generation of Palestinians. Instead, he was channeling these funds into arming his organization, so as to increase their acts of terrorism against Israel.

In 1970, Palestinian terrorist activity in the Gaza Strip intensified and provoked an Israeli response. The Israeli government ordered the highly revered General Ariel Sharon, later the prime minister of Israel, to eradicate this growing phenomenon of terrorism emanating from the Gaza Strip. Sharon, in his combative way, decided to use forceful tactics in the war against these terrorists who had found a convenient base in Gaza for their terrorist activities against Israel, even receiving support and assistance from the local community. Sharon led a large-scale military force into the Gaza Strip which included armored forces, commando units and fighter jets, which managed to eliminate most of the terrorists and to destroy many of their structures.

In September 1971, in a bloody event henceforth known as "Black September," Jordanian King Hussein expelled the Palestinian militias from his country. They then found refuge in Lebanon and re-emerged, including as the Palestine Liberation Organization.

Within a few years, these expelled militias had gained power and control over south Lebanon, from where they began extensive terrorist activity, mainly targeting Israel. Over the years, they received funds and support from Algeria, Tunisia, Libya and Syria, and from global left-wing terrorist organizations such as the German Red Army Faction (otherwise known as the Baader Meinhof Group after their two leaders) and the Japanese Red Army.

During those years, a new method of terrorism was introduced that was unknown until then, one which to this day continues to cause discomfort and inconvenience among airline passengers who are forced to go through intrusive and embarrassing searches of themselves and their belongings before boarding any plane. But the hijacking of planes was not the only terrorist activity, targets on the ground were also attacked, such as in the massacre at Lod Airport in which 25 people were killed, and the murder of 11 of Israel's athletes at the 1972 Munich Olympics.

Since the mid–1970s, Palestinian terrorist organizations in southern Lebanon have concentrated on carrying out attacks on Israeli civilians living in northern Israel. Large numbers of civilians were killed in hundreds of terrorist attacks. The Israeli army reacted strongly against these atrocities, undertaking daring operations deep inside Lebanon, some of which I took part in between the years 1975 and 1978. Sadly, these raids and operations did not succeed in weakening the terrorists, who intensified their acts of terror and artillery fire on northern Israeli families. In response, Israel went to war in Lebanon in June 1982, took over the whole of south Lebanon and expelled the PLO to the Tunisian capital of Tunis.

In December 1987, the first Intifada (uprising) by the Palestinians began. It started out as a disorganized protest against the Israeli occupation of the West Bank and Gaza, and involved the protestors hurling stones and rocks at Israeli vehicles, attacking IDF soldiers with stones and improvised weapons, setting fire to buses, and violent demonstrations. Between 1987 and 1992, 155 Israelis were killed. The Intifada lasted until the Madrid Conference in 1991 that subsequently led to the signing of the Oslo Accords in 1993.

On 13 September 1993, the Oslo Accords were signed between Israeli Prime Minister Yitzhak Rabin and PLO Chairman Yasser Arafat. In this agreement, the PLO recognized the state of Israel, and in turn Israel allowed the Palestinian leadership to control the territories of the West Bank and Gaza Strip. In signing the Oslo Accords, the PLO pledged to stop carrying out attacks on Israel. But despite the fact that this agreement promised a real chance of peace, there were several Palestinian terrorist organizations in Gaza and the West Bank who opposed it and stepped up their attacks on Israeli targets. Only a few years after the agreement had been signed, it was discovered that the PLO Chairman Yasser Arafat had cleverly deceived everyone. It was during an IDF raid on Arafat's headquarters, in the civic administration building in the Mukata'a district of Ramallah, that it became clear from documents found on his desk that Arafat was continuing to encourage terrorist acts against Israel, and funding and monitoring these himself. To create the perfect cover, these would be carried out by terrorists who were not members of the PLO. Thus, between 1994 and 1996, a series of suicide bombings were carried out in Israel, killing 224 Israeli civilians, most of them children and teenagers.

In September 2000, the second Intifada began. All the Palestinian terror organizations, including Hamas and Fatah, began using much more deadly explosives and weapons to carry out their attacks on Israeli cities. They used women and children as suicide bombers, assuming that they would not attract suspicion from the Israeli security forces and the searches conducted on them would be less stringent, or sometimes not conducted at all.

The Palestinian Authority running the West Bank and Gaza Strip did nothing to prevent this from happening, but instead, aided and encouraged the terrorists. Israel agreed to the request of the United Nations to refrain from a military response. But then, in March 2002,

Golani fighters in pursuit of terrorists in the fields of the West Bank in 1998.

Palestinian terror struck Israel again, this time in a brutal attack in which 35 Israelis celebrating the festival of Passover at the Park Hotel in Netanya were murdered. Israel decided that this was enough.

Prime Minister Ariel Sharon decided to embark on an operation in which the IDF reconquered all Palestinian cities in the West Bank, including Arafat's headquarters in Ramallah (where the documents were found proving Arafat's personal involvement in terrorism against Israel). In this sweeping operation, Sharon decided to eliminate the terrorist leaders and wipe out all the terrorist groups once and for all. And so, in addition to heavy airstrikes by the Israeli Air Force, which caused the destruction of most of the terrorist infrastructure and their headquarters, a massive incursion of IDF ground forces purged their homes and offices, arrested most of them and killed those who resisted arrest. This operation involved a combination of commando forces, intelligence forces such as Shin Bet, undercover units, and the assistance of local Palestinians who worked for Israel as informants. The targeted air strikes yielded satisfactory results as many terrorist leaders were eliminated, among them the Hamas leaders Salah Shehadeh, Ahmad Yassin and Abdel Aziz al-Rantisi. As a result of this action, the scope of the attacks on the West were significantly reduced. Nevertheless, the Palestinian terror did not end.

Between 2002 and 2005, in addition to continuing their terrorist activities against Israel, Hamas, who had by then gained power and control over the Gaza Strip, began firing Qassam and Grad rockets onto Jewish settlements in the Gaza Strip and on the towns and villages of southern Israel. The incessant firing was causing psychological damage among the civilian population of southern Israel, especially among children, who were suffering from persistent anxiety.

In January 2005, Palestinian Authority Chairman Mahmoud Abbas reached an agreement with Israel on a temporary truce with the terrorist organizations, which led to the end of the second Intifada, during which more than

Ariel Sharon, later an IDF general and subsequently prime minister of Israel.

1,000 Israeli civilians had been killed and more than 4,500 injured. Israel agreed to withdraw its troops and civilian settlements from the Gaza Strip.

If there was any hope that Israel's withdrawal from the Gaza Strip in the summer of 2005 would cause Palestinian terrorism against Israel to cease, then this was wrongly founded. Ariel Sharon, the prime minister who had made the decision to withdraw, found himself astonished by what happened after the withdrawal, which took place despite his own political principles and views as a right-wing leader. Hamas brazenly continued mounting terrorist attacks against Israel from northern Gaza, taking advantage of the fact that this area was no longer under Israeli military control. By June 2007 Hamas had complete control of the Gaza Strip. This was an intimidating regime, rife with corruption, which instilled fear and apprehension among the residents of the Gaza Strip. On the one hand, Hamas financially supported the Gazan population, who suffered from great poverty and deprivation, but on the other, Hamas arrested without trial those who showed any signs of opposition. Dozens were summarily executed; the executions carried out in the city squares to serve as a terrifying example to others not to dare oppose the regime. In the terror arena, Hamas increased the amount of rocket fire on southern Israel, and with funding and assistance from Iran, was able to improve its weaponry. The IDF responded with air strikes during which Hamas offices, makeshift buildings and factories for the production of rockets were destroyed. This led to a significant decrease in terrorist attacks compared to the previous years, but Hamas continued to rearm. Huge amounts of money and weapons were smuggled into the Gaza Strip, enabling them to keep on firing rockets and mortar shells at Israel.

Following the military coup in Egypt in July 2013 and the ousting of Egyptian President Muhammad Morsi, Hamas began sending fighters via underground tunnels from the Gaza Strip to the Sinai Peninsula, this time carrying out terrorist and guerrilla operations against Egyptian forces. Dozens of Hamas terrorists were killed in these operations, and many were arrested by the Egyptian military. The Egyptian army began a drive to eradicate terrorism in the Sinai Peninsula, and succeeded in destroying the tunnels used by Hamas to smuggle the weapons. But since then, Hamas, which enjoys very generous financial support from many Arab countries in the world, and an incessant flow of armaments from Iran, has rehabilitated itself.

On 12 June 2014, a Hamas cell abducted and murdered three Israeli teenagers. Following the abduction, there was an escalation of violence in the entire West Bank, as well as in the Gaza Strip. The IDF responded and arrested many Hamas terrorists. On 30 June, the bodies of the boys were discovered and on 23 September, the kidnappers and murderers of the boys were killed by Israeli soldiers after being located by the IDF's security forces. At the same time, there was a significant escalation in rocket fire from Gaza on Israel. The Israeli air force responded with air strikes, during which headquarters and factories for the production of rockets in the Gaza Strip were destroyed.

Between 2015 and 2016, the Palestinians began to carry out a large number of terrorist attacks throughout Israel, including a series of stabbing attacks, violent riots, thousands of cases of throwing stones and Molotov cocktails at Israeli vehicles and buses, and attacks on Jewish civilians inside Jerusalem, including a murderous attack on a synagogue in which four Jewish worshipers were killed. In these attacks, a total of 37 Israelis and another three tourists were killed. In March 2016, the first suicide bombing in eight years took place on a bus in Jerusalem, injuring 20 Israelis. Three months later, a Hamas terrorist armed with a rifle turned up in Tel Aviv and began a crazed shooting spree in the city center. Firing madly in all directions, he murdered four Israelis. At the beginning of 2017, a further 17 Israelis were killed in terrorist attacks carried out by Hamas. In 2018, Hamas terrorists in the Gaza Strip began a series of demonstrations and violent riots on the border fence with Israel, positioning Palestinian civilians and children right on the front line. During the riots, Hamas took advantage of the fact that the situation was seen by the media as a purely civilian demonstration, but this innocent "demonstration" was a cover-up. Dotted among the demonstrators were dozens of Hamas terrorists who sent rockets and incendiary balloons into Israel, as well as attacking Israeli army patrols along the Gaza border. The IDF deployed among their forces dozens of snipers, who fired at the crowd of terrorists and rioters.

Between the years 2011 and 2019, hundreds of standard rockets were smuggled into the Gaza Strip, most of which had a long-range capability of between 12 and 25 miles. Added to these were over 1,000 mortar shells, several dozen anti-tank missiles, tons of standard explosives, plus supplies of the raw materials needed for producing explosives. The primary smuggling route was from Iran to Sudan, then on to Egypt and the Sinai Peninsula, and from there to the Gaza Strip, with Iran's direct involvement in providing the arms and their transfer into the Gaza Strip. It became evident not only to the Israeli Mossad, but also to the British, American and Russian intelligence services, that Iran was the dominant supplier of arms to Hamas, to Islamic Jihad, and to any terror organization that engaged in terror activity against Israel. Syria and Iran made it clear, including in speeches made by Iranian political and religious leaders, that they would continue to fund terrorist organizations and that those organizations would enjoy extensive material backing from Iran in their efforts to arm themselves. The British, American and Russian intelligence services joined forces to thwart not only the smuggling of weapons, but also the influence of Iran in the Middle East.

Israel has invested hundreds of millions of dollars in assimilating spies within Iran and Syria, some of them locals who were recruited for espionage work for Israel in exchange for huge sums of money. The information they obtained was valuable, and was shared by Israel with Russia, America and the UK. At the same time, Israel sent warnings to Hamas through the UN to refrain from using the rockets that they had managed to smuggle. But Hamas chose to ignore these warnings and the consequences of ignoring them, that were unambiguously laid out by the UN and the Americans. In 2019, when Hamas intensified its rocket attacks on Israeli citizens, firing more than 3,000 rockets and mortars, the Israeli army decided to respond with a heavy hand. Israeli fighter jets struck a wide range of Hamas terror targets, including a naval base

IDF soldiers patrol the streets of Gaza in search of terrorists.

which contained armaments and sabotage equipment, a military compound, and a weapons manufacturing plant.

This chain of bloody events dating from 1968, the year terrorist organizations began to establish themselves, has over time become an endless conflict of a kind unparalleled in the history of international wars. The Israeli-Palestinian conflict continues to exist while other international conflicts have long ended. It seems that the road to end the ongoing hostility between the two sides is a long and winding one, with bends and bumps and sharp inclines. An unpaved road without directional signs or traffic lights.

7

The Israeli-Palestinian Conflict

On 29 November 1947, the United Nations General Assembly voted by two thirds in favor to adopt Resolution 181 (the UN Partition Plan for Palestine), calling for the division of post–Mandate Palestine into two areas, one for the Jews and one for the Arabs. Israel had agreed to the partition arrangements for Palestine and welcomed the idea of coexistence with the Arabs, even though the Arabs were to receive a larger share of the land. But the neighboring Arab countries rejected this and chose instead to go to war, initiating a bloody confrontation that became an ongoing war between Jews and Arabs extending many years into the future.

On 14 May 1948, on the final day of the British Mandate for Palestine, the declaration of the establishment of the State of Israel was officially announced to an ecstatic Jewish nation by its newly appointed prime minister, David Ben-Gurion. The following morning, Egypt attacked Tel Aviv with an aerial bombardment, and shelled the area of southern Israel bordering Egypt with artillery fire. Egypt was able to persuade other Arab states to join its jihadi war against the Jews. Syria, Jordan, Lebanon and Iraq agreed immediately, and together with Egypt, they stoked up a massive and bloody war, one that has become an ongoing bloody conflict between Arabs and Jews over the Holy Land. This was a war of existence for Jews who had been persecuted for centuries in Europe and believed that they were returning to their long-promised Holy Land. Likewise, it was for Arabs too, who had believed in their own right to Jerusalem and the entire Holy Land. In the eyes of the Jews, the partition of Palestine between the two nations was implemented legally and officially in 1947 by an international body, the United Nations. However, to the neighboring Arab countries, it was an act of appropriation and occupation of land.

During my work as a journalist in Israel in the 1990s, I made a remarkable discovery that the world did not seem to be aware of. After dozens of conversations and interviews with elderly Arabs who had been living in Israel at the time of its independence, some of them revealed to me an interesting historical detail that was kept under wraps so as not to embarrass the Arab world. Some of my interviewees had been senior figures in their communities, including town and city mayors. Age seems to change perceptions and priorities, so when people are nearing the end of their lives, they often feel the need to reveal secrets they have kept for many years, in order to clear their conscience.

Many of my interviewees divulged to me that while the neighboring Arab countries' leaders were declaring war on the Jews, most of the Palestinian citizens actually welcomed the Jews. They were well aware that Arabs and Jews had coexisted for centuries, and they were convinced that the Jews could contribute greatly to the development and prosperity of Palestine. Unfortunately, they did not have the power to do anything about their views and were fearful of expressing these thoughts publicly. They disclosed to me that the war was in fact initiated and led by the leaders of the neighboring Arab countries, and not necessarily supported by the majority of the Arab citizens living within Israel's borders, who lived and flourished there. Just from these testimonies, it became clear that most of the Arabs who had lived in Palestine during the British Mandate and during the UN partition, had coexisted with the Jews, and considered the Jews as a force for good that could only help bring about improvement to the neglected Holy Land. They were proved right when Israel not only managed to revolutionize the agricultural output of the difficult terrain but has also succeeded in becoming a world leader in advanced technology.

Even though Israel had won a surprising victory over its more powerful neighbors in the 1948 War of Independence, the war between the Jews and Arabs intensified, with neither the Jews nor the Arabs showing any signs of relenting.

From the early 1950s, armed guerrillas from Egypt, known in Arabic as "Fedayeen," started a campaign of nightly insurgencies into southern Israel to carry out murderous attacks on its civilians, including women and children. The Fedayeen terrorists were made up of a few hundred disgruntled young Arabs, who, together with their families, had fled Palestine during the 1948 War of Independence. As refugees they had settled along the Egyptian ruled Gaza Strip to the south of Israel, and in Jordan on Israel's eastern border. These were some of the thousands of Arabs who had hastily left their homes during the war, promised by the Egyptian leaders that they would be able to return to their homes in just few weeks after their powerful army had exterminated the Jews. The Egyptians promised them not only a return to their homes and the repossession of their land and property, but that they would also receive a special permit allowing them to loot all the empty Jewish homes that would be at their disposal. After Israel's victory in the 1948 war, the refugees realized that the Egyptian promises were hollow. Not only because the Jews had not been wiped out, but also that the promise of a return to their abandoned homes was now impossible. When the Fedayeen's activity intensified, the fledgling Israeli army decided to respond. Units from the Golani Brigade were assigned most of the operations to deal with the insurgency problem. The Golani's already extensive experience helped bring about good results. In the event of an incident, Golani soldiers would trace the insurgents, calculating their route and the pace of their advance from the point of penetration, then setting ambushes to surprise and eliminate the insurgents.

These early Fedayeen insurgencies heralded the unending conflict between Israel and its Arab neighbors, and especially with the Palestinian refugees, who began to avenge their situation by becoming insurgents. Over the years, Palestinian refugees formed themselves into well-trained and equipped terrorist organizations, supported financially by most of the Arab nations. The insurgencies were the opening salvo of a long-running bloody battle. They gave birth to the concept of "Palestinian terrorism" and the two major Palestinian terrorist organizations that began their fight against Israel in the 1960s, especially after Israel's occupation of the Gaza Strip and the West Bank following its success in the 1967 Six Day War.

The war of 1967 began when six Arab countries moved their armies towards Israel's borders, threatening to wipe her from the map. In addition, Egypt closed the important Straits of Tiran in the Gulf of Eilat to Israeli ships. After a tense period in which many international diplomatic attempts were made to avoid war, the Arab states refused to withdraw their forces from the Israeli borders. Feeling highly threatened by the overwhelming power of so many Arab countries assembling on its borders, Israel decided to initiate a surprise move. Within the space of three hours, Israel's air force destroyed the entire Egyptian air force. The next day, when the Syrian and Jordanian armies opened fire on Israel, the Israeli air force shelled Syrian and Jordanian airfields and managed to destroy many of their fighter jets. After just six days, the war ended in a dazzling Israeli military victory over the armies of Egypt, Jordan and Syria, and this is still considered a remarkable victory. The results of the war changed the map of the Middle East, with Jerusalem, the Golan Heights, the Jordan Valley, Judea and

IDF soldiers deal with the phenomenon of infiltration through the border fence.

Samaria (the West Bank), the Gaza Strip and the Sinai Peninsula passing to the State of Israel.

Egypt and Syria could not come to terms with the humiliation of the fiasco they suffered in a war lasting only six days, in which the army of such a small country managed to defeat them against all odds. They sought revenge. Thus, just six years after the Six Day War, Syria from the north and Egypt from the south surprised Israel by the war of 1973, known as the Yom Kippur War. Israel was not at all prepared for this war, and unlike the 1948 War of Independence and the Six Day War, it exacted a heavy toll on the country's morale, especially when the heavy numbers of casualties were becoming evident (Israel lost around 2,300 of its fighters). The Egyptian army had crossed the Suez Canal at the same time as the Syrian army were striking Israel from the Golan Heights. After several grueling days of fighting, the IDF managed to stem the invading armies and moved to counterattack and defeat their attackers. These were hard-won victories, yet on the Egyptian front the IDF managed to advance to within 60 miles of Cairo, and on the Syrian front just 25 miles from Damascus. The Egyptians had however achieved their goal of inflicting a shocking blow on Israel and bringing it to negotiations. In the 1978 Camp David Accords and the 1979 signing of peace agreements between Israel and Egypt, Israel returned the Sinai Peninsula to Egypt.

Between 1969 and 1970, in another bloody conflict known as "The War of Attrition," Egypt had tried to get the IDF to withdraw from Sinai by shelling its outposts along the Suez Canal and by increasing UN pressure on Israel. Jordan was meanwhile assisting and financially supporting the PLO, encouraging them to start a war of terror against Israel. This would be war conducted in a different way, one which would intensify over the years and continue to this day. Despite their initial encouragement of terror against Israel, the Jordanians stopped their support of the PLO and expelled the organization from its soil in September 1970 in its "Black September" operation.

In 1982, following the increase in terrorism on Israeli and Jewish targets, both in Israel and around the world, and the constant attacks on its northern communities, Israel launched an operation in southern Lebanon, targeting Palestinian terror organizations, mainly the PLO and the Abu Nidal Organization, who based themselves in Lebanon.

The PLO terrorists, led by Yasser Arafat, were well armed and trained, having enjoyed the open-armed support of Syria. The organization had based itself in southern Lebanon from which they had begun

Senior members of the Israeli General Staff at a briefing during the Yom Kippur War in 1973. Yitzhak Rabin is on the right.

launching terror attacks across the nearby border into Israel, mainly against civilians and children.

Its 1982 Lebanon War brought significant achievements for Israel. The PLO was expelled from Lebanon and established new headquarters much further away in the north African country of Tunisia, and most of the military forces of the other small Palestinian organizations were eliminated. Many terrorists were killed, thousands were arrested, and the IDF seized most of their weapons. However, the operation, which had been planned to last no more than a few days, was expanded. IDF soldiers reached the outskirts of the Lebanese capital of Beirut, and also found themselves fighting Syrian soldiers. The war lasted much longer than originally planned, deepening the polarization between the left and right in Israeli society. In 1985, after three years of fighting, Israel established a narrow security zone in southern Lebanon. It finally withdrew all its forces from Lebanon in 2000, some 18 years after it first went in, and even without a formal agreement, the international borderline between Lebanon and Israel was settled.

On 12 July 2006, following the abduction of two IDF soldiers and the firing on northern Israel from southern Lebanon, the Second Lebanon War broke out. It lasted just over a month and ended on 14 August. The war began as a limited military operation, gradually escalating into

Destruction and grief. A residential building in Lebanon, which had served as a terrorist headquarters, after it was bombed by the IDF.

a wider conflict. This time the war was against the Shiite Hezbollah terrorist organization, which was supported and equipped with Iranian and Syrian weapons.

After the 1993 and 1995 peace agreements were signed between Israel and the PLO, a vacuum had been created in Lebanon. Hezbollah had filled it with the encouragement and support of Syria and Iran. The picture that emerged was depressing. It seemed that Israel would have to continue to fight terrorist organizations, which continued to emerge.

Israel's war is no longer between countries. Peace agreements have been signed with Egypt and Jordan. Syria is engaged in an internal civil war and has forgotten Israel for the time being, and Lebanon is completely shattered, with no stable government with which any peace agreement can be signed. It seems that the conventional wars fought against Arab countries have been easier than the never-ending war with terrorist organizations. The wars with Arab countries had a schedule, allotted time periods, whereas the war with terrorist organizations is endless.

As a journalist in my civilian life, I traveled dozens of times, and over many years, to Gaza and the West Bank. There I interviewed brave locals who shared with me the truth that could not be heard in the media: that the Palestinian leadership does not want peace with Israel, that the war with Israel (a) feeds them with financial support from organizations and other countries and (b) allows them to be seen as the victims and martyrs, and thus gain the sympathy of the world. During these years, I made many contacts with Palestinian journalists and intellectuals from whom I learned about the crisis they are facing from terrorist organizations such as Hamas, which is completely in control of the Gaza Strip. For them, this crisis is a larger and more severe one than when they were occupied by Israel.

My heart sympathizes with the plight of the Palestinians, and my sympathy towards them has only grown over the years. I fought them. They were my enemy. But my aching heart still goes out to them. They live in poverty and without hope, only because they are constantly in fear of their Hamas leaders, not of the Israeli tanks. The Hamas terror organization who forced the Palestinians to vote for them. The Hamas corrupt leaders who use the many millions of dollars they receive to continue the war with invincible Israel. They build tunnels and purchase weapons, instead of creating universities, schools, hospitals, infrastructure, and most importantly, investing in education. They do not encourage their children to pursue academic studies and better their lives. Instead, they are poisoning their minds with false promises of defeating Israel, by waging a war with impossible odds. Many countries, including the United States, have realized this, and stopped their financial aid which was flowing into Gaza for many years. Even Saudi Arabia, which was Gaza's main supporter, has lately stipulated that the funds it sent to Gaza should not be used for armaments. The majority of Palestinians want to live alongside Israel, who throughout the years of occupation provided them with work and services, such as electricity and water and free urgent medical treatment. They see Israel as a solid democratic and free state; a technologically and scientifically advanced country in which a profitable future could be planned and built.

During those years when I was risking my life travelling to Gaza and the West Bank to spend time with Palestinians in order to hear the truth, I came to one solid conclusion, and this is that Palestinians want peace and need Israel, but the extremist terrorist organizations do not allow it. I felt I had to do something to help. I felt a moral obligation to try to help the Palestinians break free from the extremists' shackles that have sentenced them to a life of poverty and misery. I learnt Arabic and studied the Qur'an to help me communicate more easily with locals, to better understand the conflict between the Israelis and Palestinians, and where blame should be laid. In the eyes of my family and close friends, I was schizophrenic. To them it was surreal, because on the one hand I was a pro–Palestinian left-wing Israeli journalist, who developed close contacts and conversed with them, but on the other, I fought them as an Israeli soldier during the 28 years of my compulsory IDF reserve service. However, what bothered me in those years was not what my family and close friends thought of me, but the search for the truth. I couldn't rely on the media reports on the miserable status of the Palestinians as it was unbalanced, most of the times exaggerated and misleading, contrived to gain global attention and empathy. I discovered this when a Palestinian freelance journalist from Hebron whom I was friendly with confessed to me that some media reports in Arab countries, in the Palestinian Authority and in some of the countries of Northern Europe, are written in a non-objective and biased way and without any pretense of accuracy.

Here are two specific examples:

During the 1987 Intifada, images were broadcast around the world showing IDF soldiers firing rubber bullets at Palestinian children. The Intifada was a violent uprising during which Palestinian residents in the West Bank and Gaza Strip revolted against Israeli occupation using stones and other improvised weapons. The uprising began on December 9, 1987, and officially ended with the signing of the Oslo Accords in 1993. The images of children fleeing Israeli soldiers shooting at them were shocking, but the truth was that IDF soldiers shot at armed Palestinian demonstrators who were throwing stones at the soldiers and injuring some of them. It turned out that the images of Palestinian children fleeing had been taken from a totally different incident in another location, in which IDF soldiers had chased the children without firing on them. The biased media took two videos from two different incidents and edited them to form one clip, resulting in a false drama that made every viewer empathize with the Palestinians. Furthermore, during the investigation of the event, it was revealed that many of those spontaneous "Palestinian demonstrators" had received cash from Palestinian leaders ordering them to "demonstrate."

Another example is one in which I was involved and witnessed myself during my reserve service in Gaza. It happened near the Al-Shifa Hospital, the main hospital in Gaza. My platoon and I were on a routine patrol. We heard an ambulance siren and immediately helped clear the road from cars to allow the ambulance quick access to the hospital. When the ambulance doors opened, several Palestinian children covered in blood were taken out of it and admitted to the hospital. My heart shook. It was not a pleasant sight. My patrol commander instructed us to continue the patrol as usual. My patrol headed off in the direction of the rear side of the hospital. When we got to the back entrance of the hospital, we were amazed to see those same children who had just been taken out of the ambulance covered in blood, coming out through the hospital's back entrance, walking on their feet, taking off their blood-stained shirts and putting on fresh ones that were handed to them by three men. When we checked the stained shirts and questioned the children, we discovered that the Hamas leaders had used these children to deceive the world and embarrass Israel. It turned out that their "blood" was the blood of slaughtered animals.

My empathy is with the situation of the Palestinians, because Hamas is to blame for the sad and desperate life in the Gaza Strip, not Israel. Hamas chose the path of violence and the destruction of Israel, instead of choosing to live side by side and wisely exploit Israel's help and support, as the residents of the West Bank chose to do and who are now benefiting greatly from Israel. The Palestinians in the West Bank enjoy a life of prosperity in business and commerce with Israel and the world, low unemployment, opportunities for academic study, a profitable tourism industry (for example to Bethlehem) and in general, most of the residents are satisfied and live well. There is development and building, and in the case of the West Bank, they really use construction materials for buildings, rather than for building tunnels as routes to attack Israeli civilians. Half a million Palestinians in the West Bank make a living from working in Israel in agriculture, restaurants, industrial plants and food.

Hamas misleads the world with lies, to garner sympathy and continue receiving the financial aid they annually receive from the Red Cross and some of the Arab Gulf states. Hamas uses millions of dollars for war purposes instead of improving the living conditions in Gaza. Most Gazan residents do not agree with Hamas, but live in fear of their threatening and intimidating control.

I spent many months in Gaza and what I heard from the people was that they need Israel and that only Israel is giving them hope for a better future. Many of those who were brave enough to speak out against Hamas and revealed the truth on social media have been persecuted and tortured or executed publicly to strike fear into others. Only a small number of these courageous dissidents managed to escape from Gaza, and with the help of human rights organizations and Israel, they were able to find refuge in European countries or the United States. There have been dozens of online clips in which they revealed the truth to the world in a fearless manner, praising Israel and condemning Hamas. One of them, Yousuf Karim, the son of a hardened Palestinian terrorist, was himself a potential terrorist who chose not to follow in his father's footsteps. Instead, he confronted the truth and revealed the lie of the Hamas leadership that has cast fear over the Palestinian majority, those who are decent people who are more interested in a life of peace than endless bloody conflict.

These are the exact words of Yousuf Karim, as relayed by him in a clip found on YouTube:

> Life in Gaza is difficult and unbearable, and it's easy to think that Israel is to blame for it. But let me tell you that they [Hamas] lie to you. I was one of them. I wanted to blow up all Israeli soldiers, but then I began to read objective material from other sources in which I learnt that the ongoing terror against Israel served only the Hamas leaders' comfort, and they did not really care about the Palestinian suffering. They are all self-appointed. When I heard that Israel was being accused of apartheid, I laughed. I have never visited Israel, but from phone calls with my relatives who live there I understood that the two million Arabs in Israel enjoy equal rights, work, academic studies, business, and many of them thrive in diverse fields. They live in excellent harmony with the Jews of Israel. Some are business owners, and some are professionals holding jobs in Israeli institutions. Why is Gaza sinking into despair? Because Hamas, which controls it, has chosen violence and the destruction of Israel instead of choosing a life of prosperity alongside it. Since 2007, the United States, the United Nations, Saudi Arabia, Kuwait and the European Union have tried, and are still trying, to help Gazan residents build infrastructure and develop businesses and jobs, but they delay this support whenever Hamas fires rockets at Israel. And what does this rocket fire on Israeli civilians actually accomplish? Nothing. Hamas knows

that but keeps firing those amateurish rockets just to show the residents of Gaza that they are fighting the enemy called Israel so as to justify their status and huge salaries. Meanwhile, Israel continues to exist and prosper, and Gazans continue to suffer.

When I am asked in interviews, or during my lectures on the Israeli-Palestinian conflict, if there is any possibility of a resolution and peace between Israelis and Palestinians, I present the following possibility: peace between the two sides is possible only when today's Palestinian leaders have left the world. Today's generation of leadership is used to war because it grew up on it, hence in these leaders' eyes peace is something that is far from achievable. Compare this to today's children who will not grow up only seeing war and conflict, and will see peace as the most suitable and reasonable option. Palestinian children today are more exposed than ever to the world through the Internet where they see opportunities to succeed and make money, study or learn a profession and touch the existence that is happening in the Western world. They will strive to implement this out of self-interest and for their personal ego and wellbeing, not because of nationalism. They will also understand from history that in all the decades of conflict between the two sides, the Palestinians have never defeated the Israelis. They will ask themselves what the point is of continuing to fight.

Life in Gaza. The painful result of Hamas' stubborn terror.

8

Operation Litani

In March 1978, the Palestine Liberation Organization launched a deadly terror attack. Eleven of its terrorists infiltrated Israel by sea from Lebanon and took over a passenger bus that was traveling along the main Tel Aviv to Haifa highway. In the attack, 35 of the passengers on the bus, including 13 children, were murdered. In Israel, the attack soon became known as the "Coastal Road Massacre."

As a response to this attack, the Israeli government decided to take military action against the PLO's terrorist infrastructures located in southern Lebanon. The aim was to push the PLO northward beyond the Litani River, so they would be distanced from the vulnerable northern region of Israel. On the night of 14 March 1978, the IDF launched a vast operation in southern Lebanon, led by Infantry brigades from the 36th Division, including Golani Brigade infantry and paratroopers. Later, these troops were joined by armored corps and smaller operational units.

The Israeli forces crossed the Lebanese border and began to move northward, with their aircraft and ships helping to secure the advance of the ground forces. Within a few days, the IDF was able to accomplish its target; it had reached the banks of the Litani River and destroyed the bases of the PLO south of the river to restore a feeling of security in northern Israel. The name "Operation Litani" was chosen because the key battles took place around the area of the Litani river. Many villages and towns that had been used as headquarters by the terrorists were occupied during the operation and 300 terrorists were eliminated. The IDF lost 18 soldiers. Following the operation, the UN Security Council decided to set up an international military force, UNIFIL, to maintain order in southern Lebanon.

Operation Litani began just three months before the end of my long, grueling and challenging three years of mandatory military service. I was relieved to be still alive after more than 200 operations and some of the dangerous situations I had found myself in. But could it be that death would finally come during my very last operation, after I had managed to survive so long? Uncontrollable negative thoughts began to creep around inside me. A year earlier, a platoon sergeant in my company had been killed just two days before the end of his service. The memory of this chilling incident did not leave me during the 48 consecutive hours of preparations for the operation. I even wrote farewell letters to my family and my girlfriend.

Our task would be to take over a town and village in southern Lebanon. The town was Bint Jbeil, discovered by our intelligence to be a stronghold of the terrorists, and the village was Maroun al-Ras, which was closer to our point of departure from the Israeli border. This area of southern Lebanon was a familiar arena for us Golani forces. Every inch of it was seared into our brain; each bush, tree and house throughout the entire area. I remember that to help us endure the tedium of our four-hour shifts in the lookout posts on Mount Dov, we had devised a competition between us to determine who was able to remember the most details about the area. As we stared out endlessly through heavy binoculars over the expanse of southern Lebanon, we would conduct trivia quizzes about the names of the villages, the religious practices of the residents and the agricultural crops planted in their fields. Even today, more than 50 years after that period, it will only take me a few seconds to type out the names of many of those villages; Marjeyoun, Ibl al-Saki, Hatzvia, Bint Jbeil, Yaroun, Maroun al-Ras, Aitaroun, Ainata, Balida, Beit Yahoun and even further north, Majdal Selem, Haddatha, Khirbet Salim, al-Qalaa, ending with the historic coastal city of Tyre in the west. However, even though we knew the area like the back of our hand, we were always asked to take care when entering southern Lebanon, and to pay great attention to the smallest of details, being ever alert for surprises in the field that our intelligence unit may not have warned us about.

The most dominant terrorist organization in southern Lebanon at that time was the PLO, which had only one aim, that of destroying Israel, and in the process to constantly harass its citizens by terrorist attacks. These cowards referred to themselves as warriors, but I had encountered them hundreds of times and soon came to realize that their "courage" involved using distorted and cruel tactics in their fighting, flouting the Geneva conventions, and using civilians, especially children, as human shields. They always tried to avoid confronting an army of soldiers, as their "heroism" only extended to perpetrating their attacks on unarmed civilians and helpless children.

The main IDF force for the ground operation was a division under the command of General Uri Simchoni. This force included armored divisions, as well as infantry from my own Golani Brigade, including the 17th Battalion, which I was part of while taking a three-month sergeants' course at a base near the northern Israeli city of Karmiel. The Operation Litani ground force was divided into two and was designated separate tasks for the operation. One, under the command of Colonel Yoram Yair, included a paratrooper force as well as a tank force. The other was commanded by Brigadier General Yitzhak Mordechai, who was the commander of my force, which included the 17th Battalion and Battalions 450 and 906.

My battalion was assigned to occupy the Shiite Muslim village of Maroun al-Ras, and the nearby terrorist stronghold town of Bint Jbeil. The battle was relatively complex and dangerous because we had to avoid harming the civilian population of the village.

Another company from my battalion, under the command of Major Shlomi Bashan, captured the village of Tel Shaalbon, due west of Bint Jbeil, which turned out to be a fortified complex of bunkers with concrete covers and deep communication trenches. On the way to the target, the force found itself being fired on from agricultural fields. Major Bashan shouted the order and there was a huge burst of fire from all the weaponry of the Golani force. The ambushed Golani soldiers managed to eliminate a number of terrorist squads at close range as they

Entering southern Lebanon to begin Operation Litani.

approached the fortified mound from the north side, through a communication trench that connected the mound to the terrorists' area of residence.

Another force, this one under the command of Lieutenant General Gabi Ashkenazi, attacked the town of al-Khiam, also not far from Bint Jbeil, and occupied several outposts in the area. They found these outposts to be very well excavated and containing a huge stockpile of weapons. During the battle with the terrorists inside the bunkers, the force commander Ashkenazi was wounded. However, despite his injury, he found the strength to command his forces until the end of the fighting. Gabi Ashkenazi would later be appointed Army Chief of Staff, and in 2020 he would become Minister of Foreign Affairs in the Israeli government.

Our mission, which was to first take over Maroun al-Ras and then Bint Jbeil itself, was designed so that our force would come from the east, and another force of paratroopers and armored divisions would simultaneously approach from the west. This would help facilitate the onslaught on the target, a chain of bunkers, in particular one that was serving as the intelligence base for the terrorists.

The villages of Yaroun and Maroun al-Ras are closer to the Israeli border than Bint Jbeil, which is further north, and were thus along the route of the destination set for us. By looking at a map of southern Lebanon, in order to reach our destinations, Maroun al-Ras and Bint Jbeil, logically it would seem necessary to first conquer the village of Yaroun, then the village of Maroun al-Ras, and only then the final destination of Bint Jbeil. But our commanders, who knew better than we did, decided otherwise. They ordered us to attack the most distant town of Bint Jbeil first, and only then, possibly with the aid of other forces, conquer Yaroun and Maroun al-Ras. During a short pre-battle briefing, we realized why Bint Jbeil was chosen to be attacked before the other villages. There were hundreds of terrorists based in Bint Jbeil who, by their relentless firing, were preventing our forces from raiding the strategically important underground bunkers, built by the PLO during the Lebanese civil war, which had started three years earlier. Bint Jbeil was a symbolic base for the terrorists, and according to intelligence reports, several of the terrorist organizations' headquarters were concentrated there.

As we continued with our mission to take over the eastern part of Bint Jbeil, we came across a complex of well-camouflaged bunkers on the southern side of the city. They consisted of dozens of extremely robust missile-resistant concrete shelters with winding trenches connecting them. Following procedure, we lay down on the ground and waited for instructions. After a brief consultation with his deputy, our force commander decided to carry out an assault on the bunkers. This was despite a lack of information about the number of occupants inside, the weaponry they had in their possession, the number of trenches leading to and from the bunkers, and whether the complex was surrounded by hidden explosives. As soon as the signal was given, we began to make our move towards the bunkers. Prior to our advance, our commander sent heavy covering forces in, which included several MAG machine-guns and shoulder-fired missiles that would engulf the whole area with colossal fire. Thanks to this cover, we managed to sneak right up to the trenches, hoping that these were all were linked to the main bunkers, which would allow us to storm the bunkers from the trenches while being less exposed to the fire from the terrorists.

Suddenly, massive firing started to come at us from all the bunkers. The sound of shoulder-fired missiles and the explosion of hand grenades nearly paralyzed us. We felt protected inside the trench but had difficulty in maneuvering and shooting back at our attackers. The trenches were so narrow that it was very difficult to move inside them wearing our padded combat vests. Even to replace magazines or cartridges was difficult as the sides of the trench we were in were so close. Some of our fighters got hit and blocked the way through the trench. We had to climb over them, sometimes stepping onto their backs, a sight that would never leave me. Because we had so little room to maneuver, rescuing the wounded was extremely difficult. The idea of summoning the artillery backup that was nearby was immediately rejected. We found ourselves trapped in combat without assistance. In the knowledge that this type of combat could only be effective if carried out by infantrymen equipped with rifles, grenades and some shoulder-fired missiles, we knew we had only ourselves to rely on.

When describing such a situation in my lectures, I am sometimes asked why we did not call for artillery assistance, or for our air force jets to destroy the bunkers, instead of risking the lives of dozens of soldiers who were struggling inside those trenches and fearfully counting every second until a bullet would hit them. A reasonable question, and the answer is this:

Accuracy when bombing this kind of target is a very important component. The level of accuracy of today's artillery is much more advanced, but in 1978, the degree of accuracy was so much lower that it occasionally caused friendly fire incidents. We could have ended up with the bunkers destroyed but we might all have been lying on the ground dead or wounded. The same goes for air strikes. Even if the pilot has accurately identified the target, then drops the bomb and hits the bunker roof in the hope of destroying it, the bomb would not necessarily land at a 90-degree angle, due to the air vibrations on its way down. The bomb might hit the target's roof, but bounce off it, only to explode hundreds of feet away, which could harm our forces. Furthermore, even if the bomb hit the ground right next to the bunker, there is always the chance that the fighters inside the bunker would not be harmed due to the way the bunkers are built. The inevitable conclusion is that the conquest of such targets can only be accurately achieved by a force of infantry fighters, who can completely and reliably purge the target from close range, despite the great risk to their lives.

Our battle inside the Bint Jbeil trenches continued as we found ourselves engaged in face-to-face encounters with the terrorists. The firing was at such close range that we were able to see the faces of the terrorists. I remember one in particular who gripped his Kalashnikov tightly in both hands, shooting constantly towards us. He was a young man of about 19, with curly black hair, his face covered with dark stubble as if he had not shaved for several days. The fear of being so close to him was crippling, and I embraced every second in this horrifying confrontation that I was not hit. In every small step forward we made, I saw my body being pierced with bullets. I could not believe that I would come out alive from this hell, which seemed to be lasting an eternity. In frightening situations such as this, you start mentally saying goodbye to your friends and family, and you realize that the thing you most want in the world is to be safely at home. In battle you understand the absolute meaning of life. You are asking yourself if this was all worth it, knowing how war is a primitive act whose inevitable outcome is death and injury. It's not about power, ego raising or occupation of territory. If you conquer territory, it is eventually returned in a peace agreement, but the dead can never be resurrected, and the permanently disabled can never be put back on their feet. During each new face-to-face battle, you realize that even if you have been in dozens of such previous situations, including those in which death seemed inevitable but yet did not come, you are still desperately scared. Your body shakes uncontrollably, and your movements are threatened by paralysis, your mouth dries out, and sweat pours down from your forehead even if the weather is cold.

I kept repeating to myself, "I have to get myself out of the trench."

My combative instinct was to get out of the trench and attack the bunker from where the grenades were being thrown at us. But getting out of the trench was not going to be easy to achieve. The intensity of the fire going on outside was so frightening that my whole body was rendered immobile. I literally saw the fireballs flying straight at me. I could hear the noise they made when they hit stone or metal, and I even got

trenches, with our many wounded soldiers, the difficulty in shooting, the visual limitations, the acrid black smoke and the noise of constant massive fire, we were now able to clear most of the trenches and prepare to enter the last bunker. However, our final onslaught did not go as smoothly as we had expected it to. A further unpleasant surprise was waiting for us. A few moments before we started the assault on the bunker to conclude the battle, feeling supremely confident in ourselves and our abilities, we found ourselves attacked by heavy fire coming from another of the trenches, one which had been very well camouflaged. Not only was this trench cleverly concealed, it was separate and not connected to the rest of the trench network. It is not usual, or comfortable, for a soldier to compliment the enemy, but here I must admit it was a brilliant move on their part, as we had expected the rest of the terrorists to be found inside the bunkers, not in another trench. Thankfully, this turned out to be a one-man-band who was firing at us from a heavy machine gun. We lay on the ground until he ran out of ammunition, then we quickly stormed and neutralized him.

Towards the end of the Litani operation, the PLO and other terror organizations withdrew from southern Lebanon to the north of the country, along with a large number of their Shiite Muslim civilian collaborators. One week after the start of the operation, on 21 March, Israel's Defense Minister Ezer Weizmann ordered the IDF forces to begin the withdrawal from southern Lebanon back to Israel. The UN set up the United Nations Interim Force in Lebanon to maintain peace and order in the region, and the UNIFIL force quickly arrived and was deployed on the ground in the south of the country.

The operation was crowned a great success on all fronts. We were able to eliminate about 30 terrorists and wound nine others. Others fled to northern Lebanon. Their local headquarters in Bint Jbeil were destroyed, as well as bunkers and houses which had served the terrorists as front command squad bases. An artillery post that had continuously plagued northern Israel was completely demolished. Four jeeps, five armored vehicles, stockpiles of ammunition and other equipment used by the terrorists were destroyed, although it would have been very tempting to take them as loot if we had trucks with us. At the end of the operation, we walked the seven miles back to the Israeli border, relieved, exhausted and covered in mud.

In summing up the operation, the Army Chief of Staff, Rafael Eitan, emphasized that the terrorists had been given a valuable lesson on the IDF's ability to act and strike anywhere and at any time, and that this short operation would lead the way for similar ones in the future if they chose to continue their acts of terror.

As a result of this effective operation, a new reality was created in southern Lebanon. The PLO was pushed north across the River Litani, where it established another base which other terrorists who had been scattered throughout southern Lebanon came to join. The Christian militias, led by Saad Haddad, gained full control of southern Lebanon. These militias were significantly strengthened with help from Israel after Operation Litani, both by being supplied with equipment and the scope of their training. This turned them into a semi-regular army, first known as the Free Lebanese Army, and later changing its name to the South Lebanon Army. The SLA's goals were to clear Lebanon of the Syrian presence, to put an end to Iranian support and its attempts to take over Lebanon, and most importantly, to completely eliminate terrorism being conducted by, the groups located there, notably the PLO. The South Lebanon Army hoped that they could force the Palestinian terror organizations out of Lebanon, but this did not prove easy for them to do, and the Lebanese Christians found themselves increasingly involved in a bloody civil war.

9

The Ongoing Civil War in Lebanon

Lebanon, once the pride of the Arab world and where thousands of tourists would flock, has not enjoyed a moment of peaceful existence in the past four decades, as during this time it has found itself caught up in an endless war. The problem was, and still is, that this cannot be considered a conventional type of war, in which two or more countries fight each other for a limited period of time, followed by all parties, perhaps through the mediation of another country, reaching a ceasefire agreement.

The war in the divided country of Lebanon was a highly complex one, staged between dozens of different organizations and militias, none of which had a chance of winning. Lebanon's fate as a land of eternal wars began as early as 1516, when the Ottomans invaded and ruled for four centuries until the end of the First World War. In 1920, the Sykes-Picot agreement was signed, under which the Greater Lebanon state was established under the direct control of France. However, in elections held in 1943, politicians who supported an independent Lebanon won a large majority in parliament, which led to Lebanon's independence, its liberation coming after 23 years of the French Mandate. And so, the Republic of Lebanon was established, and for the following 40 years, a delicate balance between the Christian and Muslim citizens of the country was maintained, with the exception of a brief civil war that broke out in 1958 between the communities. This was the first civil war in Lebanon. The second Lebanese civil war broke out on 13 April 1975 as a direct continuation of previous religious and class conflicts pervading the country. It lasted until October 1989, with the occupation of East Beirut by the Syrian army, who had a significant interest in controlling Lebanon. About 150,000 people were killed during that civil war, 200,000 were injured, and around 17,500 people were declared missing or dead. A further 790,000 people fled their homes, some emigrating to Europe or the United States, and some to Arab countries that offered them shelter.

One of the direct causes of the outbreak of the civil war was the establishment of Palestinian terrorist organizations in southern Lebanon, the principal one being the PLO, the Palestine Liberation Organization. These organizations did not hesitate to enter into bloody and violent clashes against Christian supporters of the Phalangist party, and also against those Lebanese civilians, who with regard to the Palestinians' conflict with Israel, were considered too moderate by not showing any interest in their jihadi war against the Jews.

During the period of the civil war, there were many disputes and disagreements among the factions, and even massacres among the various ethnic groups of Lebanon. These groups began to further split, causing more new groups to enter the arena and make the situation even more brutal and complicated. The conflicts between the different parties, and the number of groups fighting each other during the civil war, was almost endless. During my lectures, when I am asked about the complexity and difficulty of achieving peace in Lebanon, and who exactly the warring parties are, I smile and reply that in order to answer this interesting question, I will need several hours. Just to count the number of factions, groups, parties, and organizations that have been continuously fighting each other in Lebanon for the past 45 years, I will need to take a very deep breath. Perhaps I can just mention the major ones:

> The Palestine Liberation Organization (PLO)—led by Yasser Arafat, which was composed of a large number of sub-groups, the main one being the Fatah movement.
> The Palestine Liberation Army—a pro–Syrian faction within the PLO that acted under the direction and supervision of Syrian President Hafez Al-Assad to promote Syria's interest in Lebanon.
> The Christian Phalangists—these are the Christian forces originally led by Pierre Gemayel, and later his two sons, Bashir, who was assassinated in 1982, and Amin, who succeeded his murdered brother.
> The Refusal Organizations—two groups, one of which was led by Kamal Jumblatt, most of whose power was based on the Druze religious homogeneity of its members, and the other group led by Abd al-Majid al-Rafei, which supported the Iraqi position in Lebanon.

The National Socialist Party—a Lebanese fascist party that joined the radical camp. During the war, two further major streams emerged from this party. And the list goes on and on.

Other factors in the conflict were religious groupings such as Muslim Sunnis and Shiites, and the Maronite Christians. There were also various organizations that identified with the goals of former Egyptian president Gamal Abdel Nasser, such as pan-Arab unification and the strengthening of the Arab world.

During the fighting between these groups and organizations, the Christian Maronite President of Lebanon, Suleiman Franjieh (1970–1976), invited Syrian intervention into his country on the pretext that the fighting was preventing the re-opening of the port of Beirut, through which Syria imported many of its products. Syria was happy to take advantage of this, which in terms of public opinion around the world was an official call for help by the President of Lebanon himself. In actual fact, the Syrians had no intention of providing aid and assistance to the desperate Lebanese people, who were collapsing under the heavy burden of the battles and conflicts.

In actual fact, the Syrians had other intentions, seeing an opportunity to control Lebanon. Firstly, to annex it on the pretext of a caring

Horrific scenes on the streets in Lebanon.

Ongoing chaos is accompanied by bloodshed in every corner of Beirut.

embrace, and secondly, to assist in the war against Israel through the support and arming of the terrorist organizations in southern Lebanon in their guerrilla war against Israeli civilians. And so, over a period of just three months in 1976, the Syrians infiltrated many of their forces into Lebanon and launched a war against the radical groups that operated inside the country, justifying their invasion as an effort to bring order to their divided and bleeding neighbor. As far as Israel was concerned, the Maronite Christian community in Lebanon was their only hope of purging southern Lebanon from the Syrians and the terrorist organizations. Even before they helped to formalize the Maronite Christian fighters into the South Lebanon Army, Israel was assisting them by training and arming them. Later on, a line of Maronite villages was created on the southern border with Israel, which facilitated the activity of the Maronites, as well as of the Israeli army, in its war against the terrorist organizations. In return, the South Lebanese Army assisted the IDF inside the security zone, from the time of the First Lebanon War in 1982 until the Israeli withdrawal from Lebanon in 2000. The Israeli sponsorship and support of the South Lebanon Army, and of the Maronite Christian community, was also expressed in humanitarian aid, and later, in allowing Maronites to work in Israel. Soon after, the length of the 80-mile border, both in Israel and among the Christians in Lebanon, became known as the "Good Fence."

Between 1975 and 1978, during my period of compulsory military service, the Israeli army had already adopted the Maronites and begun training them to fight. Israel was also helping them financially, equipping them with weapons and even uniforms and commando boots. In 1977, I was privileged to be one of the IDF soldiers involved in their training at our base near Karmiel in northern Israel, the base where were taking our sergeants' course.

Some 38 years later, thousands of miles away, in the United States, the hand of fate guided my path to cross with one of the Lebanese Maronites we had trained. It happened when I was sitting by the beach in Miami and enjoying an ice cream. A tall, curly-haired guy, around my own age, approached me and asked if by any chance I was Israeli. I answered yes. He shook my hand warmly and said to me in English (albeit with a strong Lebanese accent), "I am one of the Christians from Lebanon you and your army trained." After I recovered from the shock of this astonishing announcement, I stood up and hugged him. "You were tough but kind-hearted and took care of us," he added with a smile radiating across his face. The animated conversation that followed between us lasted for more than two hours.

Another unexpected complexity was added to the Lebanese civil war, which was mostly between Shiite and Sunni Muslims and Christians. This came from the Palestinians refugees in Lebanon who demanded an urgent improvement in their conditions, as their situation had been worsening because of the fighting. This was a conflict that the Palestinians themselves were not actively involved in, but nevertheless, they were suffering because of it. These were the thousands of Palestinians who had found refuge in Lebanon after they had abandoned their homes and fled from Palestine, Jordan and Syria between the years 1948 and 1956, during Israel's wars with the surrounding Arab states. The Palestinian refugees started rioting all over Lebanon, and many shops were looted. Some of the rioters were toting guns or knives and using them against the Christian militias who tried to govern Lebanon. The Soviet Union, along with Libya and Iraq, were providing weapons and economic assistance to the Palestinian refugees; not because they felt any pity for the plight of the frustrated refugees, but rather to weaken American influence in Lebanon, and to subsequently gain more control there. To help in this plan, the Soviet Union was letting Syria do their dirty work by fighting on the battlefields of Lebanon; the Syrians were in fact playing the role of a marionette dancing to the Soviet tune.

Syria had confronted the Christian militias over what they saw as their attempts to undermine Syrian political interests in Lebanon. It was at this point that the shocked Christians realized that, despite being invited in by a Christian president, Syria had in fact given their country a short-term bear hug; the Syrians had a much broader interest in Lebanon, and that interest was not in the Christians' favor. From the intelligence information that Israel passed on to them, the Christians discovered that the Syrians were striving to achieve political interests in Lebanon that would weaken the power of the Christians in the future.

A confrontation between Syria and the Christian militias was becoming inevitable. The Christian militias' resolute fight against the Syrians led to enormous bloodshed, at the end of which Syria failed to achieve its political aspirations of controlling Lebanon. The Christians saw before their eyes a war of survival, a battle for their historic home. They showed a willingness to die in battle rather than allow the Syrians to take control of their beloved country. At one point, a group of Christian militias from Beirut and southern Lebanon joined together to form a larger unified force against the Syrian forces, even though they knew the Syrians were far better equipped.

But the determined opposition of the Christians to the foreign occupier came with a cost. Hundreds were killed and there was extensive destruction of infrastructure and houses.

The Lebanese not only saw the Syrians as greedy liars, they were also offended by their attempt to deceive them and trample on their dignity and honor, and worst of all, to deprive them of their liberty.

Since 1976, Lebanon had been caught in a downward spiral of chaos and hopelessness. In January of that year, hundreds of PLO terrorists had carried out a shocking massacre of Christian militias and Maronite Christians living in the southern Lebanese town of Damour, located on the main road from Beirut to the southern border. It is believed that up to 600 Maronite Christians were killed in the massacre, the vast majority of them unarmed. This was just one among a series of massacres perpetrated not only by terror organizations and Palestinians, but also by Christian militias in all their shades throughout Lebanon, such as the counter-massacre in the Tel a-Za'atar refugee camp, and finally, the Sabra and Shatila massacre in 1982. These savage events had occurred after the Christians found themselves clashing with Syria, whilst at the same time fighting the Palestinian terrorist organizations.

The Christian militias, although well-equipped and trained in guerrilla warfare, felt helpless in the face of the strength and numbers of these organizations, and so they turned to Israel for help. This appeal for help from its Jewish neighbor state eventually led to the Lebanon War in 1982, in which the Israeli army entered Lebanon to eliminate terrorist organizations, and at the same time to force the Syrians to retreat.

The 1982 Lebanon War, in which I participated, was planned to last only a few days, and was supposed to achieve two goals: firstly, the elimination of terrorism in Lebanon, and secondly the establishment of a stable Western-style democratic government led by the Christian politician

Bashir Gemayel. But unfortunately, especially for the Lebanese people who had been enduring turmoil for decades, the reality proved to be very different. This supposed "few days of engagement," developed to a very long and deadly war that entangled Israel in the Lebanese mire for 18 years. A long painful period soaked in blood, pain and grief, during which more than 1,200 Israeli soldiers were killed, and hundreds more became disabled for the rest of their lives from their injuries. I personally attended more than twenty funerals of comrades from my battalion killed during the fighting. Each year from 1983, I would visit my wounded disabled friends, until I had no strength left to withstand my distress in seeing them in their condition, and in 2010 I stopped the visits I had been making for nearly 30 years. To see a brave warrior with the physical strength of Hercules lying like a vegetable or confined to a wheelchair became just too painful for me. Israel's second goal in that war, to establish a stable Western-style democratic government led by Bashir Gemayel, also dramatically failed.

On the afternoon of 14 September 1982 at exactly 4:15 p.m., and three weeks after he was elected as Lebanese president, Bashir Gemayel was assassinated. He was the victim of a targeted bombing whilst giving a speech to his supporters in Beirut. All fingers were pointed at Syria, who had previously made it clear that it would not accept Gemayel's rule. As far as they were concerned, his presidency would be a great obstacle in their plan to occupy and have total control of Lebanon. The Syrians not only eliminated Gemayel, but also fought all the Christian forces under him. These were comprised of several Christian militias who had united under the leadership of the charismatic Gemayel with one common goal, to prevent the Syrians from taking over their country. Bashir Gemayel's life could have been saved had he turned up at a meeting scheduled for him with Israeli Mossad officials and the commanders of the group known as the "Tigers Militia" on that afternoon at 4 p.m., a meeting that had been called to crystallize issues and discuss strategy in the war against the terrorist organizations based in southern Lebanon. Gemayel instead opted to give a pre-arranged speech to his supporters, as he had done every Tuesday before being sworn in as president. This regularly took place at Gemayel's Phalangist political party headquarters on the second floor of a three-story building in the Achrafieh district of Beirut, in front of a large group of students who had supported him during his election campaign. This time, it was to be his last speech.

For 18 years from 1982 until 2000, the Israeli army controlled southern Lebanon until it was decided by Ehud Barak, the Israeli prime minister, that the time had come to withdraw all its forces. This was a courageous decision as it flew in the face of the opinion of Israeli

IDF forces in southern Lebanon.

intelligence, who pointed out the dangers of creating a vacuum in southern Lebanon, which the terrorist organizations would surely fight over and from there continue their attacks on Israel, a prediction that turned out to be correct. Having been nourished by large budgets and weapons by Iran, the Shiite Hezbollah party was able to occupy several areas of the Lebanese capital which had previously been under the control of the rival Amal Movement, also supported by Shiite Muslims. Hezbollah's takeover of parts of Beirut and southern Lebanon helped it to emerge as a significant force. Its power in Lebanon further increased after the PLO, who had for many years been the dominant organization in Lebanon, lost most of its leaders and fighters in the war with Israel in 1982, and was then forced out of Lebanon after Israel's 70-day siege of Beirut. The PLO leader Yasser Arafat had been faced with two choices, one to leave immediately for Tunis where arrangements had already been made for his relocation there, or to continue fighting a war in which he had little chance of winning. Arafat eventually agreed to leave, but if Israel thought that this would end, or at least reduce, terrorism in southern Lebanon, it soon became clear that this was wishful thinking.

10

How I Almost Saved Lebanese President Bashir Gemayel from His Assassination

Bashir Gemayel had begun his career in politics during the Lebanese civil war that broke out in 1975. At that time, he was both a political leader and military commander as the commander-in-chief of the Lebanese Forces, which consisted of several Christian militias fighting the Muslims. Gemayel wanted to become the undisputed leader of the Christians in Lebanon who were striving for strong and stable leadership, and even sought to make the Lebanese Forces the only militant force in Lebanon. In 1980, an assassination attempt was made on him using an explosive device placed near his home. But the hand of chance rescued him from certain death, due to a delayed meeting that overran the scheduled time, meaning Bashir had not yet arrived home when the bomb exploded. Tragically, the explosion killed his 18-month-old daughter Maya. At her funeral, instead of calling for revenge, he asked his warriors not to respond. But a month later, without his knowledge or approval, the Christian militia forces under his leadership attacked Camille Chamoun's rival militia headquarters. This massacre became known as "The Day of the Long Knives," during which around 200 of Chamoun's 500 fighters were killed. The 300 fighters who survived the massacre agreed to join Gemayel's Lebanese Forces, and as a result, Bashir Gemayel achieved his goal—all the Christian Lebanese forces were now loyal to him. They were composed mostly of fighters from several Christian militias, including the "Tigers Militia" who joined Gemayel's now large and united force in their crusade for the Lebanese leadership.

The radical Tigers Militia had been blamed for originally igniting the Lebanese civil war when, in April 1975, it began conducting military operations against pro–Syrian groups. The political ideology of the Tigers Militia drew on Lebanese nationalism, based on the country's existence as an ancient nation. They viewed the modern Lebanese people not as Arabs, but as the descendants of the ancient Phoenicians, whom they claimed were the people who had laid the foundations for modern Western civilization in Lebanon. Now a cohesive unit, the aim of Bashir Gemayel's Lebanese Forces was to return the embattled city of Beirut to its former glory of being the "Paris of the Middle East," as it had been known throughout the world during the 1950s and 1960s. Israel chose to provide economic and military support to the Christian militias, as the Israelis were becoming concerned about the growing involvement of Palestinian terrorist organizations in the politics of Lebanon.

On the evening of 13 September 1982, a young man called Habib Tanius Shartouni came to the three-storey building where Bashir Gemayel's Phalangist party headquarters were located. It was familiar to Shartouni, as he was the 26-year-old grandson of the previous owner of the building, which had only been sold to the Phalangist party two weeks earlier. Shartouni's family were known for their loyalty to Gemayel and his Phalangists, and a member of his family had even served as a close aide to Bashir's father, Pierre Gemayel. Even though the building had changed ownership, Shartouni's sister had continued living in her apartment there. Habib Shartouni had been a very active fighter among the Christian militias in all their incarnations and had fought against the Syrians, whom he viewed as a cruel occupier acting solely in their own interest and spreading false promises to those Lebanese who believed them. However, over the years, Shartouni had radically changed his views and become a member of an underground network of the National Syrian Socialist Party, which espoused the vision of "Greater Syria." This party had severed its alliance with the Phalangists in favor of aligning with the PLO, Yasser Arafat's terrorist organization. Both the PLO and the Syrians were deeply suspicious of Bashir Gemayel's cooperation with Israel and could not see him as a credible partner in the militant coalition fighting against Israel. The irate Syrian President Assad hatched a deadly plan to remove the new Lebanese president, and Habib Tanius Shartouni was the chosen assassin.

Shartouni's handler in the operation was a Syrian intelligence agent who had been based in Rome and had recruited Shartouni a few months earlier. Ten days before the assassination, Shartouni was instructed by his handler to carry out the act entirely on his own, taking advantage of his family's close relationship with the owners of the building who would not suspect anything. After having been given some basic training in explosives, Shartouni went up to his sister's apartment on the third floor of the building and while she was out, placed a hidden explosive device on the floor of her living room. This just happened to be immediately above the spot where the rostrum stood in the Phalangist party's room on the second floor, where Gemayel's speech was to be given.

No one suspected Shartouni, who was not only a Christian, but also well known to the building's occupants and their security guard, being a member of the family who had owned the building. But the main reason that Shartouni would be the last person to be suspected of carrying out this destructive action, was that no one imagined this young man would ever dare to blow up a building where his sister lived.

These were the final days of the first Lebanon War of 1982. A long and draining war in which we Israeli army reservists found ourselves involved in heavy action for a continuous period of three months, something we were not at all prepared for. I was already a student at Tel Aviv University, but had been called up to join the war effort. Reservists is the term used for soldiers who have completed their three years' compulsory service in the IDF and are called up twice a year as reserve combatants for a period of two weeks each time. This time, when we were called up, we were told that our service would be for a maximum of the usual two weeks, just until the IDF forces had occupied a total of 25 miles inside Lebanon. Taking over this area would ensure the elimination of the PLO terrorists who were controlling all of southern Lebanon and terrorizing northern Israel. However, in reality, the war became more complicated, and lasted way longer than anticipated.

On June 6, 1982, two days after the war in Lebanon had begun, I found myself assigned to a reserve battalion of Golani fighters within the Galilee Division (91), under the command of Brigadier General Yitzhak Mordechai. For more than three months we were engaged in continuous fighting in the crowded and populated areas of the refugee camps in and around the Lebanese town of Sidon, mainly in the Al-Halwa camp. We encountered stubborn PLO terrorists who not only refused to surrender, but also held civilians and children against their will and used them as human shields. They simply forced their way into these people's homes and locked themselves inside with the occupants, from where they would shoot at us. I remember hearing shouts in Arabic coming out of these houses from people who insisted they were not involved in the fighting, but at the same time, shots were being fired at us. We were confused and were not sure whether to believe them or not. I was sure they were trying to deceive us. But as the shooting intensified, more shouts would be heard, this time the screams of women and children begging for their lives. We made many efforts to get the civilians out of the refugee camp, but the terrorists' commanders would not allow it, and continued to shoot at us from all directions.

There were situations in which we risked our own lives, having found ourselves shooting at buildings where there was a good chance that civilians were inside. I remember being in a close-range gunfight happening inside a large extended house, containing many rooms that

As a reserve combatant in full combat gear preparing for another battle in south Lebanon during the Lebanon War of 1982 (myself standing on the right).

were still under construction. During the shooting, I heard the sound of a baby crying. I stopped firing and moved slowly towards the sound, while shouting at the other fighters to stop firing. We slowly made our way towards the sound of the crying, scanning left and right with our fingers firmly gripping the trigger of our guns. The shooting from the terrorists inside the other rooms had also stopped. Only the baby's cries continued. When we got to the room where the crying was coming from, we saw a baby lying in a crib, his tiny faced screwed up tightly as he bawled in anguish. As we got near to the crib to pick him up and take him out of the house, we were fired on by a terrorist who was hiding in another room. We had been led into an ambush. The terrorist firing at us was not at all concerned about the possibility that one of his bullets could hit a helpless baby. One of our own snipers immediately eliminated him with a single shot in his chest. We grabbed the poor baby and handed him over to a group of local citizens who were in the area.

This is just one example out of the countless situations in which we risked our lives to avoid indiscriminate shooting. Something that has never been reciprocated by the terrorists.

On June 13, after heavy fighting, we reached the outskirts of the Lebanese capital of Beirut, along with the other forces from almost all our army units, and where we began a siege of the city that lasted more than two months, 70 days to be exact. For six weeks, fierce battles took place around Beirut, during which all the IDF forces in the area, including our Golani unit, were advancing slowly and occupying territory bit by bit, trying hard to avoid any firing engagement where there were civilians. Our aim was to tighten the siege of the city of Beirut and evacuate the terrorists from it.

Simultaneously, while we were in the thick of these blazing hot battles, cold diplomatic talks were taking place between senior politicians who sat in air-conditioned rooms, free of acrid black smoke and choking dust. In mid–August, an agreement was reached to expel the Syrian forces and PLO fighters from Beirut, including Yasser Arafat himself. The operation of expelling the PLO was carried out under the auspices of an international force composed of Americans, French and Italians, who would ensure and monitor the departure of the PLO terrorists from all Lebanese territory. The evacuation process was carried out between August 31 and September 10, 1982, and during this period, we, the exhausted reservists, began to hear that we would soon be released from duty. Rumors were flying around as we were no longer being given fighting missions.

Arriving back one day at our makeshift base in southern Beirut, I suggested to my friend Doron that instead of returning home immediately, we take a two-day trip around northern Beirut, far away from the sights and sounds of battle. We had a few days off before I would be going back to university, so I thought why return directly to the routine waiting for us back home? I was imagining exploring the beautiful country of Lebanon through the eyes of two tourists, rather than soldiers wearing uniforms and holding weapons. Doron liked the idea. We had both mastered the Arabic language, and were well trained in defending ourselves with our bare hands, or improvising something to use for our self-defense if needed.

After we had completed the military release procedures and returned our combat gear, we replaced our uniforms with the civilian clothes we had brought with us. We decided the trip would be spontaneous, taking with us no backpack nor maps. We had money in our wallets and we had enough self-confidence. Our idea was to assimilate into the local population and pretend we were two Lebanese travelers. The ability to merge into the Arab population was not at all daunting for us. We had been trained in how to do it perfectly and had also implemented it during several previous operations, mostly in Ramallah in the West Bank and in Gaza.

Since this chapter is about Bashir Gemayel and not about our trip, I will shorten the description of our expedition even though it was fascinating, and I will move on directly to the assassination of the Lebanese president. After arriving in downtown Beirut, having hitched lifts in civilian cars we paid for as if they were taxis, we found ourselves a modest hostel where we spent the night. The next day, we started walking around the city. When we got to the area of Achrafieh, we were flooded with powerful memories. We had been in this place before as it had been the scene of one of our operations, so we thought it might be a good idea to hang round there for a while, if only for the sake of nostalgia.

On the day of the assassination, Habib Tanius Shartouni had used all sorts of feasible reasons to persuade his sister to leave the building, even though she insisted she wanted to hear Bashir Gemayel's speech. Once she had eventually left the apartment, Shartouni climbed on to the roof of an adjacent building. On that day, around three o'clock in the afternoon, unaware of the drama that was about to ensue, my friend and I found ourselves in the vicinity of the Phalangist building in Achrafieh. As soldiers who were familiar with the area, we were aware of the nature of the place as a gathering venue for activists, where political discussions, lectures and speeches were held. While Shartouni was waiting on the roof for the right moment to detonate his deadly bomb, Doron and I arrived in the area of the building, where we noticed a more than usual amount of people and cars. It was as though these noisy crowds of people were making their way to a special concert in a huge stadium. But despite the large amount of traffic, everything seemed to be in perfect order, and we did not notice anything unusual or suspicious. It was only after a brief chat with two locals we stopped to ask what was happening, that we realized the event involved a prominent Lebanese figure. The Lebanese president himself. We did not want to miss an opportunity to see the new president in person, as until then we had only seen him in photos or through media reports. We approached the entrance to the building to try to get ourselves inside, but the security guards looked at us warily. They had somehow sensed that we were not really an organic part of the hordes of people who were coming to the event. We did not want to arouse suspicion, so we walked away from the entrance and stood nearby, hoping to catch a glimpse of the president's face when he stepped out of his car in front of the building. The content of his speech did not really interest us, we simply wanted to watch him up close. After all the efforts and help we as Israelis had given him in building his army, we thought we deserved to at least see him.

After half an hour of waiting around in the heat, the front doors of the building were closed and we realized that the president was already inside. Although we both felt frustrated, we nodded to each other and agreed it was not worth remaining. We would take the first steps of continuing our trip around Lebanon. A local man stopped us and asked for a cigarette. Doron, who was a smoker, offered him one, and there followed an interesting conversation about the state of the war in Lebanon, the ongoing conflicts, and of course the election of the new young president.

Suddenly, we heard a huge explosion coming from the building we had, just moments before, been trying to enter. Doron and I were sure it was caused by a gas leak, as the building did not seem to be well maintained, so instinctively raced back in order to help evacuate the injured. It turned out that Shartouni had activated the explosive device by remote control as President Gemayel had started his speech.

As we entered the building, we saw the most horrific sights, evoking a post-battle scenario. The entire second floor of the building had collapsed and everything around was reduced to rubble. We were standing among burnt corpses, in stifling black smoke, and listening to the heart-breaking cries of the wounded whose bodies were burning. I could literally see smoke rising from the bodies of both the dead and of the wounded, who were screaming in agony. We stepped slowly through the rubble; barely able to see because of the haze of smoke. Despite the difficulty of being unable to see clearly, we managed to evacuate some of the wounded and those who were starting to suffocate from inhaling the acrid smoke, focusing our attention on those who showed any sign of life and leaving the dead inside where they lay. When we went back inside again, we made our way to the far end of what was left of the hall, where the podium had stood, and where a horrifying spectacle was revealed to us. There were several bodies around the podium lying motionless on the floor.

A young girl was screaming, "This is the president! This is the president!" pointing to the body of a man entirely burnt, his face shredded beyond recognition. I reached out to him and started to press down on his chest with both my hands to revive his heart as I could feel he was still breathing, but none of my efforts were bearing fruit. Despite the first aid I provided to the elected president, I could not save him.

Bashir was killed along with his friend Jean Nader, the secretary of the party's branch in Achrafieh, plus 30 activists of the Phalangist movement. The smoke was by now beginning to choke me, and I felt faint and unstable, not only from the toxicity of the smoke but the sheer trauma of what had just happened. Two men, apparently members of the Phalangists, pulled me out and laid me down on the ramp at the front of the building. Doron rushed over to me panting and shouted, "Wake up! Don't fall asleep, wake up!" He raised me up into a sitting position and poured an entire bottle of water on my face. The whole experience was like a nightmare you were unprepared for. No one expected such a murderous attack, not even the Israeli intelligence who were active in that area. We were sure we were in the midst of a peaceful political gathering, but someone thought otherwise. Someone who did not hesitate in killing 31 people in addition to a political leader, simply because he did not agree with his views. My efforts to save the president had been to no avail, but at least Doron and I had been able to provide first aid for those with lighter injuries and help evacuate the severely injured to cars parked outside the building, from where they were rushed over to Beirut's Hôtel-Dieu de France hospital.

The explosion was so powerful that some of the bodies of the other dead, as well as the Lebanese president's, could not be identified due to the severity of their burns. It was only a few hours later, around 9 p.m. in a stark room at the hospital, that President Gemayel's body could be identified. This was thanks to an Israeli Mossad agent who had been in almost daily contact with him, due to the highly tense atmosphere in the area following the election. The Mossad agent recognized Bashir's wristwatch that had miraculously remained almost intact and the white gold wedding ring he was wearing. In addition, he found inside his jacket pocket other means of identification, a letter from his sister Arza, who was a nun, and a congratulatory letter on the occasion of his election from a mayor of one of the towns in southern Lebanon.

Gemayel's funeral was held in Kafka, a small village near Achrafieh. His supporters, who refused to believe that their leader was dead, chanted throughout the ceremony, "Long live Bashir." He was just 34 years old at the time of his presidency and assassination.

A week after his assassination, Bashir Gemayel was succeeded as Lebanese President by his brother, Amin Gemayel.

Over 30 years later, at an event in 2014 held at the British parliament in London, I met Amin Gemayel and we naturally spoke about the tragic murder of his brother. Although Amin was not present at the bombing of the building, he remembered every minor detail of the incident that he had been given on the evening of the assassination. We talked and shared our different recollections of that painful drama. Throughout the conversation, Amin did not stop thanking me and my friend Doron for what we did that afternoon. He appreciated the fact that we had risked our lives for people we didn't even know and had no interest in. Then he shook my hand and warmly hugged me.

Amin Gemayel served as Lebanese president for six years until

Amin Gemayel and myself at an event held at the British parliament, London in 2014.

September 1988. During this period, his government ricocheted back and forth between relying on the West, especially the United States, and succumbing to Syria's growing interference in Lebanon's internal affairs. Through the mediation and efforts of the United States, Amin agreed to sign a peace agreement with Israel, and on 17 May 1983, the Israel-Lebanon Agreement was signed, which contained several encouraging areas of normalization between the two countries. However, despite the signing of the agreement, Amin refused to implement its terms, as he had signed it merely to satisfy the Americans, whom he was at the time heavily reliant on.

After a series of terrorist attacks targeting U.S. soldiers sent to Beirut, the U.S. withdrew its troops. Gemayel then found himself in the arms of Syria, who pointed a gun firmly at his head. As a result, in March 1984 the fragile agreement with Israel was rescinded. The Israeli delegation continued to operate in Lebanon for several more months, but Syria's deepening involvement in the country soon became evident. During his tenure as Lebanese president, Amin Gemayel had tried to work for reconciliation between the opposing factions but was forced to comply more and more with Syrian dictates. Thus, he appointed Rashid Karami as prime minister under pressure from the Syrians, whose forces then returned to Beirut. Initially this was only a small force, but in February 1987 around 7,500 Syrian troops marched into western Beirut. Amin Gemayel was given a clear indication by the Syrians that he should not even think about continuing his tenure of the presidency. He also received threats on his life and his family, leaving him no choice but to flee Lebanon for Paris.

In 1995, following the assassination of Israeli Prime Minister Yitzhak Rabin, Amin went to the Israeli embassy in Paris to sign the condolence book. After this gesture, he was banned from returning to his native Lebanon. However, in 2000, after many significant changes in Lebanese politics, and in the light of the withdrawal of the Syrian presence and its forces, Amin decided it was time to return to his homeland. Since then he has been one of the prominent leaders of the Lebanese Christians.

A few weeks after the assassination of Bashir Gemayel, Habib Tanius Shartouni was captured and imprisoned to await his trial. His capture was mainly thanks to Israeli intelligence, who were able to provide helpful information about him. However, in 1990, under the auspices of the Syrian invasion of East Beirut, he managed to escape from his Lebanese prison, where eight years after the murder, he was still awaiting trial. It turned out that the reason for not bringing Shartouni to trial was a technical one. There was simply no court. Lebanon had been in so much chaos that it was not even able to manage its vital institutions with any degree of stability. Shartouni's escape from the dilapidated Lebanese prison had been thanks to the Syrian presence, as the man who carried out the assassination of Lebanon's president in the name of Syria, was freed by that country's emissaries. Only in October 2017 did the murder case reach the court. After a full year of pre-trial hearings and 35 years after the assassination of Bashir Gemayel, the Lebanese court sentenced his killer Habib Tanius Shartouni to death in absentia, as well as Nabil al-Alam, who was convicted of involvement in the murder.

Bashir Gemayel's assassination caused great concern in Israel. The day after his murder, IDF infantry entered Lebanon to capture key points in western Beirut, so as to prevent a bloody confrontation between Christian Phalangists and Muslims. Two days after the murder of Bashir, on 16 September 1982, Phalangists entered the Muslim refugee camps of Sabra and Shatila, where their fighters carried out a pitiless two-day massacre of its occupants. Hundreds of Muslims living in the Sabra, Shatila, and two more Palestinian refugee camps in western Beirut, were killed. This was not the first massacre during the Lebanese civil war, as it had already been preceded by other massacres, such as

President Bashir Gemayel's successor Amin Gemayel with United States President George W. Bush.

those in the town of Damour and the Tel a-Za'atar refugee camp. Unlike its predecessors, however, the massacre in Sabra and Shatila provoked a significant reaction from around the world. It turned out that Syrian President Hafez al-Assad agreed to help the Christian Phalangists to carry out the massacre in order to embarrass Israel, assuming that the world would blame Israel for it because of the IDF presence in West Beirut. The Israeli infantries did not in fact enter the Sabra and Shatila refugee camps but remained around their perimeter. Indeed, the Syrian plot succeeded, as the massacre provoked strong condemnation of Israel around the world and a demand from Israel to immediately withdraw all its forces from Lebanon. The Lebanese government released a statement confirming that a total of 460 people had been killed in the Sabra and Shatila camps; 320 of them had been Palestinian civilians, and the rest were Lebanese and Syrian.

As if the murder of Bashir Gemayel and his little daughter Maya were not enough, in November 2006 fate struck the Gemayel family once again. Pierre Gemayel, the 34-year-old son of Amin, a brilliant and charismatic politician, who served as Lebanese Minister of Industry and aspired to the presidency, was shot and killed in Beirut. Pierre was known as one of the fiercest opponents of the Syrian occupation of Lebanon, and never hesitated to voice his outspoken views about this. Just a few years earlier, he had taken the bold step of returning to Lebanon from exile in France, where his entire family had moved to following the Syrian takeover. Pierre's death caused great fear to seep into the heart of this dynastic political family, the destiny of whose members was to be killed on the altar of leadership of a divided and conflicted state. Their fate was reminiscent of that of the American Kennedy family.

11

The Lebanon War
of June 1982

In the summer of 1982, Defense Minister Ariel Sharon had presented Prime Minister Menachem Begin with a plan for a limited operation in Lebanon to put an end to the constant terrorist attacks against northern Israel from southern Lebanon, and to eliminate the terror organizations' operational capability by destroying their headquarters and underground structures. Little did Sharon, nor the prime minister, realize that a can of worms was about to be opened.

The plan was to capture a wide stretch of land, extending to 25 miles into Lebanon, just beyond the Litani river. At the same time, the Israelis would take over the Beirut to Damascus road in the east, which was being used by Syrian forces to enter Lebanon, although it was not in the plan to reach the Lebanese capital of Beirut. The goal was to rid the designated area of terrorists' nests and, together with the UNIFIL forces, keep southern Lebanon free of terrorists and the Syrian forces that were encouraging and supporting them. But in reality, as the "limited" operation progressed, the IDF advanced a far greater distance, due to the discovery of numerous well-fortified terrorist bases hidden within the civilian population. In practice, we the fighters found ourselves advancing much deeper into Lebanon, well beyond the distance of 25 miles in the original plan. We gained control of the coastal towns of Tyre and Sidon, after fierce house to house battles where we came face to face with PLO terrorists who were embedded in these urban areas, and using civilians as human shields. What began as a 25-mile Israeli military operation against the activities of Palestinian organizations based in Lebanon, led to us becoming embroiled in a war with the Syrians, to the Israeli occupation of most parts of Beirut, to the establishment of Hezbollah and to a bloody 18-year defeat in the Lebanese mire, which claimed the lives of 1,216 IDF soldiers and injured countless others.

The plan to eradicate all terrorists from southern Lebanon was laid on the table of both the Israeli security council and political Cabinet months before its actual implementation in June 1982. Prime Minister Begin praised the plan but suggested waiting for the right timing to carry it out, so as not to create hostile global public opinion which would accuse Israel of invading Lebanon. On 3 June 1982, three members of the Abu Nidal terror organization ambushed Shlomo Argov, the Israeli Ambassador to the United Kingdom. One of the three terrorists, Hussein Ghassan, shot Mr. Argov in the head as he was getting into his car after a banquet at the Dorchester Hotel in London. Argov was not killed, but he was critically injured and remained in a coma for months. This was the timing Israel had been waiting for.

After many discussions in the Israeli Cabinet, it was agreed to deploy an extensive military force which would enter Lebanon from its south to eradicate the terrorist threats from there once and for all. Prime Minister Menachem Begin, together with Chief of Staff Rafael Eitan, and with the encouragement of Defense Minister Ariel Sharon, recommended to the Cabinet to approve Sharon's plan to invade southern Lebanon. Those attending this meeting agreed that the objectives of the operation were threefold:

1. The elimination of the terrorist organizations' headquarters throughout Lebanon to remove the constant threat to the citizens of northern Israel.

Waiting for the order to enter southern Lebanon.

2. To hit and cause severe damage to the Syrian military force. The Israeli Air Force would destroy the Syrian armaments and missiles in the Lebanon Valley, thus ending the Syrian influence in Lebanon and its support and arming of terrorist organizations.
3. To help the Christian militias end the civil war within Lebanon, and in the establishment of a westernized Lebanese state with a stable regime that would agree to sign a peace agreement with Israel.

At the same Cabinet meeting, Ariel Sharon revealed that he had been in contact over the recent months with a Christian leader in Lebanon named Bashir Gemayel, who was planning to run in the forthcoming presidential election. The Mossad, which had begun developing these ties a year earlier, had been helping to strengthen Gemayel's status in Lebanon. Sharon, who was a dominant force in the Cabinet meeting, recommended the Israeli government help prepare Bashir's path to the presidency. Sharon saw him as the most favorable candidate due to his Westernized views, and as someone who would potentially sign a peace agreement with Israel, whom Gemayel did not regard as the Zionist enemy to be eliminated.

On June 4, 1982, the day after the assassination attempt on Ambassador Argov, the Israeli Air Force attacked terrorist concentrations in southern Lebanon. This was a softening and weakening assault in order to prepare the way for us, the ground forces.

This happened after my three years of compulsory service which I had completed in 1978. I had become used to the life of being an ordinary citizen, focusing on planning my future and studying at university. It never occurred to me for a moment that I would return to fight on the soil of Lebanon that I knew as well as the back of my hand. A soil that had been left scorched and bleeding from both internal and external wars, a constantly burning soil whose flora had ceased being green. Just the thought of being there again as a warrior, not as a tourist, began to send shivers down my spine and generated a feeling of disgust. "I'm only 25 for God's sake," I told myself. I wanted to laugh, dance, celebrate, party and enjoy the wonderful relationship I had with my stunningly beautiful and intelligent girlfriend. I was not at all happy to have to deal again with those familiar fears and anxieties of war. A war that was going to be carried out mostly by infantry fighters in face-to-face battles, inside dark rooms, in homes that would surely be inhabited by innocent civilians. I did not want this anymore. But my hands were tied. I must obey orders, and yes, strange as it may sound, I was willing to die for my constantly attacked country.

I had been assigned to a reserve battalion composed of fighters aged between 22 and 29, men of my age group, who found themselves again being sent into Lebanon's fields of fire. This time, we were joined by young Golani Brigade soldiers, who were stationed in the Golan Heights for defensive operational activity. My reserve battalion also joined with the forces in the Galilee Division (91), which consisted of brigades and battalions of infantry and artillery, plus platoons of engineering and sabotage forces, intelligence personnel and medical teams and combat and transport helicopters.

The invasion of Lebanon began when we, a substantial combined IDF force, crossed the Lebanese border and headed north, through the southern part of the Lebanon Valley, towards the town of Damour. In the blue skies above us, we noted the presence of Israeli fighter jets that instilled confidence in us. The waters of the Mediterranean were also being utilized, with our navy ships transporting some of our infantry and their equipment towards the beautiful shores of Tyre, Sidon and Beirut, in order to accelerate the progress of our forces as much as possible to the areas where the terrorists had fortified themselves.

There was a feeling in the air that we, the reserve fighters, wanted to complete in this short war what we couldn't during our compulsory service during the years 1975 to 1978. And that was to finally eradicate the terrorist infrastructure in Lebanon. Although we found ourselves stuck in this new conflagration for three consecutive months, we all felt a deep responsibility towards the Israeli citizens living in the north of the country, who were the real victims of the

Me on a break during the Lebanon War. Mount Hermon is in the background.

terror from Lebanon. The incessant bloody terrorist attacks, that not only caused loss of life, injury and anxiety, but also completely disrupted these people's entire daily routine. We knew that these desperate people were pinning their hopes on us, the Golani fighters, who had defended them for more than 30 years.

The war began.

On June 9, as we made our way north towards Sidon, we unexpectedly ran into Syrian commando and armored forces, as well as a group of PLO terrorists who were sheltering like cowards behind the Syrians. We realized that the Syrian force, which was well trained and equipped, would prevent us from advancing north of the Litani river to complete the 25-mile distance we were expected to achieve. This hurdle led to fierce and uncompromising combat between us and the Syrian commandos; heavy battles in which we lost dozens of fighters who showed exceptional courage and devotion to the mission. I must admit that the Syrians fought with much more professionalism and bravery than their terrorist comrades did. We had to call for aid from our Air Force. In retrospect, I can assume with certainty, that without the help of our fighter jets, we would not have won the tough battles against the Syrians, even though in the eyes of our commanders, we fought with heroism and exceptional professionalism. It's hard to compliment the enemy, but I feel the need to be loyal to my inner truth.

However, despite my thoughts on the professionalism of the Syrians, the result in the field did not flatter them. The battles between our air force and the Syrian commandos, as we progressed north deeper into Lebanon, embarrassed the Syrian president Hafez Al-Assad. Around 20 Syrian artillery and air missiles were destroyed, and 47 Syrian fighter jets were shot down by the Israeli jets over the Lebanon Valley. This was an astonishingly brilliant operation during which not a single Israeli jet was lost, and emphasized Israel's absolute air superiority over the Syrian Air Force. According to senior Israeli Air Force officials, this battle was considered one of its most important ever operations, and one that significantly shaped the IAF's character.

After vanquishing the Syrian commandos, the combined IDF force managed to reach the Beirut-Damascus road. Some of our forces entered into the city of Beirut itself to eliminate the PLO's main bases located there. Meanwhile, my own force moved westward towards the coastal town of Sidon. We remained there for many weeks engaged in continuous fighting in the crowded and densely populated refugee camps around the town, mainly in the Ein al-Hilweh camp. The battles were, as we had expected, complicated by the presence of Lebanese civilians and children, who were trapped between us and the terrorists, who were shooting at us from their houses. It was assumed that these civilians were held captive in their homes against their will by the terrorists, who took advantage of the fact that Israeli soldiers would not shoot in the direction of anywhere they suspected the presence of unarmed people. The moral dilemma inside the notorious Ein al-Hilweh refugee camp was now doubled and even further complicated. Rumor was spreading among our fighters that in this particular camp, not only were the terrorists using civilians as human shields, but there were also children, who had agreed to pretend they were being held against their will in return for considerable sums of money. This was proved to be correct after external, non–Israeli sources examined incidents that had taken place in the two years prior to the Lebanon war. We were confused by this and forced to fight at a slower and more careful pace than usual, and to shoot as precisely as if the target were under a magnifying glass, tactics that were causing us to further endanger our own lives. "I wonder if the outside world knows about these situations," I pondered to myself. I doubted it. The world only sees the bodies of Palestinians civilians but does not know which side sacrificed them, and most importantly, which side was careful not to shoot them.

On June 13, after our complex and extra-cautionary fighting in the Ein al-Hilweh camp, we arrived at Beirut along with some of the other forces from our division. We were ordered to besiege the city. During

Final preparations at the base before entering Lebanon.

this 70-day siege, we endured fierce battles some very crowded residential neighborhoods, where it was difficult for us to distinguish between the enemy and innocent civilians, since everyone was wearing civilian clothes. The cowardly terrorists chose not to dress in their combat fatigues so they could deceive us, as we, from our long experience with them, knew for sure that they possessed uniforms. Yet, despite the challenging limitations of fighting with civilians nearby, and the mounting numbers of dead and wounded among our force, we continued to tighten our grip on the city of Beirut and clear the terrorists out of the city, eventually forcing Yasser Arafat and his PLO to leave Lebanon. During the course of the fighting, Beirut Airport and many buildings throughout the city were destroyed.

At the end of these three months of fierce combat covering almost all areas of Lebanon, thousands of terrorists from all the terror organizations established in the country were killed. The IDF lost 368 soldiers. The organization that suffered the most losses was the PLO. In the light of the resulting situation, especially after it became clear to Yasser Arafat that he had lost more than a thousand of his fighters and most of his infrastructure had been destroyed, he expressed his readiness for negotiations. The United States was required to mediate and called for the PLO to withdraw completely from Lebanon. Arafat, for his part, agreed to negotiate in an attempt to rescue his forces from this political disaster; an attempt that resulted in the arrival of an international force which evacuated the PLO fighters to the Tunisian capital of Tunis.

In mid–August, an agreement had also been reached to expel the Syrian and Palestinian forces from Beirut, a move that left the city under IDF control until the area could be stabilized by diplomatic means. While waiting for the evacuation process to be carried out, the Lebanese Christian leader Bashir Gemayel was elected president on August 23. Israel saw his election as a political breakthrough and Israeli Defense Minister Ariel Sharon stated that the signing of a peace agreement with Lebanon was imminent. Gemayel himself did not get to sit in the presidency for long. By September 14, Gemayel had been assassinated. By way of revenge, Christian Phalangist militia entered the Palestinian refugee camps of Sabra and Shatila and killed hundreds of local Muslim civilians. During that volatile period, we, the exhausted reservists stationed at our makeshift base in southern Beirut, were receiving hints that we were about to be sent home and released from duty, perhaps as early as September 13. While waiting for our discharge, we were patrolling and protecting the locals from Muslim militants who were willing to kill anyone who looked Christian.

In our understanding as fighters, the main reason for the war in Lebanon was the elimination of Palestinian terrorism. However, there were other principal objectives that had been agreed by the decision makers at the political and security level, as well as the United States. Something that was not shared with us at the time. After all, we were merely the pawns in the chessboard of the powers that be.

The First Reason

It transpired that this related back to the bloody Lebanese civil war in 1975 between the Christians, and a coalition of terrorist organizations and Muslim radical groups, which had ultimately led to the collapse of the Lebanese government and its army. This had created chaos and an existential threat to the Christian populations in northern and southern Lebanon, and to the Christian political hegemony. Israel had looked on the Christian militias as a partner in the war on terror and had therefore armed and assisted them. When the terror from southern Lebanon intensified, Israel felt that the Christian militias would not be capable of fighting the terrorist organizations alone, hence the invasion of south Lebanon with the aim of eliminating the growing terror infrastructure there.

The Christian militias saw these Muslim terrorist organizations as a cruel external enemy who had no historical grip on Lebanon. And so, they desperately wanted to expel them from Lebanese soil, an interest they had in common with Israel.

There was another symbolic motive as to why Israel chose to assist the Christian militias. This dated back to 1948 and the early months of the young Jewish state, when the Christians who ruled Lebanon had helped to smuggle weapons and equipment through southern Lebanon into Israel in exchange for sums of money. Czechoslovakia in the days of its Communist leader Marshal Tito, as well as France and Britain, had agreed to sell Israel obsolete weapons that were stored in warehouses after the end of World War II. Israel, which had just been established, desperately needed these weapons to deal with the threat from its three belligerent neighboring Arab countries. Delivering these weapons via the sea or by air was impossible. The only viable option was to smuggle them to Israel by land, and the only friendly adjacent soil Israel had in those days was Lebanon. In those years, the Christians completely controlled Lebanon, and Beirut was known as "the Paris of the Middle East," with millions of tourists visiting it each year to enjoy its beautiful beaches, luxurious hotels and vibrant night life.

The Second Reason

After 1975 (and up until 2005), Syria deepened its presence and influence in Lebanon, taking advantage of the punishing civil war that had disrupted the Lebanese establishment. The Lebanese army was easily crushed due to the defection of fighters and officers, who had gone to join the dozens of different militias and groups fighting each other for the control of Lebanon. Syria understood very well how to fill the vacuum by asserting her presence and promising to help return order to Lebanon, but in actual fact, Syrian intentions were not solely to help the fractured country, but to take control of it. Syria had proclaimed many times that historically the land of Lebanon had actually belonged to her since the dawn of history. However, Israel was not interested in historic territorial claims, nor in the ownership of Lebanon. Israel simply wanted to ensure peace and security for its own citizens.

Israel was aware of Syria's support and encouragement for the terrorist organizations that attacked her, hence Israel's intention was to weaken, even if just temporarily, the Syrian presence and influence in Lebanon, and if necessary, to remove all Syrian forces from its soil, either militarily or by diplomatic efforts. Despite Israel's warnings, the Syrian influence in Lebanon did managed to weaken the Christian militias, and strengthened the power of Lebanon's Shi'ite Muslims, who were Syria's dependents and doers. This subsequently led to the birth of the brutal Shi'ite terrorist organization Hezbollah, which filled the void created in southern Lebanon after the 1982 war once the two dominant terror organizations, the Abu Nidal Organization and the PLO, had disintegrated. While the members of Yasser Arafat's organization were deported to Tunisia, the ANO fighters fled east to Iraq. Once there, its founder and leader Abu Nidal set up another terrorist organization after having major disagreements with Yasser Arafat. In August 2002, Abu Nidal was assassinated by Saddam Hussein's soldiers in Baghdad.

The Third Reason

On April 29, 1981, the Syrians deployed long-range SA-6 surface-to-air missiles to the Lebanon Valley. These missiles had the capacity to reach any corner of Israel and beyond. Israel felt seriously threatened and could not countenance this aggressive move by Syria. A crisis was beginning to unfold. The presence of the Syrian long-range missiles obstructed the Israeli Air Force's ability to control the airspace of south Lebanon and to continue its mission to clear up terrorism in the area. The IDF's ground forces were now also limited in their protracted actions against terrorist organizations, not only around the Lebanon Valley, but all over the south of Lebanon. What made the situation worse, and prompted great concern on the Israeli side, were the public statements by Syria encouraging terrorist organizations throughout the whole of Lebanon to intensify the armed struggle against Israel, and that they, the Syrians, would be happy to support them with unlimited financial resources. Israel's Cabinet was convened at night to discuss the Syrian threat. One of the ministers expressed concern that a war on the Syrian front could only be a matter of hours. The Israeli army began preparations for war.

At the same time, U.S. President Ronald Reagan sent his special envoy Philip Habib to the area to try to (a) persuade the Syrians to remove the missiles from Lebanon, and (b) persuade Israel not to invade Lebanon and certainly not to attack the Syrian missiles. But Syria stubbornly refused to accede. Not only did they close their ears to what the U.S. envoy Habib presented to them, but they continued to issue explicit threats against Israel. In one of their threats, they even suggested they would welcome a comprehensive war with Israel in order to take advantage of the opportunity to conquer the Israeli-held area of the Golan Heights.

Although the Syrians did not fire one of these missiles at Israel, they left them in place for many months to pose a threat to Israel. A year after they were positioned there, they were another reason for Israel's invasion of Lebanon.

The Fourth Reason

The heated situation that had risen from the Syrian missiles in the Lebanon Valley led to a further flourish of diplomatic activity. Thus, on July 24, 1981, after many weeks of negotiations, the American mediator Philip Habib succeeded in breaking down the stubbornness of the PLO terrorists. Their activities were stilled through a ceasefire agreement between Israel and all the terrorist organizations in Lebanon, especially the PLO. Sadly, it turned out that this agreement was a smokescreen, as the terrorist organizations had no real intention of implementing it. They had agreed to the ceasefire to buy themselves some time to reorganize and re-arm. After the Israeli success of Operation Litani in 1978, when the PLO's morale and operational capacity was totally undermined, Arafat and his organization had nonetheless managed to equip, rearm and re-establish itself in southern Lebanon. Now they enjoyed the support of Syria, Iraq and Iran. Arafat chose to violate the 1981 cease-fire agreement after he "discovered" a loophole in it, which he cunningly exploited. The agreement was proving to be problematic in the way it was being interpreted.

The signed document was aimed to ensure a state of non-combat between Israel and the PLO, and that its terms would to all territories. It was about the cessation of hostilities, no matter in which geographical location. Thus, while the Israelis argued that the PLO should be banned from mounting attacks against Israel from any country, Arafat's interpretation claimed that the terms of the ceasefire agreement was valid for its attacks on Israel only from the soil of Lebanon, and still allowed the PLO to attack Israel from non–Lebanese territory, such as Jordan or Syria. Moreover, although Arafat explicitly undertook that he would condemn any act of terrorism against Israel, it turned out that his promise was false. He constantly refused to condemn many of acts of terror that were carried out from south Lebanon.

Emboldened by the ambiguity of the agreement, the PLO began to encourage terrorist activity from Syrian territory, and renewed their terrorist attacks against Israel, this time with increased force and the use of more sophisticated weapons. Israel saw this as an example of Arafat's duplicity, and felt not only betrayed, but also threatened. This signaled the first steps leading to the 1982 Lebanon War.

A moment of planning before the onslaught.

The issues outlined above left the State of Israel with no choice but go to war in Lebanon.

However, before the Israeli cabinet would agree to enter Lebanon to conduct a full-scale war, the IDF tried to deal with the terror issue by conducting a series of short military actions. These involved a series of raids both in southern Lebanon and in the capital Beirut (many of which I took part in with my battalion) during which we targeted and destroyed the terrorists' bunkers, at the same time eliminating some of their senior leaders, aided by precision bombing by our air force's fighter jets. But these actions failed to completely paralyze the terrorist activity. Syria's deepening involvement in Lebanon and support of the terrorist organizations, with the collusion of Iran, made our short military actions less effective.

We were still constantly having encounters with terrorists and nearly every night we had to infiltrate southern Lebanon to carry out raids on terrorist targets scattered throughout the area. We were aware of the new weaponry the terrorists were using, thus most of our raids were to target their locations and destroy their armaments and artillery. It turned out that the terrorist organizations, which for years had only been using bazookas and Katyusha rockets for attacking Israel, had received a generous gift from the Syrians. As part of its unlimited and broad support, the Syrians provided the terrorists with new weaponry, including cannons that had far-reaching artillery capability. This method of attacking Israeli population centers by the use of artillery has since been adopted by other terrorist organizations, and would go on to be used by Palestinian organizations operating in the Gaza Strip and then by Hezbollah in Lebanon. These attacks not only caused panic and large numbers of casualties among Israeli civilians, but also completely disrupted their daily lives to the point that a significant number of Israelis in the northern region were forced to abandon their homes.

During one particularly bad period, we found ourselves engaged in fighting the terrorists for three consecutive weeks, sometimes having to use guerrilla tactics. In such cases, they had the advantage over us because they were familiar with the topographic conditions in the area of operation. But we learnt that guerrilla warfare doesn't always have to be to the advantage of the terrorists. This type of engagement can also serve to benefit the attackers as long as they are able to call on their personal skills and not just the weapons at their disposal. We proved this when we came under fire, including from close range, and defeated the terrorists by way of tricks and deception. Sometimes we had to stop ourselves from bursting into laughter during the battle itself when we saw the terrorists' reactions to our wily stunts. Encounters with these amateurish fighters could make us laugh, but on the other hand, they caused us great stress and misery. Not only were we in intense combat activity and not able to sleep more than three hours a night, we were saddened to hear the continuing news about the wounded and killed from the civilian population of northern Israel who were suffering incessant shelling. From my past experiences of engagement with them, I can say that I did not consider these terrorists to be brave warriors or admirable fighters. On each encounter, they would flee the battlefield, or surrender immediately, or worse, use children as human shields. I can only count a few cases where I saw any of them behaving remotely like fighters and squaring up to us, the armed soldiers. Their "heroism" manifested itself by dominating the weak in society, the civilians, children and unarmed women.

When it was found that none of our raids and operations had succeed in eliminating the terror from Lebanon, Israel escalated its response and sent fighter jets to bomb terrorist bases throughout the whole of southern Lebanon. However, despite the extensive destruction of the terrorists' headquarters, both by Israeli jets, and us, the ground forces, the attacks on northern Israel did not diminish. The invasion of Lebanon by a massive combined force was inevitable.

As a freelance journalist at the time, I took advantage of the access I had to protocols from political Cabinet discussions that were not defined as confidential. In one of them, I discovered that in the intensive discussions that the Israeli government had on the issue of the invasion of Lebanon, most members of the government were not happy about it. Most of them, including the prime minister, tried all diplomatic means to prevent a full-scale war in Lebanon, one which they feared could turn out to be a catastrophic bipartisan international war in the area. They were fearful of setting the whole area on fire. Instead, Israel preferred to solve the problem in Lebanon through prudent diplomacy, something the terrorist organizations chose to reject. These organizations showed no sign of ceasing their fight against Israel, and worst of all, they repeatedly declared that their main goal was the elimination of the Jewish entity and the Israel's destruction. These uncompromising pronouncements, which were accompanied by severe terrorist attacks against Israel, were hugely alarming for the Israeli Cabinet. Hence, going to war was deemed to be not only a necessary step, but the right approach for the leaders of the state that was under constant threats.

In the event, the 1982 Lebanon War did bring about some significant achievements. The Syrian army in southern Lebanon was hit hard, the PLO was expelled from Lebanon and established its new headquarters in Tunisia, far away from Israel's borders, and most of the military forces of the smaller Palestinian terrorist organizations were eliminated. Many terrorists were killed, thousands were arrested, and the IDF seized most of their weapons.

I cannot close this chapter on the Lebanon War without sharing with you a tragic drama, the chance of its occurring being perhaps one in a million.

In war, there are many heart-breaking situations involving loss and enduring pain, but we seldom encounter tragedies caused by improbable coincidences, such as for example two close family members dying in the same battle. The following story and its sequence of events, including all the stages that took place during the 24 hours in which the drama unfolded, is an especially rare one; an unfortunate coincidence that resulted in a devastating human error.

The story concerns two Israeli soldiers with exactly the same name, both of whom were aged 19, and who happened to live in the same street, in the same neighborhood, Talpiot in Jerusalem, just a few houses away from each other. These two young men were both killed in action during the same week, in the same battlefield location of the Ein al-Hilweh refugee camp during the Lebanon War. The name they shared was Yuval Harel. One was Yuval Harel who served in the Armored Corps, and the other was Yuval Harel from the paratrooper's force.

The tragedy in this sad story was not about the coincidence of

During a battle inside Lebanese territory.

two killed soldiers having the same name and living in the same neighborhood. It is about the way their families learned of their death when military representatives came to inform them about their beloved sons.

Yuval the paratrooper was killed on Thursday, June 10, 1982, at 12:55 p.m., when Israeli Air Force jets erroneously bombed his force on the eastern side of Ein al-Hilweh. Thirty-four Israeli soldiers were killed by this terrible catastrophe. I was only 100 yards away from the incident and could hear the bomb landing, followed by the pitiful screams of the wounded. My platoon could do nothing to help them since we were engaged in an intense face-to-face battle against dozens of armed terrorists in the crowded alleyways of the camp. Yuval was a soldier in the force of paratroopers whom we were fighting alongside in the refugee camps around Sidon. In Ein al-Hilweh, we were fighting inside the south section of the camp, while Yuval and his force were in the eastern section. They too became involved in a difficult and complex battle due to the overcrowded conditions of the camp and the large number of civilians out on the streets, as they were reluctant to stay inside their shattered homes and there were no shelters where they could find protection. Many of these people were being used by the terrorists as human shields, as they knew the Israeli soldiers would not shoot if unarmed civilians could be endangered. Only half an hour after the bombing, we were shaken by hearing from one of our paramedics about the death of Yuval and the other 33 soldiers. The news spread fear and concern among us. How could our revered Israeli Air Force make such a deadly mistake? Our unit was in deep shock and our morale, and confidence in our own air force, descended to our boots. Would we be the next unit to be attacked from the air by our own fighter jets? Nonetheless, we continued with our mission, fighting in the hellish conditions of the crowded camp.

The other Yuval Harel, from the Armored Corps, was by this time already dead. He had been killed two days earlier on Tuesday, June 8 at 2:30 p.m., when a missile hit his tank as it was breaking through into the terrorist strongholds in the same camp.

On Wednesday morning, June 9, an IDF team who are specially trained for the sensitive role of breaking the news to a family of the death of their loved one, had been sent to the Talpiot neighborhood in Jerusalem, to inform the family of Yuval Harel from the Armored Corps who had been killed the previous day. When the team arrived in the neighborhood, unaware of two families carrying the same name living so close by each other, they were mistakenly directed by neighbors to the home of the wrong Harel family. This was in fact the home of the paratrooper. Thus, they imparted the terrible news to the family of Yuval the paratrooper, who at that time was very much alive. His family began to mourn.

However, when they returned to their base, the team realized to their horror they had gone to the wrong house, which was by sheer coincidence the home of a soldier with the same name also fighting in Lebanon. The team immediately rushed to the Harel family home to apologize, and to inform them that their son had not been killed, and that they were meant to inform the other family named Harel, who happened to live down the road. The family let out a sigh of relief, but mingled with grief as they knew the Harel family down the street. The team then went to the family of Yuval Harel from the Armored Corps and informed them of the sad news.

Meanwhile, the war in Lebanon continued to take its toll. On Thursday June 10, the other Yuval Harel, the paratrooper, was killed. This tragedy, already shocking, now worsens.

On Friday, 11 June, a different team was sent to Talpiot to bring the sad news to the paratrooper's family, who were still recovering from the shock of having been erroneously informed about their "son's death." When the team knocked on their door, the family screamed at the army officials saying that there was a mistake, and that a different team had already visited them and mistakenly informed them of the death of their son, and that they had meant someone else living down the street. But the team, who were already informed about the terrible circumstances of the mistake, told the young paratrooper's family with tears in their eyes, that this time, it was not by accident nor by error. They had come to inform them that their son Yuval had in fact been killed too.

The two soldiers from the Talpiot neighborhood of Jerusalem, who in life had shared the same name, were buried near to each other in the same row of the military cemetery on Mount Herzl in Jerusalem. About a year later, a son was born to another family named Harel living in the neighborhood. He was named Yuval, after the two fallen soldiers.

Several documentaries and songs have appeared in Israel over the years to tell this remarkable story. One film relates a minor, but telling, incident from Yuval's (from the Armored Corps) life. When he was just four years of age, the Harel family was living in Canada as his father was working there temporarily. One day Yuval became separated from his parents in a crowded shopping mall. With great resourcefulness, little Yuval managed to locate the "Lost and Found" office in the mall. Once inside, the tiny boy grabbed the announcement microphone and addressed his father in Hebrew: "Dad, I'm at the Lost and Found."

Throughout all the years that have passed since then, and even today, I have not been able to stop thinking about what this family went through on that day.

12

The Undercover Mista'arvim

Mista'arvim is the generic name for the undercover units operating in the IDF. In 1986, General Ehud Barak raised the idea of establishing a modern and more sophisticated "Mista'arvim" undercover unit called "Duvdevan." Duvdevan was the first unit to be much improved on the previously less professional undercover units operating since the 1940s.

"I want us to form a unit whose fighters will look, talk, and dress like Arabs, and ride their bikes around the streets of the Gaza Strip and West Bank as casually as if they were on Dizengoff Street in Tel Aviv, conducting quiet acts with a pistol hidden underneath their clothes," Ehud Barak told his senior commanders during a General Staff meeting to discuss an effective and stealthy way of combatting the escalation of terrorism from Gaza and the West Bank.

By stating "quiet acts," General Barak was referring to individual combat, face-to-face, with very close contact with the enemy, without the aid of large weapons. A small combat unit, which could strike without the need for large and noisy forces, such as artillery, tanks, or fighter jets. Ehud Barak was one of the most highly decorated soldiers in Israel's army, having taken part in many battles and combat missions. Despite his high rank and the esteem he was held in by the military, he had nonetheless taken part in operations posing as an ordinary soldier, and on occasions had been disguised as a woman, a teenage boy, and as a vegetable seller working at a stall in Jenin's market. In 1999, this "vegetable seller" went on to become the tenth Prime Minister of Israel.

Mista'arvim are trained commandos who operate undercover by posing as Arabs, both in their appearance and by speaking fluent Arabic. They assimilate among the local Arab population to capture wanted terrorists, gather information and help other combat units when fighting. They dress as Arabs, are fully conversant with the customs and etiquette of Arab society and are able to recite Muslim prayers by heart. Their Arabic is so fluent, that they even learn to speak it in the appropriate dialects and accents. Refining the accent may sound a minor detail but is crucial because the Arabic language has many different accents and dialects, which vary from one Arab country to another, and from one neighborhood to another in those countries. Furthermore, even the Palestinians, who are the main enemy with whom this unit interacts, have different types of accents. The Palestinians living in Gaza speak with a totally different accent from those who are from the West Bank. While assimilating among the local Arab population, the Mista'arvim are commonly tasked with performing intelligence gathering, law enforcement, hostage rescue and counterterrorism, and to use disguise and make up as their main weapons to accomplish their missions.

The Mista'arvim operated away from the public eye, maintaining uncompromising secrecy, hiding the true nature of their dangerous work. Preparation for a specific undercover action usually begins when intelligence information is received about a particular person or persons, who are involved in terror activity and wanted for interrogation by the Israel's intelligence. Or their undercover action would be to kill terrorists who are about to carry out an attack on Israel. In the second stage, several experienced Mista'arvim who know the area well from previous "visits," are sent to search for and sniff out important clues and information about the wanted persons. Another reason for choosing experienced ones is that they will already be familiar in their guise as "locals" to some of the civilian population, and even to local police and

Israeli undercover activity among Palestinian rioters. The Mista'arvim undercover agents are wearing white hats to prevent being shot by friendly fire.

security personnel, and therefore will not cause suspicion. There was an operation in which a very senior officer in the unit was sent, something not usually done in battles or in war, as he happened to be very well known among the locals as a distinguished "Muslim businessman," and because of his familiarity with the entire area. The third step will be carried out according to the results of the information obtained. If the information was insufficient, the operation to capture the wanted terrorists would be postponed for another time, but if the information was concrete, then the unit's fighters would be sent to carry out the mission, using us, the infantry fighters, as an auxiliary and backup force.

In formal terms, the undercover unit is called Mista'arvim. However, during operations and radio communication, or during the planning and training stages, they would be known as "the Colored" (referencing their civilian clothes) and we, the commando backup force who wear the military uniforms, would be called "the Greens."

Another dangerous mission the Mista'arvim undertook was to assimilate among a crowd of Palestinian protesters, pretending to "support" the protests as if they were demonstrators. They dressed as local protestors by wearing kaffiyehs around their necks and vigorously waving Palestinian flags. Hidden under their clothing as a precaution would always be a pistol. Their presence at public demonstrations can help the Israeli military and the "Shabak," Israel's intelligence and security service (known as "Shin Bet" during the 1950s) to identify protesters they wished to arrest and interrogate. During their uprisings, when Palestinians in the West Bank or Gaza would take to the streets and start throwing stones and Molotov cocktails, the fighters of the Mista'arvim would skillfully merge into the rioters. They would find and arrest wanted terrorists, particularly those whose status and role obliged them to take a prominent part in such demonstrations. Despite the danger of such an action, putting their head directly into the lion's mouth, these are welcome opportunities for the Mista'arvim to obtain a definite identification and successfully apprehend their targets among the crowd of demonstrators. These brave undercovers excelled in their assimilation ability, utilizing their acting talents and high self-confidence over the three or more consecutive hours of "participating in a demonstration," despite being acutely aware of the mortal danger they were in if their identities were to be exposed. Seemingly, a dangerous undertaking like this, placing themselves in the heart of a hostile crowd which could at any moment lead to their being brutally lynched, seems crazy, but the men of the Mista'arvim were born to be abnormal.

The word Mista'arvim comes from the Arabic term "Asta'areb," which describes a situation where non–Arabs assimilate into an Arab environment and adopt its customs. Historically this refers to the Musta'arabi Jews, Arabic-speaking Jews who had lived in the Middle East since the beginning of the Arab rule of the 7th century. In order to integrate into Arab society, these Jews dressed as Arabs, spoke their language, and adopted their customs. And thus, allowed themselves a more comfortable, sociable, conflict-free life with the Arab community. Many years later, during the 1940s, Jews who lived in Palestine, during the British Mandate, used the "Asta'areb" to form several underground organizations and counter-movements to fight the British occupation.

During an activity within a hostile crowd, whether to capture or kill a wanted terrorist, or simply to gather information, the fighter, being only flesh and blood, will naturally feel the fear seeping into his heart. As with anything that carries such danger, at first, the fighter may feel anxious and stressed, convinced that everyone is watching him and examining his moves, and that he is the focal point of all that's going on around him. The fear of being exposed is always there. This is why a high level of alertness, and a massive surge of adrenalin, are prevalent while the fighter is in route to the target, and whenever he arrives at a new location. Because of this, the exposure of the Mista'arvim fighter to the area is introduced gradually, so he can carefully acclimatize himself to the situation around him and begin to gain confidence. The most critical moment in an operation is when the disguised fighter transforms himself from a passive local citizen into the functioning fighter who has to arrest, or shoot the wanted terrorist; the inconspicuous Clark Kent morphs into the Superman role. The moment of transformation begins with an agreed signal directly from the commander in the field, or from the Command Squad stationed on location or back at the base. At this moment, the surprise factor is invaluable. The fighter has to be the first to act and gain the upper hand, being the one who creates chaos in the arena, exploits the confusion and performs the mission. Agility is also important. If fighters are exposed and cause a commotion to happen around them, they must be immediately on top of it and lose no time in reacting. Every minute counts, as there have been many occasions that fighters who were exposed have been stabbed or lynched. I have witnessed those horrifying situations many times when we, the "Greens," were called on to rescue Mista'arvim who had been exposed.

Problems can arise when there is an excess of self-confidence among some members of the unit, perhaps following a series of successful operations. Their commanders are well aware of this possibility and are constantly instilling in the fighters not to become complacent, but rather to keep their instincts and senses fully honed, as well as their readiness for rapid action.

A fighter from the Mista'arvim undercover unit catches a wanted terrorist while we, the "Greens," secure him.

I can testify that overconfidence and excessive complacency barely existed among commando units like us. We were trained to avoid this by being exposed to many different situations and scenarios. It was imprinted on our brain that a calm, quiet and seemingly comfortable situation can quickly change, as it could simply have been the calm before a storm, a storm that can spell personal disaster for a soldier or a national catastrophe for the country we are protecting. Even after many days of seeing no sign of suspicious activity on our border patrols and other missions, we were always far removed from any feeling of complacency. We did not need our commanders ordering or instructing us in this. We had learned this in the earliest training stages of our service, in those three months which would determine whether we would remain or be removed from the unit. I remember a particularly annoying exercise to test our readiness for action. On cold nights, we would be woken from our beauty sleep, ordered to get dressed in full combat gear within 60 seconds, and await our orders outside, shivering and shocked by the panic of waking up, half dozing, but nonetheless, ready to storm any target.

Adherence to this concept of constant alertness was uncompromising among all commanders and fighters. It was embedded within us. The level of individual and company readiness was so high that sometimes in training we felt we were involved in a real battle, performing with such perfect precision that it gave the feeling of authenticity. Yes, I got very upset when I was forced to get out of a warm and deep sleep, and sent out into the freezing cold of the Golan Heights in mid–February, only to discover it was just an exercise to strengthen my alertness, and train me to be ready in a minute to perform my role as a commando fighter. However, it did not take long for such miserable feelings to subside, due to the atmosphere of seriousness, maturity and responsibility pervading among us the fighters. The resentment of being woken in the middle of the night would usually pass once we were standing erect, dressed and in gear, listening out for the command to get moving. What guided our thoughts was that great sense of national responsibility, the feeling of being on a sacred and supreme mission. I was after all training to be a combat soldier who would be taking an active part in the protection of civilians, as well as the national security of the country I was ready to die for.

During my reserve service in the 1980s, I had the pleasure of taking part in the activities of these special Mista'arvim fighters. Although it was a minor part, at least it gave me the opportunity to see up close their awe-inspiring activities. This was during the Palestinian Intifada (uprising) of 1987, when I was already in my reserve service period. My company was stationed in Ramallah and Hebron, where most of the violent activity by the locals was concentrated. We were attacked with stones, Molotov cocktails, and even gunfire. The outbreak of the first Intifada, in December 1987, was the culmination of a lengthy set of circumstances during which many factors of distress and frustration had been accumulating, and which eventually erupted into rage. The first Intifada proved to be a turning point in Israel's policy in the West Bank and Gaza Strip. Security officials did not initially recognize that this was in fact the beginning of a widespread and ongoing popular uprising, nor that these local riots were limited in scope and timing. Once the characteristics of the new struggle were identified, Israel, as a democratic state which was a signatory to international treaties, found it difficult to decide what steps to take in terms of the ethical and moral codes in dealing with the sudden violence by civilians. During this uprising, the level of activity of all the intelligence and undercover units was very high and extremely intense, higher than that of the ground forces, as it was necessary for them to cover all civilian riots throughout the West Bank and Gaza Strip. The Mista'arvim fighters would return to their base after one dangerous activity and would immediately be called to another.

Because of the collaborative operations my platoon and I had with the Mista'arvim during that period, I was able to learn about this unit from almost every angle. Being a commando fighter myself, I was able to analyze their combat methodology to the point where I could read their thoughts at critical moments during a dangerous situation. Over time, I befriended some of them, in fact five of them became long time close friends of mine during our reserve service as combatants, both on the operational and personal level, as we were all pretty much the same age, talking voraciously about our shared passion for music, football and beautiful girls. Nevertheless, I felt I was not one of them. To me, they were special fighters, crazy guys with rare abilities. They were men who were easy to admire and draw inspiration from. One of my five friends was Moti. I once asked him to describe the feeling of being in close-range contact with terrorists, so I could compare this with my own. This is what he told me, "In one operation, I was very close to a terrorist who was about to carry out a deadly attack in Jerusalem. Before I shot him, I took five seconds to think about the powerful feeling to be this close to a living person, who in a few seconds will no longer be alive. A living creature, who will not be able to carry out his evil plot to kill innocent children and civilians. It was a supreme feeling that gave me a tremendous sense of satisfaction and a sense of being God."

I could easily relate to what he said. Although when I was in situations like this, I did not have the opportunity to think about the death of the terrorist I was about to shoot at close range. If I had not shot first, then he would have shot me.

I have to admit that I sometimes harbored feelings of jealousy towards the Mista'arvim. I so wanted to be part of them. The level of risk and challenge they experienced on each of their missions, even the most minor, definitely attracted me, even though in some of the operations in which we cooperated, it was us Golani commandos who acted with the greater heroism. On one occasion, it was men from our unit who saved the lives of two Mista'arvim whose cover had been exposed, and were at the point of being lynched by locals in one of the crowded streets of Ramallah. In some operations we not only saved the lives of some of our Mista'arvim comrades, but also achieved results that advanced their mission far beyond expectations. Nevertheless, I have always felt that the role of these undercover fighters was more fascinating, exciting and dangerous than my role as a commando combatant. I felt that the fear I experienced in hundreds of situations and combat activity within my battalion was not quite the same fear as that experienced by the fighters of the Mista'arvim.

While I could feel protected by fighters from my platoon during combat, knowing I was fully equipped with an automatic rifle, grenades, and a shoulder-fired missile, and with backup when necessary from fighter jets, tanks and artillery, the fighter of the Mista'arvim is armed only with a pistol, acts almost alone, albeit with perhaps another five or six Mista'arvim accomplices and perhaps with help from a distance from us the "Greens." Still, the level of danger is undoubtedly higher among the undercover fighter compared to ours.

The skills needed by a Mista'arvim fighter varies from situation to situation and from operation to operation. He is actually an actor, performing not to a cultured and receptive audience in a relaxed theater venue, but exposing himself to an audience that could end his life at any moment, whether it be with a knife, gun, or by lynching. Each fighter undergoes a counter-terrorism course, training in petty warfare while remaining undercover, and is taught the speedy and clinical use of hot and cold weapons (hot meaning a gun or pistol, and cold meaning a knife or sword). Fighters also learn how to fall back on the techniques of "Krav Maga" (a combination of boxing, wrestling and martial arts developed by the IDF), fluency in the Arabic language, disguise and, when necessary, makeup. Other crucial competences are surveillance and ambush, navigation, and how to move about naturally and calmly in the midst of a crowd without arousing suspicion, especially in areas where almost all locals know each other. For this, training takes place in commonplace locations, such as a large market, a bustling street, a town center square and in cafes and restaurants. The use of cosmetic products for disguise is taught by a professional makeup artist, and the acting lessons are given by a professional acting coach, these two experts in their respective fields having been granted a high security classification by the state. Each of the fighters has his own set of costumes that he uses for disguise depending on the type of the mission and location. They are trained to transform themselves very quickly, as they could be called upon to act with minimal time to plan or prepare for the action. In some situations, the martial art of Krav Maga turned out to be a very valuable weapon for these fighters, sometimes more than a knife or pistol. There are situations where a fighter from the Mista'arvim will not be carrying a weapon when he is surrounded by, or face to face with, the enemy. These are the situations where he knew he would be subjected to a body search as he entered the target area, whether he was going into that area to gather information or lay the ground for an assault by an IDF force who were waiting a short distance away. If he is to go unarmed, the fighter sent in would be one with substantial body strength and physicality, and with exceptional skills in the noble art of Krav Maga.

These fighters are trained to confront an armed terrorist with a pistol, or just with their bare hands. Each one of the fighters comes to know the enemy area they are assigned to as if they were born there. They learn the name of each intersection and square. They check out all the restaurants and cafes and can even recommend which one serves the tastiest food. Their mastery of the language means they can listen out for the latest gossip circulating around each village, such as who is about to get married and who is the meanest person in town. If they need to be mobile, they would be sure to drive the make of vehicle that is most popular in that town. The fighters move around in civilian vehicles but change the license plates depending on the location and the mission. Unlike "Green" soldiers, an undercover fighter has been granted a special military permit allowing him to operate in civilian clothes and with an unshaven appearance.

Aside from physical fitness and excellent health, fighters of the Mista'arvim are required to have unique personal qualities and character traits such as remarkable courage, patience, alertness, self-confidence and charisma, and his natural acting skills ensure the fighter will play his role as convincingly as possible. It is like sending a spy into the depths of enemy territory; hence he must have the ability to improvise and invent solutions in a second, especially in stressful situations where death seems inevitable. The use of various disguises provides the fighter with some degree of protection, even if it is momentary. They can be disguised as an old man, a tourist, a student, a taxi driver, but the most preferred one is as a woman.

"Why a woman?" I once asked my friend Moti.

"To be disguised as a woman in the Arab sector is very safe," he smiled surreptitiously. "There is a custom in the Muslim world for a man not to look at a woman's face in public places. Picture this, the target I am following in order to eliminate him, is sitting at a café in the town square. I approach the café disguised as an ordinary middle-aged Muslim woman. I'm carrying on my head a basket full of vegetables, which is a normal sight on every Muslim street. But inside the basket, in amongst the vegetables, is my loaded pistol. Do you think he, the target, would suspect anything? He would continue to happily drink his coffee, even as the woman walks right by him. Then, at the perfectly timed moment, the basket 'falls' off my head. As expected, locals would come up and offer to gather up the vegetables scattered all over the ground. I'm also picking up my vegetables, except that I, unlike the nice gentlemen who have come to my aid, am the only one who knows that among the peppers, cucumbers and tomatoes, there is also a pistol wrapped in a paper bag, which is marked in Arabic with the word 'flour'. I grab the 'flour bag', pull out the loaded pistol and shoot my target."

Moti had an amazing resemblance to an Arab, even before he donned his disguise. This appearance of his not only contributed greatly to his cover being convincing, and thus reducing the danger of being exposed, it also helped him to be granted more operations than the other fighters, something he was really pleased about. Moti was a patriot who was willing to risk his life to save innocent civilians from Palestinian terrorism. Aside from being very funny when he showed us his talent at mimicry, Moti had extraordinary courage. Describing someone as exceptionally brave, to us, as commando fighters who do not know what fear is, can only be applied to someone extraordinary. Moti was indeed special.

After having studied Muslim prayers and the entire Qur'an, in addition to mastering the Arabic language in an Egyptian dialect similar to that spoken in Gaza, Moti was ready to be infiltrated into the midst of the Gazan population. He was sent to the Jabaliya refugee camp, an area swarming with terrorists' nests. There he would amble along the streets in his civilian clothes, looking just like a local, not even armed with a small pistol so as not to arouse suspicion. In these situations, the fighter's physical abilities are rigorously tested, and most importantly, his ability to act calmly, to maneuver, deceive, utilize and improvise. While in Jabaliya, he started building close and friendly relationships with young locals by frequenting the mosques and cafés. To do this, he played the role of being an extremist who avidly supported terrorism and was willing to be a martyr, to kill the Jews at any cost. Once he felt his cover had been accepted and he was part of the community, his next task was to conceal micro-transmitters in offices and houses where he knew discussions about terror and extremism would be taking place.

The Mista'arvim unit was established with the understanding that a unique and cunning method of warfare was necessary to deal with the many security incidents in the Gaza Strip and the West Bank, especially among a dense civilian population. The unit's motto of "Combat by using tricks will prevail" implies its diverse range of activities.

The unit's activity has not ceased and continues to this day. It operates within the 89th Oz Brigade, a commando brigade set up in 2015 and dedicated to special operations, with the Mista'arvim unit functioning in both a visible and disguised manner among the local Arab population. In 2001, 2005 and 2016, the unit was rewarded with a commendation by the Army Chief of Staff.

13

My One Collaboration with a Mista'arvim Unit

My collaboration with the Mista'arvim had started well before General Ehud Barak raised the idea in 1986 of establishing a unit within the Mista'arvim called Duvdevan. This was not because we were the outstanding fighters, the elite of the army, but simply because of coincidence and timing. It was during my compulsory army service between 1975 and 1978. My platoon collaborated just once with a unit called "Sayeret Rimon," at that time a combination of a combat infantry and an undercover unit, which operated intermittently from 1970 to 2005. Sayeret Rimon had been established at the initiative of the head of Israel's Southern Command, Brigadier General Ariel Sharon, when terrorism from Gaza was intensifying. Its role was to eradicate terrorism in Gaza, while cooperating with the security and intelligence units, and with other commando units such as that of Golani and the paratroopers. Sharon appointed Meir Dagan, later head of the Mossad, to lead it. Here is the operation in which my platoon and the Sayeret Rimon unit joined forces back in 1978:

In the winter of 1978, just a few months before the end of my three years' mandatory service, a raid was assigned to the Sayeret Rimon, to diminish the ongoing terrorism in Gaza. We, the Golani, were chosen for this mission to be the backup "Green" force.

The target: Two houses in the Al-Shati refugee camp in Gaza.

The main objective of this operation was to eliminate more than 20 terrorists, as well as destroy or confiscate weapons that were in their possession. They were housed in a large basement in one of the houses, at the southern end of the camp, located in the northern Gaza Strip, not far from the sea. According to the information we had in our possession, the group of terrorists who were operating from this house were the ones that had been murdering Israeli citizens who visited Gaza. The operation's secondary objective, which was assigned to us the "Greens," was to raid another house in the south of the Al-Shati camp to capture two wanted terrorists living in the house and bring them to Israel alive, at most slightly injured. This way, they could be grilled in order to get further important intelligence information out of them. Although we were aware during the pre-operation briefing that our role in the mission would be smaller than that of the Sayeret Rimon, we were happy to be part of the operation as we felt privileged to fight alongside these special Mista'arvim colleagues.

At first, we did not really understand why we were chosen to be the "Green" force in this operation, as most of our activity had historically been taking place up north, in the south Lebanon area. We did not assume that we had been chosen for the mission because we were the best commando unit in the IDF, on the contrary, we were mediocre compared to the three other elite units at the time. It was only during the pre-briefing that we realized we were selected for the mission only because at that time we were becoming part of the landscape of the Gaza refugee camps, due to the timing of our rotation of duties between units.

Throughout the years 1977 and 1978, because of many terrorist incidents in the West Bank and in the Gaza Strip, the IDF's four infantry forces (including my own Golani force) operating on the northern border, in the West Bank, and in Gaza, would alternate their activities and missions to prevent burnout and complacency among the soldiers. For example, after two to three months, the unit serving in Gaza would be exhausted and lose the element of sharpness, so would be switched back to manning the northern border, and those who were stationed on the northern border would be sent to Gaza. Those who had been serving in Ramallah would be replaced by those who served in Hebron, and so on. We, as one platoon of the company, happened to find ourselves based in the Al-Shati refugee camp for several weeks, sharing the activities in Gaza with the rest of my battalion. Thus the target, the Al-Shati refugee camp, was by now very familiar to us. We knew every alley, street and pathway in Al-Shati and its surroundings. The operation I am about to describe was planned to be carried out in exactly the same week that we were still on our shift in Gaza.

After the 1967 Six Day War, when the Gaza Strip came under Israeli control, most of its residents accepted the new situation and found themselves benefiting from it. Tens of thousands of Gazan Palestinians found employment opportunities in Israel, and business owners from the Gaza Strip were happy to do business with Israelis, and welcomed them to their premises. However, a small minority of the Gazan population did not look favorably on this situation. These were a fanatical group of terrorists who preferred to starve, as long as they could continue their fight against Israel. They did not care about the improvement of the economy in Gaza, or the contentment of the workers who had found a source of income in Israel. They only saw an "occupying enemy" who needed to be intimidated. They threatened the thousands of Palestinian employees to stop working in Israel, and even went as far as killing some of them. Then these terrorists, who were not yet well organized, turned their attention to Israelis who were visiting Gaza to shop or do business. This caused a significant decline in the many businesses in Gaza, and some sadly closed down. The terrorists were not at all worried about the bankruptcy of local businesses and consequent job losses that led to the weakening of their economy. Instead of reducing their activity, they intensified it by expanding their terrorist activities beyond the Gaza border, infiltrating Israeli cities and killing civilians. Between 1970 and 1976 more than 900 Israelis were murdered in these acts of terror. An incident that particularly shocked the Israeli public was the 1971 murder of the children of the Aroyo family, which included their two children. This family was visiting Gaza when a 16-year-old Palestinian threw a hand grenade into the family's car. What was astonishing about this incident was that, trapped inside their burning car, the family had screamed and begged the locals for help, but the Palestinians stood by and watched as the two children burned to death.

This distressing incident put the Israeli government in a difficult dilemma. On the one hand, Israel was content to provide thousands of jobs and business opportunities for Gaza's two million residents. However, on the other, Israel found itself vulnerable and constantly threatened. Surprisingly, the Israeli army did not respond to the Aroyo murders because the government would not approve it. The Israeli public took to the streets and made their voices heard in a loud protest of several days. One of their placards read, "It is the government's remit to provide security for its citizens." One of the journalists covering the protest reported that he had received anonymous messages from civilians, telling him they were about to attack the residents of Gaza themselves, and that the wording on that placard was a hint. The Prime Minister urgently convened the Cabinet, and after a short and purposeful discussion, they authorized the army to act. Thus, in 1972, Brigadier General Ariel Sharon was tasked by the Israeli government with eradicating terrorism in Gaza. He deployed military forces to the Gaza Strip that included infantry units and tank companies and recruited locals from Gaza to cooperate with Israeli intelligence to quickly root out the terrorists' nests and eliminate them. Sharon went into the Gaza Strip himself, spearheading his forces and directing the operation that lasted several consecutive days.

In addition to the operational actions against the terrorists, Sharon used the stick and carrot method on the population: in those areas where terrorism was not allowed to operate, the local civilians received encouragement and financial support from Israel, helping their businesses to flourish and providing jobs. In contrast, areas where the civilians entertained terrorism did not receive any of these. However, in spite of the goodwill gestures from the Israeli government, and the heavy-handed response by the IDF, terrorism from Gaza did not diminish, and attacks on Israel continued. In the diplomatic arena, it was clear that none of the efforts made by the UN and other countries around the world was helping in any way to reduce the terrorist activity.

Left with no choice, in the years between 1972 and 1979, the IDF embarked on a series of raids throughout Gaza, especially in the terrorist strongholds of the Sajaiya, Al-Shati, and Beit Hanoun refugee camps, and in the coastal area, where the terrorists operated from a fishing village not far from the Al-Shati camp.

Once all the necessary pre-operational preparations were completed, the green light to start the operation was given. A team of five men from the Sayeret Rimon's Mista'arvim undercover unit were sent into the Al-Shati refugee camp to interact with the locals to gather information on the two targeted houses and the two wanted men. Once embedded in the Al-Shati area, the undercover fighters began to mingle among the local population, befriending some of the men who regularly came to sit in the cafés for coffee and to smoke the much-loved Nargila pipes. One of the Israelis managed to charm some of the older men who were happy to talk to this engaging young stranger, who was pretending to be a Palestinian from Hebron fleeing the Israeli army, and who was supposedly taking refuge in the safety of Gaza. These older locals, who suspected nothing, proudly spoke of the presence of two Palestinian heroes who had chosen to live in their suburb. Although the local men didn't know the exact address of the house where the two were staying, this piece of information was sufficient for the Israelis to use as a critical starting point.

Meanwhile, soon after the Shabak security service (by this time the widely used acronym for the Shin Bet) had provided the exact address of the house to the chief operational commander back at the base, it was passed on to the Sayeret Rimon's commander. He immediately sent two members of his Mista'arvim team, who had been busy mingling among the local population, to that address. When they reached the property, they started collecting all kinds of useful details about it: its external structure and features, the color of the façade, the number of windows, where the main door was located, whether the roof was flat or sloping, if there was a garden and entrance gate, and, importantly, if there were any security people to negotiate. They also managed to establish the number of occupants of the house and if there were any children among them and studied the two terrorists' daily and nightly routines and movements, even noting their regular sleeping place. They also needed to work out a safe escape route out of the area in case something went dangerously wrong in the crowded streets of Al-Shati. When their intelligence gathering mission was completed, they were asked to return to base. The force commander however, remained in the area close to the target, waiting for us fighters to arrive, when he would then lead us in the assault. He also needed to keep his eye on the house to make sure there were no changes, such as the arrival of Gazan security forces, terrorists, or any other change that would require a revision to the plan.

After we received clearance that all the Mista'arvim information gathering team had left the immediate area, we, a combined force of 18 Golani and Rimon fighters began making our way towards Al-Shati in two separate groups. To minimize suspicion, the nine Rimon fighters had dressed in civilian clothes and were travelling in a civilian truck, which claimed to be owned by a fruit and vegetable company transporting its agricultural workers. We, the Greens, made our way in a large blue transit van to meld into the environment of the camp. This type of vehicle, a 1966 Volkswagen Split van, with its capacity of 10 passengers, was commonly used by the locals for transporting people around the city or groups of workers to and from Gaza. Even though we wore our green uniform, we deliberately left our helmets back at base. Instead, we were wearing hats of the kind worn by Middle Eastern Arabs. In doing so, we were seen from the windows of the van to passers-by as innocent local passengers going about their daily business. To conceal our combat vests and rifles upon arrival at the destination, we all wore long, oversized coats. Now we looked like local citizens. It was my first time in such attire during an operation or raid, and I childishly felt like I was some senior mega-spy in an enemy territory.

Order of action: Approaching the two houses in the Al-Shati camp quickly but quietly, with our radio mode switched to silent. Due to the impossibility of communicating with the rest of the team, we each had to rely on our accurate recall of all the details down to the smallest one, and on our memory of the features, color and size of the targeted building, including the number of floors, entrances and windows. An excellent memory is one of the combatant's most important attributes, along with the many others that had been identified long before joining the unit, back in the days of high school. On this kind of mission, we normally make copious notes while we are being briefed. However, when leaving our base for the mission, we are ordered to leave all our notes behind and be totally reliant on our memory.

When we arrived near our targeted house, we calmly climbed out of the van, while the driver kept the engine running, waiting for us as if he were simply a taxi driver. The Sayeret Rimon fighters reached their destination before us and hooked up with their commander who was waiting for them in the field.

According to the plan, we were to capture and bundle the two wanted terrorists with their faces covered and their hands cuffed under the back seats of the van, so they would not be seen through the windows. The operation commander would be sitting in the front seat to supervise the getaway from Gaza. Myself and another fighter would sit on the heads of the two terrorists, pointing our guns in their faces, and calming them down in fluent Arabic. The rest of our team would watch through the windows with their fingers poised on their triggers, ready to act on any unexpected eventuality as we drove back to our base.

But the plan went badly wrong.

As we piled out of the van at the designated address, two menacing looking dogs ran towards us barking loudly. Despite the dogs being huge and intimidating, we weren't as scared of them as worried about losing

Al-Shati refugee camp.

the element of surprise of our mission, and worst of all, of being lynched by the hundreds of locals who were shopping in the main street, just 100 yards away.

And then something happened which put our well-constructed plan into serious jeopardy. One of the dogs attacked Gidi, a member of our team, and sank his sharp teeth deep into his leg. It happened very quickly. We didn't know what to do and how to respond. No one suggested, or even considered the option of opening fire on the dogs. Such a senseless move could cause a devastating response. One of us had to make a snap decision; there was no time to think anymore. I decided to take the initiative and to come up with a creative idea.

When we had climbed out of our van into the street, I remembered having noticed a butcher's shop selling meat products. I glanced back and indeed the shop was there, only a few yards away. I ran to the shop and grabbed two large chunks of raw meat that were sitting draped over the counter, probably waiting to be weighed for a customer. I raced back into the street and threw the chunks of meat towards the two dogs. The dogs pounced on the meat and forgot about us for a while. In those few seconds, without being instructed or ordered what to do, our team dispersed itself around the front of the house as if we did not know each other. I was the only one capturing the attention of passers-by and fortunately none of them suspected anything. Everyone seemed to be convinced that these were just noisy dogs, happy to be with a generous man who was feeding them expensive cuts of meat. I breathed a sigh of relief while maintaining eye contact with the rest of my fighter comrades. The shop owner, who had chased me down the street thinking I was a common thief, was also moved by my generous gesture in feeding stray dogs with cuts of meat that some residents of that street could not afford to buy for their own families. He stood so closely behind me that I could feel his quickened breathing and then said to me, "What a wonderful thing to do. I can't decide if you are crazy or drunk, but one thing's for sure. It's going to cost you seventy lira." It was hard not to burst out laughing but somehow I managed to stifle my laughter. My colleague Yossi, who carried his wallet with him wherever he went, approached the shop owner with a smile, pulled out a 50-dollar bill and said to him in perfect Arabic (with a well-honed Gazan accent), "Forgive my friend, he just loves dogs and wanted to feed them. Here, please take this." The shop owner accepted the cash with a beaming smile, as he was delighted to get fifty dollars for two pieces of meat that probably cost far less. (At that time the exchange rate of the lira was four lira to one U.S. dollar.)

During battle, you have to be able to think "outside the box." If you think or act according to what you have learned in training, you may find yourself injured or killed. I am referring to the type of battle that has been complicated by unexpected factors, such as an ambush, or because of incorrect intelligence data. On this particular occasion, in the busy street of Al-Shati, we were experiencing an incident where a pair of street dogs had unexpectedly attacked us. This is where the individual soldier's capability comes into play. Imagination and a creative way of thinking are most needed in those situations. Being able to remember a small detail like the presence of a butcher's shop, and then utilizing it, along with the imaginative idea of snatching a piece of meat and using it to silence the dogs, helped us handle this unforeseen episode in a much better way than shooting at the dogs.

The sequence of events concerning the two dogs that I have just described probably took no longer than two minutes. But these were two minutes that seemed like an hour to us. We looked around and were relieved to see no one had gathered around us. Everything seemed to calm down and no one in the street had suspected anything unusual was taking place. However, in spite of the fact that we had not raised any suspicion, we now had to make a crucial decision on whether to abort the mission and return to the van, whose engine was still running, or to complete our mission. We all looked to Dan, our commander, for a decision. I could easily read what was going on in his mind and felt sorry for him, as we understood the huge predicament he was in. I could sense that the whole team were experiencing the same thoughts, the same split-second hesitation, and weighing up the consequences of either decision. But the decision had to be made in situ and within our group in a matter of a few seconds.

Would it not be the best course of action to postpone the operation and return to the van waiting to take us back to the safety of our base? What if we had now already lost the element of surprise and the two terrorists were waiting for us behind the front door of the house we were about to enter, both of them armed and ready to attack? If the decision had been mine, and I am sure the rest of the fighters felt the same, I would continue as planned and complete the mission. If we were to give up now, it would mean that we had failed to complete a simple mission we been sent to do. More importantly, we would have failed at our first chance to cooperate with an undercover unit, and may consequently not be given any further opportunities. Besides, how could we look at ourselves in the mirror and call ourselves commando soldiers? Every commando soldier knows that no matter whether the likelihood of surviving the inferno is small and unrealistic, no matter the number of bodies and the rivers of blood around you, no matter the terrifying thunder of the explosions, the soot filled smoke and the acrid smell of burnt bodies, you must stick to your mission, calmly focus and carry out what is expected of you. You must remain cool and level-headed, even if you have been badly injured or you have lost contact with the rest of your unit, so that your judgment and your ability to interpret the reality will help you to handle the situation better.

The dogs were content to continue eating their tasty free meal and the satisfied shop owner returned to his customers. We kept looking to Dan, our team commander, waiting for his order. The decision was made without a sound, just by a nod of his head. Much to our surprise and relief, none of the locals showed any sign of being suspicious of us.

We continued to make our way towards the entrance of the house. The house belonged to a family of five people (parents and three teenagers), who felt honored and proud to take in the two terrorists, considered by their community as jihadi heroes. We knew that at this time of day the family had a set routine of getting together for lunch, and that the lunch always took place in their dining room on the second floor of the house. We entered the house through an unlocked front door (a normal occurrence in Arab households), and once inside, we pulled out our pistols and quietly climbed to the second floor. But when we got there, we were perplexed and rather worried as we found ourselves facing five doors. According to the intelligence we had received, there should have been only two brown doors on the second floor. Again, a speedy decision was needed. Not only were there more doors than expected, some of them were painted in different colors. Could we be in the wrong house? Could it be possible that our unquestionably reliable undercover colleagues had not managed to get all the information correct? Dan, our commander, didn't hesitate. This time he exercised his instinct. He barged through the left-hand door, while we followed him. Once inside, we were delighted to find that we were in the right house.

Among the surprised occupants who were enjoying a delicious looking lunch were two familiar faces, the two faces we had embedded in our brain from the first moment we began the preparations for the operation, from the photos of them we had been shown during the briefing.

Suddenly, one of the occupants of the house came out of the kitchen. We didn't want to take any risk. Pini, one of our team who had attached a silencer to his pistol, shot him in the leg. This was simply to neutralize him as we did not see any benefit in killing him. We shouted in Arabic to the occupants to remain seated around the table and place their hands flat on the table. We then ordered the two wanted men to stand against the wall and raise their hands. They responded promptly and without any objection. We cuffed their hands and covered

Inside the target house, trying to determine which door to open.

each of their faces with a white cloth. Within seconds we all ran down the stairs into the street. The whole operation had lasted no more than four minutes. We climbed back into the waiting van according to the pre-arranged plan, and drove away at a normal speed, towards the exit from Gaza, back to base for a post-battle brief.

In 1971, Sayeret Rimon gained recognition when its fighters had managed to eliminate 12 senior terrorists in Gaza. To do this, the commandos had disguised themselves as survivors of a wrecked fishing boat that had supposedly sailed to the Gaza Strip from Lebanon. After this incident, it was realized that commando fighters, apart from mastering the skills of infantry combat, could also turn themselves into successful undercover operatives. And so, without it being designed or pre-planned by any of the unit's officers, Sayeret Rimon became an early model for the future Mista'arvim units. It led to the establishment of the rest of today's undercover units, including Duvdevan, which are now all referred to as Mista'arvim. As to its modus operandi, this was not originated by Sayeret Rimon, however, Sayeret Rimon was the first in the IDF that operated both as an undercover unit, trained in intelligence and espionage, and as an infantry commando unit that also specialized in guerrilla warfare. This made Sayeret Rimon an excellent model for the establishment of all the Mista'arvim units of today's IDF.

14

Inspiration—How I Healed Myself from PTSD and Anxiety

When I was asked to describe my PTSD and anxiety, by a friend from my platoon when we were talking about his injury and mine, I said this, "The problem with anxiety, compared to other illnesses, is that you live and feel it all the time, at almost every moment. It is with me when I smell, hear, see, feel. When I smell a piece of meat grilling on the barbecue and see its rising smoke, I smell the burnt corpses with smoke still swirling round them that I saw during battles. When I hear shouts or sirens, or fireworks exploding, I hear echoes of the explosions of shells and grenades. Anxiety is something I feel on a daily basis as long as I am active and alive. This is in addition to the terrifying uncontrollable thoughts that take me to dark and scary places."

What led to my post-traumatic stress disorder (PTSD) was the accumulation of all the horrific scenes I experienced during the many battles and operations I took part in as a commando fighter. I saw at close hand destruction and burning corpses, but it was mainly a result of those near-death situations I encountered in massive explosions or in face-to-face battles with terrorists, during which I had more than few terrifying moments. I was still young, full of plans for the future, and could not accept the idea of being mentally ill and financially supported by the army welfare, and possibly needing medication for the rest of my life.

It was in 1984 that I first started to suffer from severe anxiety attacks, and was informed that I was suffering from a condition well known to combat soldiers all over the world. After a thorough examination of all the combat situations I had been in between 1975, the day I enlisted, and 1984, when I was diagnosed, I could not put my finger on one specific event which had perhaps caused me to contract this disorder. There were long conversations and further tests by my then psychologists, who were in contact with military sources that provided them with information about my activities. They were especially interested in the years between 1980 and 1984, when I was already a combat reservist taking part in hundreds of intense combat situations, the peak being the 1982 Lebanon War, where I had witnessed horrific scenes of corpses and explosions over three consecutive months. I was told that such a disorder does not necessarily happen from just one event, but can be from a sequence of events occurring over several months or years. From this I realized that the disturbing phenomenon residing within me and causing me so much disturbance was probably acquired throughout those nine years from 1975 to 1984.

When I was about to be discharged from combat reserve service, the psychologist suggested to me that the best treatment would be to continue my combat service in order to overcome my fears. He explained that there was a case in which a soldier who was shell shocked was brought back later in the day to the battlefield he was in, and this helped prevent the development of PTSD. Taking his advice to heart, in spite of already having had nightmares and crazy thoughts, I continued my reserve service for another 20 years.

I decided to study the topic in depth. I wanted to learn more about PTSD and anxiety out of my personal insight that if you discover the source of a problem, then the way to find its solution might be achievable. When you analyze the problem, and break it down into sections, you will then be able to understand it much better. The more you understand it, as well as its causes and sources, the more effectively you will be able to handle or treat it. And so, the first thing I learned was that during an anxiety attack, the brain distorts reality, and injects into our consciousness a different interpretation for our thoughts. We then start thinking that something bad is about to happen. We feel we are about to die, or being on a verge of insanity. In some situations, we feel apparent disengagement from reality, a feeling of alienation and non-belonging, and a sense of watching oneself from the outside. These thoughts cause confusion within our consciousness, and this leads to panic attacks. The more I studied, the more I realized that these imaginary and false thoughts are not physically harmful at all, and most importantly, they can be controlled. Later I discovered that the source of these anxiety attacks is a disruption in the balance of chemicals in the brain, due to the psychological symptoms of those negative and terrifying thoughts I have described.

When these terrifying thoughts come, the brain receives a false warning of impending danger, and quickly prepares itself for dealing with a threat through a state of "fight or flee." It is this sudden preparation of the brain that causes the chemical balance to be disturbed. For example, on a ship, as long as the passengers are spread out in all areas of the vessel in a balanced way, then the ship sails smoothly. However, in the case of panic following a sweeping wave or an attack on the ship, if all the passengers rush to one area in the back or front of the vessel to find shelter, this would cause a dangerous imbalance in the ship, and its sinking would be inevitable. For healthy people who do not suffer from anxiety, this imbalance can be transient, a temporary glitch in their lives when they encounter situations such as a serious car accident or finding themselves too close to a huge fire. However, for people with anxiety or PTSD, the situation is compounded by additional physiological symptoms, such as sweating, body tremors, dizziness, rapid and strong heartbeat, blurred vision, shortness of breath, all of which aggravate the situation.

PTSD and anxiety are psychological conditions I told myself, and psychology is all about thoughts, so maybe I can change the way my thoughts unfold or control them by diverting them to other situations and places. Realizing this, I started studying alternative techniques for relaxation such as meditation, deep breathing, and any practice connected with thought diversion and the use of imagination. I found myself searching for any mind activities that could change the content of the thoughts presented in the brain at that given moment. Activities that could push those frightening thoughts into a totally different path and location, changing their scenario and even their colors. This was the turning point of my personal journey of self-healing from the terrible disorder called PTSD, a journey that has borne the fruits of success. The understanding that those terrifying thoughts were no more than a distortion of reality created by my own brain gave me the strength to fight by diverting my thoughts elsewhere, to a happy situation, or to a calm environment, like a beautiful and quiet beach. In addition, the realization that trying to block out my illness with alcohol or drugs would only bring momentary relief, and that the answer lay inside my head, in my own thoughts, contributed greatly to my fight. Thus began the process of my self-healing without medication and without expert and educated psychologists telling me what to do in such situations. This process led to the amazing revelation that each of us has hidden powers inherent in his soul and embedded in his essence, and all he has to do is give them expression. The ability to think of creative solutions, to think outside the box, not to be held captive by what the doctors automatically recommend, are all traits for which I had been accepted to serve in a commando unit all those years before.

Since 2018, I have been helping those similarly suffering from anxiety, and I hope that in this chapter I can help others. In this chapter, I will share with you the process I went through to heal myself without any medication from post-traumatic stress disorder, in the hope this can help others who suffer from all kinds of anxiety to try to heal themselves, or at least reduce and minimize its attacks and control them. This can be also helpful for the partners or other family members who live with someone who suffers from anxiety. But just before I detail the treatment ways that have been proven to be effective, I would like to relay some background to this phenomenon.

Post-traumatic stress disorder is an ongoing stress response to a traumatic event and can be brought on by any stimuli that could be reminiscent of that event. Many people will experience a significant trauma during their lifetime as a result of war, a serious accident, sexual assault or other life-threatening event. However, if these symptoms persist for more than a month after the event, then it will be diagnosed as post-traumatic stress disorder. My PTSD was manifested in several ways: disproportionate panic attacks, a feeling of losing my sanity, a sense of disconnection or alienation from others, an inability to feel positive emotions, anger, irritability or aggressive behavior, self-destructive and risk-taking behaviors, constant alertness but trouble in concentrating, and difficulty in falling asleep or being able to sleep through the night. And the most frightening of these manifestations was a strange feeling that I was detached from myself, that I was not part of any existence or reality, a kind of derealization.

Anxiety is a reaction of our brain to certain situations and is essential to us as human beings. Without anxiety, the human race certainly would not have survived. Anxiety pushes us to strive, to be sharp and focused in order to achieve an important goal or to instill a dream. In addition, it acts as a warning mechanism against danger and causes us to be careful and take protective measures, such as escaping from a fire, or undergoing medical tests when new symptoms are felt. But on the other hand, anxiety can be experienced in our backyard. This is when it becomes a disorder or illness, when it is chronically present and impairs the ability to function in daily life. Anxiety disorders are a collective name for a range of sub-disorders such as: panic attacks, social anxiety, obsessive compulsive disorder, post-traumatic stress disorder, general anxiety disorder and more. Anxiety affects thoughts, behaviors, bodily sensations and can impair personal and social relationships. A study by the American Association of Anxiety Disorders compared people diagnosed with anxiety disorder with people who do not. Many of the anxiety disorder participants who took part in the study testified that they do not believe they deserve to live in a healthy society, make friends or get married. Indeed, a relationship with a person suffering from anxiety can be no easy task at all. Only those who live with such a person can really understand what the difficulties are. These difficulties can manifest themselves on several other levels, such as social, economic, occupational and any situations that require contact with others.

I once remarked that anxiety is like a wave on the sea. When it hits us, it is better to just let it envelop us within it and drift away for a short distance, rather than to fight it and be dragged exhausted underwater. Although this sounds like a highly philosophical approach that does not offer a practical way of coping, it actually makes a lot of sense. Sometimes we need to let our thoughts sink into an imaginable void, and not rush to address any problem as quickly as possible and out of stress. You will be surprised to find out how much the anxiety level of your life can drop if you simply decide, if it's possible for you to do so, that you will wait a few minutes before you start dealing with crises or problems that life presents to you. You can then start solving the problem and deal with the stress, instead of fighting it and, in doing so, only aggravate your situation.

Anxiety and post-traumatic stress disorder are each a condition that is very difficult to deal with within our human limitations. From my personal experience of both, I can describe a crippling attack of fear that causes discernible physical symptoms. The problem with PTSD is that it involves not only the people who suffer from it, but also those who surround them, such as work colleagues and family members. Whenever I felt a wave of anxiety attacks, it felt like an uncontrollable process that conveyed in my mind flashing images of violence, fire, tension, corpses and approaching death. There would be a weird loud noise in my head, and I could not understand how it found its way into my mind while I was at home, at work, and nowhere near a battlefield.

It was only after studying the topic by reading dozens of books (pre–Google and the internet era), that I started to understand that these were invisible and uncontrollable flashes, and that they wormed their way to my consciousness when a minor unimportant trigger would occur, such as a brief argument, or a feeling of momentary chaos; normal situations in relationships that usually reach an end in a short time with understanding and a hug. In those routine situations, I would get a different picture. I would see fire and smoke, I would hear noise and violence that was happening deep inside my brain, invisible to the outsider. I remember it as a feeling of a fierce inferno surrounding my whole head.

The conventional medical approach is based on the assumption that among PTSD patients there is an imbalance in the level of neurotransmitters in their brain; an imbalance that can be adjusted by drugs which increase the level of serotonin and inhibit its absorption and breakdown levels. Such drugs were used for 24 years to treat the anxiety I suffered from but in my case, they didn't help. In fact, they only served to alleviate my situation by confusing me, and displaying a different reality in my head than what was real. The drugs also caused me to run away from the problem by taking the easy way out, instead of facing it head on and dealing with it. This is not even to mention the addiction they caused me over the years. I was taking a selective serotonin reuptake inhibitor (SSRI), plus the medication sertraline (Zoloft), both of which were approved by the Food and Drug Administration for PTSD treatment. In addition, I took Diazepam, Amitriptyline, Phenelzine, and antidepressants such as Paroxetine or Mirtazapine. When I realized that these medications were not preventing the anxiety attacks, I started looking for other ways to deal with my problem. I felt that there had to be another way to treat psychological conditions, and ones which did not require surgical intervention.

From my experience I can recommend methods and techniques to deal effectively with anxiety. However, I would first like to suggest that in addition to my recommendations, when feeling a spate of acute anxiety attacks, it is advisable to also take appropriate medication in combination with psychotherapy, but just for short time. Medication cannot totally cure PTSD or anxiety, as these conditions usually return after stopping the medication. Psychological treatment is designed to bring about long-term changes in thoughts and inclinations to prevent the effects of anxiety that impair the quality of life. In an anxiety attack, the brain can sometimes distort reality and give it different interpretations, different appearances, causing confusion that leads to panic attacks.

But studies show that these imaginary and false thoughts are not harmful to you and do not physically threaten the body. It all depends on your reaction to these thoughts. If you direct and control them and convince yourself that these are just hollow thoughts and that there is no danger to your body, then in a while these thoughts will disappear. This is what a relaxing medication such as Diazepam does when it is used during an anxiety attack.

Here are some recommended ways to deal with anxiety that I discovered for myself while studying and observing the processes I was going through:

Thought Diversion

I'll start with something simple that will surely seem amusing and you may not take seriously, but believe me, it works. To soothe an anxiety attack, pop an ice cube on your tongue. The cold of the ice cube gives the body a physical shock and helps the brain to stop getting lost in its distortion of reality by dealing with the sudden temperature change in your mouth. Instead of being lost in thoughts about things are not in any way harming you physically, your mind suddenly focuses on the cold discomfort in your mouth. This is what I call thought diversion, and is at the core of dealing with anxiety, which I discovered over time while studying this subject.

While your mind is concentrating on the cold on your tongue, and performing the principle of thought diversion, the body is simultaneously dealing with the feeling of cold. Your body sees this as a problem that needs to be addressed immediately. When we enter the "fight or flee" state, the body devotes more energy to the processes necessary for its survival, and along the way also puts us in alert. The ice cube causes dryness in the mouth that makes it start to produce saliva. Because the ice cube encourages the body to produce saliva, it actually calms the thoughts that have caused your anxiety attack. This can also apply when sucking something sharp tasting such as a slice of lemon or eating something hot and spicy.

Cognitive Behavioral Therapy

If we can change the way we think, we can change the way we feel. If we can do both, then we are able to change the outcome of things. By using this ability, you can help clear away any frightening thoughts which cause anxiety and depression. If we understand that our brain sometimes distorts reality in a way that causes us to perceive it, or its consequences, incorrectly, then we should address the brain and its thoughts by cognitive behavioral therapy. This is a method of treatment based on the assumption that thought patterns influence behavior, and that emotional disorders originate in distorted thought patterns. The example I have just given, in which you use both your imagination and concentration to direct your thoughts to the coldness of the ice cube or the acidity of the lemon slice, can also be applied in redirecting the brain's distorted thought patterns to the kind of thoughts that you want and feel comfortable with. In doing so, you are actually returning your thoughts to their normal state. By controlling and redirecting those troubling thoughts that originate in distorted thought patterns, you are in actual fact shaking their ground and weakening their influence on your behavior. Therefore, if your behavior during an anxiety attack is reckless, anxious, obsessive, desperate, panicking, then with this method of weakening the influence of those frightening thoughts, your behavior will cease to be in panic mode, and you will not feel threatened by any of the distortions in thinking that lead to anxiety.

Make Changes in Your Behavior

A change in your thoughts and behavior can happen quickly, much more so than you might think. From time to time, our mind wanders to places and situations against our will. For us, there is no control over the brain, but we have the ability to change its patterns of direction by our ability to imagine, an ability that is exclusive to humans. In doing so, you divert the direction of the thoughts that are leading you to distorted places and menacing situations. By diverting your thoughts' direction, you are making a change in your behavior, therefore, those negative thoughts disappear. They are no longer fulfilling a function, and this immediately affects your actual, physical behavior, which will be free of negativity and fears.

Use your imagination and a high degree of concentration to tilt negative thoughts that can lead to anxiety. It takes commitment to do so; not just every day, but every minute and second. Erase from your mind and consciousness any notion that it is easier to believe in the negative than in the positive. Believe in the positive, be proactive and implement it at every opportunity you have in your daily life, not just theoretically in your thoughts.

Work on building a strong mental response mechanism that will help you to control and direct your thoughts. This will help you calm down and fend off anxieties, which are the result of the distortion of reality created by the mind. Say loudly to yourself in the mirror every day that all those negative beliefs you have adopted and embraced throughout the time you have suffered from anxiety are illogical, false and bear no connection to reality. This can only be achieved if you work on a strong and positive response mechanism that challenges the negative. When the anxiety attacks happen, direct your thoughts to a happy event in your life that you remember well, and concentrate on all its details down to the smallest one. By doing this, you can recreate the whole event and focus on all its beautiful details, including the people who took part, the delicious food, and every good thing that was part of the event.

When your brain focuses only on negative thoughts and memories, fears and worries become intensified. When this mental distortion occurs, you begin to lose control over your thoughts and let them lead you. When that happens, they take you to dark places and situations that bring back bad memories or fearful experiences you had. That's how my personal anxiety developed. If this had been explained to me then, when it all began, I would have stopped letting my thoughts lead me to those terrifying situations and bloody events I had experienced on the battlefield, and thus, I could have spared myself from PTSD.

This is why I am writing this chapter. I wish to warn those who are at the starting point of this terrible illness. With all due respect to modern medicine and to the esteemed doctors and psychologists, I state here one unequivocal fact. Your mind deceives you! If you suffer from PTSD or anxiety, or both, I am directing this fact to you, to spare you the suffering I went through for years, simply because I followed the doctors' instructions and swallowed amounts of drugs that did not help. Stop now! Do not go down the path that I blindly followed, just to find out that it was in vain. This is the fundamental principle for you to acknowledge so you can start healing yourself.

Other Recommended Ways

You can also employ a method known as Mindfulness. Our attention is a flashlight you can direct to wherever you choose. Mindfulness exercises reduce anxiety and depression and improve working memory. Focused attention exercises cultivate your brain's ability to concentrate on one single object, something that is tied to your sensory experience. One can take for example one's breathing: focus all your attention on the sensation of breathing, the coolness of air moving in and out of your nostrils, your abdomen moving in and out. Another focused-attention exercise is the body scan, by taking that flashlight and directing it systematically around the entire body. Start by focusing your attention on your toes, taking note of whatever sensations might be there.

A technique I have also found effective to neutralize my anxieties I have called "write and realize." It is quite simple to do. When you feel attacked by a wave of anxiety, take a pen and a sheet of paper and write down a list of all the anxieties, negative thoughts, fears, scenarios, situations or events that are going through your mind at that moment. Then read what you have written, reading the lines slowly and aloud, and if necessary, repeating the reading one more time. When finished, put down the paper and look around you. You will then realize that none of the things on that list have happened. There was no fire, no blood on the floor, no fainting and no death. You will immediately realize that none of those horrifying events you have described on your list occurred in reality, they were only in your imagination, in your thoughts, as a result of the distortion of thoughts by your mind. You will smile awkwardly when you realize this. I speak from my experience. When I did it for the first time it did not work, it was only when I persevered that I saw results, followed by a slight change starting within me. By drawing up lists of events and then realizing they were not happening, I learned that anxieties do not exist in reality but only in our thoughts, and thoughts can certainly be controlled by us. But how?

Here's an example:

Your thoughts send you a desire to murder your hateful neighbor who, for more than a year, has been annoying the whole apartment building with his selfish behavior. Would you get a pistol and kill him? Of course not. What stopped you from murdering him? The control of your thoughts. You were able to change your thought pattern and control it. This is the ultimate proof that we can control our thoughts if we want to. Surprisingly, over time, you will realize that everything you have written on your list as a negative thought or fear can be similarly controlled. Therefore, when you write them down, you will over time train your brain to recognize them as unnecessary thoughts, and so the brain will stop transmitting them to your conscious mind. You will be the ultimate guide and the leader of your thoughts. This could be a significant achievement on the way to your self-healing from anxieties. In time, with perseverance and practice, you will understand that what triggers those anxieties was nothing but irrational, imagined, exaggerated dramatic thoughts that were created in your mind due to the bad memories or experiences you had in the past. If you instill this and concentrate on using your imagination, these types of thoughts will gradually disappear from your life, and with it the anxieties that affect your mood and your ability to function, your quality of life and the people around you.

Sharing your thoughts and feelings with others, or with a sheet of paper, can be a powerful way to deal with restlessness, worries, stress and anything that puts you into a state of anxiety. It's proven. This is why many support groups have been set up. Luckily, being social animals, we are also surrounded by friends, family, spouses, in addition to the support group we may regularly visit.

Thoughts shape reality.

I am referring to moods and emotions, not the kind of thoughts about having a million dollars in my bank account. For example, a positive thought causes a calmer life and reduces stress and sadness, whereas a negative thought causes stress, fear and worries. There is a very fine line between thoughts and reality. If you start thinking about a pain in your hand, chances are that after a short time you will really feel discomfort in the area of your hand. If while traveling by train or bus, you are thinking about a delicious ice cream that you would love to have when you get home, then most likely as soon as you get home, you will feel a pang in your stomach that is a longing for something sweet. These are just two common examples of one important principle. Although they are intangible, thoughts can shape our state of mind, our moods and emotions in reality. In an anxious state, terrible thoughts pass through you and you draw worrying situations in your mind. When this happens to you, erase those thoughts immediately and force yourself to think of another, more relaxed scenario, like working on the garden or dancing at a party. Tell yourself that these horrible thoughts can happen in reality so it is best that I get rid of them quickly. This is despite the fact that in general, in understanding the elements of anxiety and its causes, these thoughts will not happen in reality because they are false and exist only in your imagination.

The root of human thought is composed of two basic elements. The mind and the consciousness. The mind and its thoughts are two different things. "I think, therefore I am," argued the philosopher Rene Descartes, and for this thinking two things are needed: brain and mind. The mind can exist without consciousness, but consciousness cannot exist without the mind, and in any case, both have tremendous powers. The brain has enormous powers such as memory, learning, imagination, humor and more. Consciousness also has enormous powers and sometimes has the power to overcome the mind and defeat it, and in doing so is helping us deal with unwanted thoughts that harm or frighten us. For example, a person who fears negative criticism, but dreams of becoming a singer. However, this person is affected at the same time by the fear of performing in front of an audience, a fear that is created in his brain. At the same time, his desire to instill his dream comes from his consciousness. The significant understanding that he is affected by two different forces embedded in him can help him use one force to overcome and defeat the other force. If he convinces himself that the fear of criticism, or the anxiety that will attack him when he is on stage, is a false and unreal fear that is invented by the mind, but does not exist in his consciousness, then he can overcome it by his consciousness, from which he draws the power needed to defeat the mind. In other words, he gives positive meanings to negative thoughts, thus overcoming the fear and anxiety and fulfilling his dream and plan.

The human brain has a natural tendency to think negatively and to think of the worst possible scenario. This is probably a survival mechanism, but can sometimes do more harm than good. This may sound strange, but the conclusion is that we need to look for certain dangers in our lives in order to activate the survival mechanism inherent in us, the same survival mechanism that sometimes causes damage in situations where it can help save us. How strange.

Nevertheless, negative thoughts are not always serving that survival mechanism. Most of the time they harm us. Although the world is full of events over which we have no control, we certainly have control over our own actions and thoughts. A negative mood makes it difficult for us to think clearly, so we may adopt a child's perception of thought that is characterized by black or white. In fact, the only person who is against you is yourself, since the choice of how to respond to the existing situation is yours alone.

Thoughts can be controlled! It has been proven. If you choose to think negatively and create unnecessary worries in your thoughts, then you will realize that worries only create more worries. The more you think about something bad, the higher the chance that it will happen or in particularly bad cases, happen again. If you go through a day full of small accidents or stressful events, the more you think about them the more likely they are to double themselves and intensify their destruction. If you choose this path, you will find that you have accumulated large amounts of negative thoughts that are the definite recipe for anxiety. Stop telling yourself that you are miserable and suffering and about to die, or lose your business, or your wife. It will not lead you to a positive result. Instead of thinking of something painful, frightening or depressing, think about how the problem can be solved or the situation improved.

During PTSD attacks, your mind instills in you a strong belief that the reality you see is incorrect, and at the same time distorts what's really happening to you by embedding a completely different reality in your thoughts. This can also happen to those who do not suffer from PTSD or anxiety. For example, an elderly person may have lost his self-confidence and thinks that his mind is no longer functioning as it used to, or fear that this is the beginning of Alzheimer's disease. Thus, because of his fragility and insecurity, he tends to believe any reality or thought that his mind presents to him.

By controlling your thoughts through thought diversion and by cognitive behavioral therapy, you will be able to interpret the reality to the way you wish to see it, and not the way your mind wants to. Your mind deceiving you during an attack is easy because of the tendency of the average person to think negatively rather than positively. Few are the people in this stressful modern society who live and think positively all the time. So, remember that whenever you apply the method of diverting and controlling your thoughts, always do so while calling up good memories from your past to your consciousness.

This mind distortion during a PTSD attack is actually an auto-generated action, not triggered by an external event or witnessing something distressing that is happening, such as a car accident or devastating fire. Because you are surrounded by anxiety, you subconsciously surround yourself with dramatic events that are not happening at that moment and relate them to you. Sometimes you even amplify them as a cry for help. And what kind of help are you looking for in those seconds? A chemical medical miracle which you convince yourself when swallowed will help you escape the threatening inferno. And that is the trap you are caught in and start drowning in; a trap that you have dug by your own actions. The addictive use of drugs, which in some cases make the illness worse. It is not far from the truth. I have been there.

In conclusion, in order to succeed in achieving all of the above, you need a key for success.

My motto for success is this: If you train yourself to think that achieving success is a critical thing like breathing air, or consuming necessities like food and water in order to stay alive, then the road to seeing success will be easy and short. Success is driven by your will alone. The stronger and more persistent your desire and will along the way, the more success becomes achievable.

If we start from the premise that what causes PTSD, and/or any anxiety attacks, is the deception of the brain that distorts reality and infuses incorrect information into our consciousness, then, in order to redeem yourself from PTSD or anxiety attacks, you must train yourself to think that the brain is misleading you. The belief that your brain instills in your consciousness a twisted and distorted reality, can be a mantra for you to repeat every day, and not only during an attack. If you do this regularly, this ammunition will help you during the attack with an efficiency that will surprise you.

I define PTSD and anxiety attacks as purely psychological problems. Dealing with psychological problems that do not require surgical intervention can only be achieved through mind and thought control, and consciousness monitoring. To deal with it successfully, you must find a key, and that key is in your head. If I succeeded in doing it, then you can too.

15

Moral Dilemmas
During Battle

During war, soldiers and commanders often find themselves dealing with another battle, one involving ethics and human principles, often referred to as a moral dilemma. In this chapter I would like to present three examples of moral dilemmas I have personally experienced:

After a long face-to-face battle in Beirut, I voluntarily carried a wounded terrorist on my back to get him medical treatment. He was the very same enemy soldier who, just a few minutes earlier, had been trying to kill me.

In the 1982 Lebanon War, we encountered a horrifying phenomenon where Lebanese children were facing us with Russian RPG missiles.

Taking a possibly fatal risk when deciding whether to allow a child or a pregnant woman to pass through a checkpoint, even for critical hospital treatment, knowing that there have been many deadly incidents previously in which an "innocent" woman or child had blown themselves up with explosives hidden on their bodies, taking with them the lives of both soldiers and civilians.

Saving the Life of an Enemy Under Fire

This incident took place in 1981, and the scene was the large Palestinian refugee camp of Ein al-Hilweh, located near the city of Sidon, 18 miles south of Beirut. My company was assigned a mission to clear a ravine near Ein al-Hilweh from a group of terrorists who were continuously firing at us. The exchange of fire was intense, as the terrorists were hiding in small caves and crevasses in the rock and it was difficult for us to accurately identify the source of the shooting. We had to use the M72 LAW, a portable one-shot 66-mm anti-tank missile, something

179

we would normally only use for attacking sturdy buildings, or tanks and armored vehicles. But we had no choice. The stubbornness of the terrorists, despite the many losses among them, and their continued firing at us from the ravine had almost exhausted us. But we were equally stubborn. We knew that these terrorists were planning to establish themselves along the entire ravine, which was an important strategic point in southern Lebanon. Some of the terrorists emerged from the top of the ravine and began running away northwards. Two of them lay on the ground and fired missiles towards us, serving as a covering force for their fleeing comrades. The term "covering force" can refer to soldiers, tanks, artillery or jets who fire on the enemy to protect friendly troops when they are advancing, retreating or operating on the battlefield.

A short battle ensued in which we fired at the two with precise waist height shots fired from the M72 LAW weapons. The mission to purge the ravine was nearly completed, even though we had not been able to eliminate all the terrorists. Our consolation was that we had at least taken over the ravine, and from there were now in a position to completely eradicate the terrorists and their activity from it. We began to make our way down the sides of the ravine, while firing single bullets to deter any remaining terrorists as we carefully scanned every inch.

Suddenly, there was a huge explosion. The sky was filled with a huge sheet of white light, which shrouded everything. Small rocks that had been hurtled into the air from the force of the explosion began to slowly fall from the sky. The shooting stopped abruptly and there was a deathly silence. The terrorists thought we had all been killed, and we assumed they too were all dead. None of us could work out what had caused the unexpected and horrifying explosion. Only in the post-battle briefing did we find out that it was the blast of a large explosive device that had been hidden by the terrorists in the ravine. Apparently, one of the terrorists had still been hiding inside one of the caves down in the ravine. He emerged and activated the explosives to make his mark as a suicide bomber.

Lying prostrate on the stony ground, I patted my body several times to check if I was alive, then slowly raised my head to see what was going on. I could not see anything clearly. Nor could I distinguish which of the wounded and dead lying around were from our forces and which were the enemy. I got to my feet, and when it became clear to me that I was not injured, I ran to the wounded man who was closest to me, lifted him onto my back and started running eastward, away from the brutal scene of carnage. I could recall that east of where we were was the main road that led south, to Israel, and north, to Beirut. I had neither the time, nor wherewithal, to think about the identity of the wounded man I was carrying on my back, while the echoes of explosions and shots were following me so closely.

The fire behind me intensified. It turned out that more terrorists, equipped with shoulder-fired missiles and numerous hand grenades, had arrived the in the combat area. I kept on running with the wounded man on my back. I expected at any second to be hit by a bullet that would fell me. The shots were becoming so close that I could see stray bullets and stones ricocheting off the rocks. A small rock even hit me in the stomach. Despite the pain from this, plus my fatigue, I continued running with the wounded man on my back. What kept me going was the trust being placed in me by this suffering human being that I would bring him to a place of safety, so I needed to continue with all my might towards the main road. My hope was that there would be a helicopter or military truck waiting there to rush him to the nearest hospital.

After about 700 yards, when I realized I was out of range of the fire, I stopped. I laid the man on the ground facing upwards, took a flask of water from my combat vest, splashed his mouth and face, and tried to communicate with him to see if he was alive.

To my concern, he did not respond. I continued to try to revive him. After few minutes, his eyes flickered open and he whispered in Arabic "Shukran" (thank you). I jumped to my feet and aimed my weapon at him. The shock that this man was in fact my enemy almost caused me a heart attack. My body was already stressed by my heavy panting and accelerated heartbeat caused by such a dangerous and strenuous run. The man looked at me imploringly and said in Arabic, "Please have mercy on me in the name of Allah." "Why should I have pity on him?" I murmured to myself. "He almost killed me." I was distressed and confused. I was just a 23-year-old; I had no strength for such a moral confrontation. I had seen blood and hundreds of burnt bodies and come out safely from a tough battles and dangerous shooting incidents, but I had never encountered such an ambiguous situation. Nor was there anyone next to me to advise me on what was the right thing to do. I also did not have much time to think, because all the time explosions resounded all around. I watched him mumble words in Arabic that had one meaning: a plea for mercy. I had to decide.

While I was trying to figure out what to do, I continued to dab him with water, cleaning his injury as well as I could. Nevertheless, I could not clear the confusion in my head. If I shoot him, I might have to carry that feeling of guilt in shooting at an unarmed human, and my conscience would haunt me for the rest of my life. On the other hand, I couldn't ignore the thought that this human was a terrorist that might

In the heat of battle.

return to the terror arena after he recovered. I was facing a serious dilemma. Suddenly there was the noise of yet another huge explosion, followed by another and another. I lay down on the ground, but at the same time I knew I had to get myself away from the range of the fire. I noticed a hill about 300 yards to the east, which would be a safe direction to head in, due the presence of Israeli forces there. I got up, and before I could start running, the man on the ground begged me to take him with me. "Please don't let me die here," he said in Arabic. I did not know what to do. Being already aware of his heavy weight, I had the fear that his weight would slow my run towards the hill for a temporary shelter. I felt helpless, unable to control and manage my thoughts and decisions. I was sweating profusely and the noise of the explosions was deafening. I remember that even my vision began to blur. Years later, on a visit to my local clinic due to a persistent headache, the doctor explained to me that there was a link between stress and vision, which can cause a temporary impairment in one's ability to see clearly and distinctly. The wounded terrorist kept begging me not to leave him there helpless and unarmed. My thoughts were vague, and in the background were the echoes of the explosions. The noise of war. The smell of war. I had to make a rapid decision. In order for me not to abandon him, I would have to use greater-than-usual mental powers, meaning to erase from my mind the identity of the wounded person lying beside me. I owed it to my conscience and to the values I was educated in. I felt this was beyond my abilities. I found myself wrestling with my thoughts. How could I think about saving someone else, when I could hardly save myself in this inferno? Let alone the fact that this person was an enemy terrorist, who had been trying to kill me and my friends just half an hour ago. This was the craziest situation I had ever encountered in my life, and remained so during all my long years of service filled with battles and dangerous situations.

Suddenly there came another loud explosion, this time even closer, and at that moment, all the confusion and the wrestling of my thoughts vanished. Instinctively, my conscience and compassion took over. As if on automatic pilot mode, without him having to beg or ask me to, I picked him up, placed him over my right shoulder as we had practiced, balancing his body weight evenly to make it easier for me to carry him, then I started running wildly eastwards towards the hill. The hill was quite a distance so it took me a while to get to there. During my run, with the echoes of the explosions in the background, my convoluted thoughts suddenly came back, as if my mind was determined to make the rescue task even more difficult for me. Why should I rescue him under fire and risk my own life to save his? Would he have done the same for me? Why don't I just dump him in the field? But every time I thought of throwing him off me, I thought about him being a human just like me. What madness, I thought, how crazy wars can be, how irrational. I started screaming loudly so as not to break down and give up. I shouted nonsense; meaningless, illogical sentences, just to keep up my physical strength and not to fall. Then, after all the physical and mental effort I had mustered, I arrived heavily panting and sweating at the main road where Israeli forces were positioned waiting to enter the city of Sidon. I was sure there would be a medical team amongst them, or at least a paramedic. I laid the wounded man down on his back, told him in Arabic that he would be fine here, and that Israeli soldiers would take care of him. He nodded and again whispered, "Shukran."

I looked at his face and asked him his name. With a calm expression he responded, "My name is Azem Salim, I'm from Beit Hanoun in Gaza." Then he grabbed my hand in an anxious way and asked me, "Will your friends treat me the same way you treated me?" I smiled and placed my hand on his shoulder to calm him down. "You can be sure that from here you will be fine. We are the Israeli army." I left him and went to find the commander on field to report a wounded man and his identity. The commander, who was also the doctor in charge, looked at me indifferently and said, "It's all right, we will treat him as if he was one of us."

I took one last glance at the bleeding man lying on the ground, the man who was considered my enemy, but during the last hour, he became in my mind a man just like me. Then, I started running back towards my company. The noise of the battle still echoed in the air, black smoke and thick dust that made my vision difficult. I arrived unharmed and immediately joined my comrades who were still engaged in the damned war.

The fundamental dilemma in the case I have related, was not whether any human life should be saved if at all possible, as I believe that in every human being, the instinct to save a life is pre-programmed and embedded. Therefore, to me, the question of whether we act on impulse to save life is not a weighty issue in which diverse views need to be expressed. But if this is so, to what extent should you increase the risk to yourself to save another life? The dilemma in my case was complicated at least sevenfold. It was not simply about saving the life of an enemy who had already surrendered. In such a case the dilemma does not exist, as I am committed to honor the Geneva Convention, as well as the values embedded into me in my military service. The dilemma was about saving the life of someone who had just been trying to kill me. The dilemma was further exacerbated when I saved his life while risking my own, carrying him while I was being fired on for 700 yards, when my own physical strength was slowly ebbing away. The fear of dying from the continuous fire during the rescue was remarkably less than the confusion and frustration that caused my mental state to unravel during those dreadful moments.

I admit that I had been worried in carrying an enemy who could perhaps decide to strangle me, but from the moment I dragged the wounded man away from the fire zone, I knew I was doing the right thing. Once you are on the inside of the event, and the adrenalin is coursing throughout your body, you act in automatic mode. Miraculously, in those moments, the fear dissipates as if swallowed up by the earth. Feelings and emotions are also temporarily out of the picture. All that is left swimming front of your eyes is the urge to apply the combat practices you have learned, and get safely out of the situation. Evacuating a wounded combatant from the fire zone is part of this. You do not involve emotions and do not waste time on checking the identity or rank of the wounded person in need of immediate evacuation.

Shooting at Armed Children During War

Throughout the Gaza Strip, the Hamas militant organization has used civilians, and especially innocent children, as human shields. I remember one particular event that took place there when we were conducting a routine patrol, when a Hamas terrorist fired a rocket at us from the roof of a residential building. He quickly fled the scene while we chased him, but as he ran away, he spotted a group of children and shouted to them to run with him. When those children joined him, we immediately stopped firing. When we captured him after a problematic chase through crowded alleys populated by civilians, we asked him why he had taken those little kids with him. He looked at us with a mocking, dismissive smile, and said, "We were told that you Israelis are not capable of shooting children. You are cowards."

Two days later, we stopped a Palestinian boy running towards us shouting "Allahu Akbar," the Arabic phrase meaning "God is the Greatest." Because we could see he was unarmed, we did not shoot at him, but he was getting ominously closer to us still frantically screaming the dreaded words "Allahu Akbar," so often the precursor of a deadly suicide attack. The patrol commander suspected that maybe this boy was carrying an explosive belt and ordered us to take shelter. Meanwhile, another patrol force from my company arrived on the scene behind the boy, ran towards him and from behind pushed him to the ground. A search of his body found no explosives, just a large knife and an unusually large plastic key. During his interrogation, he confessed that the key had been given to him by his terrorist handlers from the PLO's organization. They had told him the key was to open the gates of heaven for him and for his family. Only two months later, when undercover fighters captured the same terrorist who gave the boy the promising key to the gates of heaven, did his investigation reveal the meaning of the act. He admitted that in doing so, they wanted to achieve victory in the arena of world public opinion. They assumed that we, the soldiers, would shoot the child who was attacking us, thus showing the world how the Israeli army shoots at children. How cruel.

Despite condemnations from the United Nations, Amnesty International, and many human rights organizations around the world, terrorist organizations have not stopped using children in their violent activities. It was Fatah that originally began to implement this cruel practice, when they trained children to fearlessly shoot deadly missiles at us. Although there were many Palestinian mothers who opposed and condemned the phenomenon, or expressly forbade their children from taking part in an act of martyrdom, Fatah continued to exploit children and teenagers by teaching them how to fire missiles at IDF forces, while promising them that they would be safe as the IDF will not shoot back at them. Sadly, the UN and Amnesty International did not act decisively against this phenomenon of child exploitation.

During the 1982 Lebanon War, we encountered situations where we had to make a decision within seconds on whether to shoot back at those armed 12-years-old boys, or to run and hide. The option of not shooting back is unfamiliar to us as commando fighters, as we are trained to face up to an onslaught, not to run away from those firing on us. But the adversaries we were facing were just teenage children trained in the firing of formidable RPG missiles. These were very difficult situations, both in terms of the ability to make the right decision instantaneously, and in terms of the outcome of such unusual confrontation. One still haunts me from that terrible period. A particularly nasty incident where the accurate firing of an RPG missile by a boy who looked around 11 years old succeeded in killing an Israeli soldier. He was an unusually daring Palestinian boy, full of self-confidence and bravado, filled with certainty he would not be in any danger having been told that Israeli soldiers do not shoot children. He brazenly stood in front of us and aimed the RPG towards us. We did not believe this kid would really pull the trigger. Besides, we genuinely believing he was holding an empty unloaded missile so we did not take him seriously. But we were wrong. He fired the missile at us, and managed to take down one of our soldiers, whose whole body shattered into pieces from the missile fired at him from such a short range. The boy was shot and killed on the spot. In the interrogation of his family, it turned out that the boy had been very active, having been inspired by his uncle, a senior terrorist with blood on his hands, and wanted by the Israeli security forces. His mother admitted that she had witnessed her son's conversations with his uncle, but did not take this seriously and did not believe that the boy would commit an act like this. She explained that in one of the conversations, she had overheard the boy had received instructions from his uncle on exactly how to fire the missile. On that phone call, the boy had been asking his uncle precise technical questions about the missile; which button to press, how to aim the missile and so on. Knowing this kind of missile myself, I can say it is very easy and pretty straightforward to operate. All you have to do is aim and pull a trigger. Just make sure no one is standing close behind you.

The RPG, is a manual anti-tank missile developed and manufactured by the Soviet Union in 1962. It subsequently became the most common weapon in the world for use against tanks and in the demolition of buildings. Its features have made it a preferred weapon for guerrilla organizations and irregular militias, who fight against an organized army that has an armored corps equipped with tanks. The RPG is widely considered to be a simple but effective, reliable, and inexpensive weapon, and is comprising a simple elongated hollow tube with just one button to press. The user inserts the tail of the missile into the hollow tube, pushes the button and fires the missile. Its disadvantage is the tremendous noise it makes, and also the dangerous fireball that shoots out of the back of the hollow tube when it's fired.

Judgements at Checkpoints

Compared to being sent to the battlefield, the checkpoints I helped to man during my military service in Gaza and the West Bank, were effortless in terms of the physical aspect of being there. However, they were hard to endure mentally and morally, due to the sensitivity of the task we were forced to perform. At the checkpoint, we were forced not only to prod and probe the body of the average Palestinian seeking to cross the border into Israeli territory, but also to penetrate his soul, by the invasive tests and personal questions. In some situations, it was exacerbated by the way the Palestinians responded to our invasive checks and personal questions, leading many times to violent clashes between us and irate civilians. In my understanding, this was in a large part due to the culture gap between the two sides. In Palestinian culture, insulting someone or causing them offence can result in murder, while in Western countries, an insult or offence does not often lead to physical confrontation, as the "offended" will simply ignore what has happened. This is how we, as Israelis, assumed that the Palestinians would respond. We hoped they would understand that we were only performing our duty to protect our citizens, as they would surely know about the many previous cases in which terrorists had passed through the checkpoint unchallenged and gone on to carry out terrorist attacks in Israel. Some of them, mainly mature adults, did understand the need for our "invasive checks and personal questions." They realized from experience that the degree of scrutiny of a person coming through a checkpoint can differ from person to person, and there were times when we did not check at all. Sometimes we performed random checks on selective persons or vehicles, which could include a performing a full physical examination of all a vehicle's occupants and their belongings.

Between 1980 and 2004 hundreds of Palestinian children and teenagers were arrested after attempting to smuggle explosive belts and weapons across into Israel. At that time, they were exploiting the less rigorous checks and searches by the IDF at the Israeli checkpoints and security fences in the Gaza Strip and in the West Bank. We, the soldiers, were faced with difficult dilemmas at least ten times a day. But the problem was not only dealing with one type of dilemma. During a battle, the phenomenon of the moral dilemma rarely emerges, but at checkpoints the dilemmas encountered by the soldiers are two-fold, as they

One of our tasks was to man a checkpoint around the West Bank.

are both moral and practical dilemmas. In this situation, they are even more frequent because of the thousands of Palestinian commuters passing through the checkpoints daily, some to work in Israel, some to take advantage of free medical treatment, and some conducting errands for the Ministries of Defense and of the Interior, both of which government bodies are responsible for issuing passes and work permits in Israel for Palestinians.

Our task at the checkpoint rarely ran smoothly and free from mistakes and misconceptions. It was always an ambiguous procedure, in which we had to make good use of our innate senses and instincts, much more so than our combat abilities. We had to make instantaneous decisions based on the right judgment as to whether to approve a pass, or put the person involved through a thorough search and examination. These would be people who were showing signs of nervousness, or who refused to answer our questions. The situation can be likened to the tough security screening we may go through at airports of certain countries, except that at the airport the examiner is not facing a possible threat of death by the examinee.

We found ourselves caught up in situations where our judgment was subject to confusion. Inside ourselves, we would be wrestling between the conflicting matters of personal conscience, national security, and the duty of a soldier to obey orders. The double dilemma that prevailed among us soldiers, which personally bothered me in particular, was the statistical fact that most of the civilians passing through the checkpoints were decent, hard-working people. Seemingly this sounds like a satisfactory situation, but in reality, it made our task even harder. The acknowledgment that most of the people we encountered were decent and had no malintent often made our searches less thorough, and thus, in some terrible instances, our gesture of good faith turned against us if one of these seemingly innocent people violated this trust and blew himself up along with us. During my many years of service, I have seen more than one case in which human limbs crashed at a checkpoint where Palestinians with bad intentions were allowed to pass.

Seeing a sick crying baby in the arms of his mother, feverish and screaming in distress, brings out my emotion as a human being that this baby is helpless and in need of help, whether he is Palestinian, Jewish or Christian. But in the more rational area of my brain, I imagine that his mother could be carrying explosives underneath her floor length Arabic dress. As a soldier, I am caught in the vortex of a swirling dilemma. On the one hand I want to act humanely, but on the other hand I would have a crisis of guilt if it turned out that my humanity allowed a terrorist to cross the checkpoint and kill civilians or soldiers. it is incumbent upon us as members of a moral army, and also as human beings, to treat with compassion and humanity a pregnant woman, a feverish baby needing to get to hospital, an elderly man, or a handicapped person in a wheelchair. However, applying these values was not as easy as it sounds and, in some cases, it brought about enormous difficulties dilemmas.

On March 24, 2004, Hussam Abdo, a 14-year-old boy sent by Fatah's Al-Aqsa Martyrs Brigades, was caught wearing an explosive belt at a checkpoint near Nablus. During interrogation, when asked why he had agreed to such an act that would mean his certain death, he responded, "Because I was promised that I would not be searched by the Jews."

A month later, a 12-year-old Palestinian boy with an explosive belt was arrested in Hebron while on his way to blow himself up in front of a patrol force of Israeli soldiers. Just ten days after this, another 12-year-old boy was arrested in the same neighborhood of Hebron, carrying inside his schoolbag an explosive weighing five kilos. During their interrogation, they all said the same thing: "We were promised we will not be searched."

By March 2006, dozens of Palestinian children and teenagers had been arrested after attempting to smuggle explosive belts and weapons through Israeli checkpoints and security fences. In a number of cases, the detainees admitted that their actions stemmed from a desire to win the sympathy of their relatives, rarely expressing any remorse for the act they intended to commit. In a particularly shocking case in October 2016, IDF soldiers arrested two Palestinian boys who were 8 years old. These tiny boys were armed with knives and sent by Palestinian terrorists to carry out a stabbing attack in Israel, assuming such young children would not raise any suspicions when passing through the checkpoint.

In 1987, during the Intifada uprising in the West Bank, I allowed a disabled person to pass without performing a routine search on him. I made every effort to complete his crossing as quickly as possible by limiting the process to only asking him to show me his ID card. I then helped him by pushing his wheelchair through the checkpoint and I handed him a bottle of water. In retrospect, it turned out that I had made the wrong call in applying the values of compassion and consideration towards a disabled or sick human. This "handicapped" human, turned out to be a heartless bomber who was carrying a lethal explosive underneath his wheelchair. It was only thanks to the vigilance of the checkpoint commander who was more experienced than me, that a substantial disaster was averted when he managed to neutralize the "disabled" terrorist before he could launch the explosive. I was, of course, punished for my negligence by my battalion commander. My punishment was working one full day in the kitchen back at the base.

Although not trying to justify my dangerous mistake with the "disabled" terrorist, I explained to my platoon commander that I was a Golani fighter specializing in adrenaline-fueled commando battles, and was not experienced in spending hours policing an often-tedious checkpoint. Then, to my relief, he changed his tone of voice towards me, and even hinted to me that he sympathized with my logical explanation. It turned out that I predicted a psychological element that was not yet known in my great army. Only from the mid–1990s, did the army begin to train officers to provide mental psychological assistance to soldiers on duty at checkpoints.

In 1983, years before the Intifada, we came across another case in which we showed consideration for a pregnant Palestinian woman. It was at a checkpoint located northwest of Jericho. When we allowed the pregnant woman to pass, it turned out that the "fetus" in her womb was in fact a bomb. Three kilos of explosives were wrapped in a piece of cloth that convincingly shaped her belly to look like that of a pregnant woman. Fortunately, the female soldier at the checkpoint who insisted on conducting a search of the pregnant woman's body, prevented the explosives from being activated. The "pregnant woman" began to cry and direct all the blame on to her handlers, whom she claimed had threatened her and forced her into doing what she did. None of us believed her. She was later tried in an Israeli military court and sent to five years in prison. During her interrogation, after she broke down, she surprised the investigators when she revealed that ambulances are often used for smuggling. Palestinian Red Cross ambulances were allowed to pass through the checkpoints without any inspection. This privilege was exploited by terrorist organizations in the West Bank who smuggled explosives and wanted terrorists to and from the Gaza Strip. After searches of several ambulances where explosives and weapons were found and seized, it became very clear that these ambulances were not being used for altruistic, lifesaving activities. The Israeli security decided to scrap the exemption from searching ambulances, even those dealing with emergencies, which unfortunately delayed the transporting of genuinely sick or wounded patients who needed urgent care.

In the years following the Oslo Accords of 1994 and 1997, a wave of terrorism took place throughout Israel that included a series of numerous suicide bombings. These young suicidals managed to fool some of the checkpoint's soldiers and carried out deadly attacks in which 1,450 Jews were killed. In response, even more checkpoints were set up.

The Hague Convention of 1954, as well as the four Geneva Conventions drafted and signed in Switzerland between 1864 and 1949, set out the ground rules of proper conduct between armies and nations in time of war, but these seemingly do not concern Palestinian terrorist organizations. They do not respect any of these conventions and continue to commit war crimes contrary to international moral codes, by using children and civilians as human shields, and in some cases sending them to conduct terror attacks, assuming they will not raise any suspicion.

16

1976 Operation Entebbe

Many legends have been linked to the IDF's unknown operations around the world. One of the best known took place at the airport in Entebbe, Uganda, over 2,000 miles from Israel.

On the morning of June 27, 1967, an Air France plane carrying 240 passengers took off from Tel Aviv to Paris. It was hijacked by two German terrorists from the Revolutionary Cells urban guerrilla group and two Palestinian terrorists, who were members of the Popular Front for the Liberation of Palestine terror organization, otherwise known as the PFLP. There were 248 passengers and 12 crew members on the plane at the time. Among the passengers were 104 Israeli nationals, and 56 Jews from other countries. The objective of the hijackers were the Jews and the Israelis only. The terrorists forced the plane to land in Benghazi, Libya, where it was refueled, and then took off for Entebbe airport in Uganda. Once it landed at Entebbe, two more Palestinian terrorists came on board to join the group of hijackers. Uganda's President Idi Amin ordered 200 of his military forces to surround the plane to also assist the hijackers.

On Tuesday 29 June, the hijackers demanded the release of 53 imprisoned terrorists, 40 of whom were detained in Israel, including the Japanese Kōzō Okamoto. They also sought the release of five terrorists detained in Kenya, eight anarchists imprisoned in Germany, Switzerland and France, as well as a US$5,000,000 ransom from the French government. They threatened to kill the hostages if their demands were not met.

Israeli Prime Minister Yitzhak Rabin urgently summoned the Army Chief of Staff Brigadier General Mordechai "Motta" Gur, and the head of the Mossad intelligence agency to his office. Meanwhile, the Israeli intelligence agencies had already swung into action. They were able to closely monitor the hijacked aircraft using the technology of those days, and quickly discovered that the plane had changed its route and was making its way to Benghazi Airport in Libya, instead of its intended destination of Paris. After refueling in Libya, the plane took off for Uganda. Once at the plane's final destination, Entebbe, the hostages were taken off the plane and led into the stuffy, neglected old airport terminal, which was no longer being used as the airport had recently built a new one.

The atmosphere among the members of the Israeli Cabinet as they discussed the matter was unbearably tense. The room was full of cigarette smoke, as both Defense Minister Shimon Peres and Prime Minister Yitzhak Rabin were notoriously heavy smokers. Some of the ministers suggested rejecting the hijackers' demands outright, others thought it was better to release terrorists with blood on their hands than to abandon a hundred helpless Israeli citizens to be killed. Defence Minister Shimon Peres was the only one to strongly push for a military operation to rescue the hostages. Apart from him, neither Prime Minister Rabin, nor any of the other ministers in that smoke-filled and crowded meeting room, including the Army Chief of Staff himself, felt able to support such a bold and unfeasible option. They were not overly enthusiastic about a dangerous rescue operation so far away from home, an operation that could possibly have no chance of success. Having been a senior military officer before his political career, Prime Minister Rabin felt conflicted and under pressure. On the one hand he did not want to surrender to the terrorists' demands, but on the other, he did not want to risk the lives of the hostages in the event of the failure of such a dangerous and impossible mission. As an army veteran, Rabin held the view that soldiers are obligated to risk their lives as a requirement of their job, but not the lives of civilians who have not been trained to fight.

As the Cabinet ministers continued to verbally wrestle with each other, not able to make a unified decision and struggling to find a consensus that all would be comfortable with, one of the Prime Minister's assistants entered the room with a note in her hand. The room fell silent. The ministers, who were thirsting for any new piece of information or unexpected developments in the hijacking, stared at the woman as she stepped towards the Prime Minister and put the note down in front of him. All the Cabinet members were watching their Prime Minister with eager anticipation as Rabin slowly read out, "The hijackers have separated the Israelis from the non–Israeli passengers." The Prime Minister continued reading from the note, "The Israelis have been taken to a small hall adjacent to the main arrivals hall where the other passengers are being held. All the non–Israelis will be released and flown to Paris tomorrow."

The Cabinet ministers were stunned. They all understood the significance of this separation. Some of them were Holocaust survivors, and the announcement of this enforced separation mentally transported them back to the Nazi extermination camps, when Jews had been separated by the Nazis twice. The first time had been when Jews had been isolated from non–Jewish citizens around the Nazi occupied European countries, and then again on their arrival at the camps when Jews who could be used for slave labor were separated from those who were too young or infirm to work. These people would be immediately marched away to be murdered in the gas chambers. This resonation had also affected three of the hostages who were Holocaust survivors when listening to their names read out in the distinctive German accents of the hijackers Wilfried Böse and Brigitte Kuhlmann. The chilling separation reminded them of the horrifying days of the Holocaust.

After separating the Israeli passengers from the non–Israelis, the hijackers offered the captain of the plane and all his crew members a chance to join the freed passengers and fly with them to Paris. Captain Michel Bacos, along with his loyal Air France crew, refused the hijackers' offer of being released, strongly feeling their responsibility to remain with the captive passengers.

Wilfried Böse, who was surprised by the captain's response, ordered the captain to obey his instruction and join the freed passengers. Captain Bacos was resolute when he stood up and looked straight in the eye of Böse and told him, "I refuse to leave my Israeli and passengers behind in Entebbe. I have already gathered my crew together and told them that under no circumstances will we leave this terminal for freedom while many of our passengers are still being held here against their will and while guns are pointed at their heads. All my crew members have agreed to this." Encouraged by the bravery and admirable leadership of their captain, the crew immediately joined him and did all they could to comfort and encourage the Israeli hostages, trying to make them feel supported at this difficult and distressing moment. One of the Palestinian terrorists ordered the Air France crew to return to their seats, but the courageous captain shot him a contemptuous look, making it clear that he and his crew intended to stay with their passengers wherever they were taken. Once this decision had been accepted by the astonished hijackers, Bacos walked over to the Israeli hostages, hugged them, and accompanied them into the area they were now being ordered into.

After the jarring news of the separation of the Israeli and non–Israeli passengers, preparations for a hostage rescue operation by the Israeli military began to roll. Senior army officers sat for many hours

The old terminal at Entebbe where the hostages were held.

exchanging ideas to come up with a rescue operation. These were all commando officers with substantial experience. They knew that embarking on a complex operation on hostile soil far from home had to be carried out in a way that was bold, imaginative and daring. They also knew that those who would ultimately decide whether to embark on a military operation would be the members of the government, so they had to present them with the most convincing and compelling rescue plan. It was clear to the architects and planners of the operation that they were going to be doing something never before attempted. Unlike other operations, where they had had time to prepare, this one was not only a long way from their base, but neither did it allow the commandos enough time to build a model to train on.

During the preparations for a hostage rescue operation, my unit learnt that we were probably going to be part of it. We were flown from our base in the Golan Heights directly to Sharm-el-Sheikh, in the Sinai Desert, were we were going to train for the operation. We could have trained in much better conditions at our own base, but the choice of Sharm-el-Sheikh was to save on the flight time of the potential mission as we would be closer to Africa.

During the flight, we were instructed not to talk about the

preparations for the operation in any way to anyone, including any soldiers we might come in contact with in the area.

It was a pleasant low-altitude internal flight, during which we enjoyed the beautiful scenery and orchards, sights that were infinitely more pleasant than the fortified fences, weapons, and armored vehicles, which were our daily sights in the Golan Heights. Our journey south ended among the ruins of a deserted army base used by the Israeli navy. We began training on a disused grounded aircraft that for this situation was used to replicate the hijacked Air France plane. The compound of the former army base represented the Entebbe airport area, while the now empty weapons storehouse substituted for the terminal where the hostages were being held. The entire facility was re-arranged and set up according to the information the Israeli Mossad had received from the freed non–Israeli hostages when they were questioned by French and Israeli officials on their arrival in Paris.

We as soldiers, were unaware of the arguments, disagreements and deliberations that were going on among the decision makers in the Israeli government. However, the surprise visit of our Commander in Chief, the Army Chief of Staff, Motta Gur himself, provided us with a clue. Only after the operation, reading the countless media reports, interviews, analyses of the operation by experts including retired generals, did we understand that Commander-in-Chief Gur had not been 100 percent in favor of the operation. His visit to us in Sharm el-Sheikh was to be the key factor in his decision for or against the operation. On the morning of Saturday 3 July, he had asked to be flown down to the Sinai Desert to see for himself the training and exercises being carried out by the commando forces, and to assess the operational capability of the fighters who were about to be sent on the rescue mission. He would also closely examine the rescue plan itself, whether it was viable and had a chance of success, or was too complicated and dangerous to carry out.

By the end of his short impromptu visit, the Chief of Staff had found himself surprisingly impressed with the operational capability of his commando fighters, and in particular the tricks they were planning to use to fool the Ugandan sentries. Chief of Staff Motta Gur now fully embraced and supported the rescue operation.

The senior army officers who were assigned to plan a rescue operation, came up with four options. Defence Minister Peres, as the only one encouraging military action in Entebbe, was trying to convince some of the Cabinet members who were still hesitating to support this view. He asked the Cabinet members to at least listen to the four possible options for a hostage rescue operation, which had been prepared by senior military personnel. For the next three hours, the Cabinet members listened intently to the four options that were presented by Brigadier General Dan Shomron, who was the chief architect of the plans and who would go on to be appointed as the commander of the Entebbe rescue operation. In presenting the plans to the Israeli Cabinet, Shomron was accompanied by Lieutenant Colonel Moshe "Muki" Betzer and several intelligence officers. The Cabinet members agreed. Ten minutes later, they followed up Shomron's presentation with a stream of questions, probing the details of each plan.

The four plans presented were:

Dan Shomron. Commander of Operation Entebbe, later Israeli Army Chief of Staff.

Plan Number One

The Israeli government would inform the hijackers that it had agreed to release the prisoners held in Israel. Once the date and time was confirmed, a force of 40 Israeli commandos, dressed in orange shirts like those worn in prison, would arrive at Entebbe on a direct flight in a civilian plane. On entering the terminal, the skilled Israeli commandos would each draw a pistol from behind their backs, eliminate the seven unprepared and shocked hijackers, and rush all the hostages outside to the waiting plane that would have kept its engines running to ensure a speedy departure.

Plan Number Two

In collaboration with Israeli Mossad agents based in Uganda, a group of 35 paratroopers would be dropped on to Lake Victoria, picked by a large fishing boat arranged by the agents, and once ashore driven to Entebbe airport to storm the terminal and free the hostages. They would be flown to Israel by a waiting Hercules plane, planned to land at the airport at exactly the same time as the onslaught on the terminal.

Plan Number Three

A force of 20 fighter commandos would fly to the Kenyan capital of Nairobi. Mossad agents would arrive two days earlier and hire a yacht for the commandos to sail across Lake Victoria from its Kenyan shore to Entebbe. The commandos would be wearing colorful summer clothes, some even in swimsuits, to appear to be a group of holidaymakers, in the event of them being spotted by the Marine Guard of Lake Victoria. The force would aim to arrive on the shore near Entebbe late at night, change quickly into their combat uniforms, pick up their weapons and begin marching toward the airport, just over a mile away.

Plan Number Four

A large, combined commando force of 400 of the best IDF fighters would be flown to Entebbe on four large Hercules planes. The first plane would carry an assault squad from the Sayeret Matkal commando unit plus a team of Paratroopers; the second would bring a backup force from the Sayeret Matkal unit; and the third would carry a force from the Golani Brigade. The fourth Hercules would serve as the command-and-control base for the operation. Two Boeing jets would also be sent, one serving as the Air Force command station which would circle Lake Victoria, and the other as a temporary hospital which would remain on the ground at Nairobi airport in neighboring Kenya to deal with any casualties.

For most of the panel around the table, the first plan seemed the most attractive and practical, and pretty straightforward. In this plan, the fighters would enter the terminal hall as welcome guests of the hijackers, who would not be pointing their guns ready to shoot. The Cabinet members believed they had received a clever and creative plan that had a great chance of success and most were willing to agree to this. However, Brigadier General Shomron told the Cabinet members that he was more interested in Plan Four. The reason was that inside the terminal there was also a large presence of armed Ugandan soldiers. To overcome these soldiers, as well as the hijackers, using a small pistol would not be enough. The commandos would need to have much more powerful weapons, such as automatic rifles and grenades, and possibly even missiles.

There was a momentary silence in the room. The Cabinet members and Prime Minister Rabin understood the logic of the Dan Shomron's explanation and asked him to elaborate on plan number four. Shomron pinned a hand-drawn map on the wall which showed the details and stages of the plan. According to this plan, the operational force would be flown to Entebbe in four large Hercules planes.

The first plane would carry the Sayeret Matkal commando force led by renowned commando fighter Lieutenant Colonel Yonatan "Yoni" Netanyahu, who would storm the old terminal and release the hostages. They would make their way towards the terminal using two BT40 Land Rovers and a black Mercedes sedan. The Mercedes was a ruse to deceive the Ugandan guards into thinking it was a surprise visit of President Idi Amin in his presidential car. This plane would also carry 35 Paratroopers led by Lt Colonel Matan Vilnai, to take control of the nearby new terminal and the air traffic control tower, and to mark out the airport's runway with battery powered lights that would be necessary in the event of any power failure.

On the second plane would be members of the Sayeret Matkal securing team under the command of Shaul Mofaz. They would assist the combatants to storm the terminal by securing the front area of the building and eliminating the old terminal's watchtower.

The third aircraft would be use as the evacuation aircraft and would carry the Golani Brigade team commanded by Uri Sagi. Its mission would be to serve as a combat reserve force, and to quickly lead the hostages to the aircraft.

The fourth aircraft would be serving as the command-and-control base for the operation, under the Operation Commander Brigadier General Dan Shomron and his team.

To complete the deception, the Israeli Mossad provided a cover for the landing aircraft to look like they were regular civilian passenger planes. In addition, they managed to outwit the Ugandan air traffic controllers by integrating the arriving aircraft into the Entebbe airport schedule. The two Boeing planes, one serving as an improvised hospital, and the other as the Air Force command station, would take off well before the four Hercules.

On Saturday, 3 July, Prime Minister Rabin summoned a small group of Cabinet ministers for an urgent and top-secret discussion at his family home to make the final decision on whether to go ahead with the plan. Time was running out as the hijackers had threatened to start killing the hostages on Sunday 4 July. At 2:00 p.m., the Army Chief of Staff Motta Gur (who had just arrived back from his visit to our training base in the Sinai), Foreign Minister Yigal Alon, Defence Minister Shimon Peres, Minister of Transport Haim Bar-Lev and Interior Minister Yosef Burg all arrived at Yitzhak Rabin's house.

According to the original plan presented, about 400 fighters would be flown to Entebbe. However, Prime Minister Rabin expressed concern about risking such a large force to participate in the operation. As a former military man, he did not see the need for a large number of well-trained commandos to rescue hostages from a single building. He recommended sending no more than a hundred. Finally, after discussions with the military personnel, it was decided to reduce the number of fighters to only 200, about half the amount planned. A rumor began to circulate among the preparatory forces about the decision. While we waited anxiously on the burning Sinai sands, this rumor was verified. A strange feeling crept over me, which was one of disappointment. Being one of the youngest fighters, only 19 years old, I began to feel that I would not be among the lucky ones that would soon be flying down to Entebbe. Indeed, during the afternoon, Ron Shechner, the company commander of our glorious company C of Battalion 12, the most decorated battalion in the whole Golani Brigade, approached me. Knowing him so well, I could sense bad news from the expression on his face.

"It's been decided that not so many fighters will be needed for the mission," he said quietly while placing his hand on my shoulder as if to comfort me.

"I know I'm very young, but...," I mumbled.

"No, it has nothing to do with your age," he replied. "They want to prioritize the officers."

"OK, that makes sense then," I said.

"Anyway, you will be missing nothing," he continued. "Our task is only transporting the hostages," he smiled. Then he explained that we, the rest of us fighters, would remain in Sharm-el-Sheikh to serve as a backup and aid force, ready with all our combat equipment to be flown to Entebbe if needed. It turned out that both in the political Cabinet and the top command of the army, there was a reasonable fear that the forces being sent to Entebbe would encounter difficulties. There could be unforeseen eventualities, such as the arrival of a large force from the Ugandan army, a possibility that was as yet uncertain. There was also a fear that an entire battalion of the Ugandan army could be stationed not far from the airport, possibly in the city of Entebbe itself, and would be sent to the terminal to confront the Israeli forces.

During my two years in company C, I was the liaison for my tough company commander Ron Shechner, becoming almost his right hand throughout all the operations and training took part in over the course of a year. I was his "kashar," the Hebrew term for the fighter in a company whose job is to carry on his back a large radio device called 77PRC (no longer used today). I had to stay close to the commander to pass the handset of the device to him when he was called or wished to use it to pass on instructions to his men, or report to the chief operational commander. There develops a close relationship between the company commander and his kashar, as it requires many hours spent together. My responsibilities as kashar were of course in addition to my function as an ordinary fighter and member of the combat force.

When Ron saw the disappointment still etched on my face, he looked at me and said, "Hey, remember that you are a fighter in C company in the 12th Battalion of the celebrated brigade called Golani." He continued, "The 12th Battalion, to which only the best and most excellent fighters are admitted, the battalion renowned for its acts of heroism in the conquest of Mount Hermon and the Golan Heights in 1967, and then again in 1973 for its inconceivable bravery."

I nodded and shook his hand, wishing him luck and a safe return.

He then tapped me on the shoulder and said, "Go and have some coffee. I promise you will be attending the post-combat debriefing after we get back."

This was at least some kind of consolation for me. If I was to be excluded from taking part in the operation, I thought, then at least I would be able hear it first hand and have the feeling of being there too. Post-combat debriefing after a battle or operation allows us to draw lessons on how to act on the battlefield in the future. The investigation is based on gathering all the details and facts about the specific operation, while presenting all the stages of its procedures to the senior commanders so that they are able to understand what transpired. The process is not intended to pinpoint culprits or lay blame but to uncover what really took place, so as to improve and streamline the combat activities of both the individual fighter and the planners of the operation.

The debriefing takes place immediately after the operation, when the details are still fresh in the combatants' memory and can be recovered quickly and accurately. Investigating operational events and the learning process is an important component in building an army. Being present at a debriefing session can contribute greatly to the retelling of the story as the attendee hears about the event from all aspects, including successes and failures they may not have personally witnessed. This helped me greatly over my years of lecturing and participating in panel discussions, but I never realized then that one day I would need this material for a book as I do now so that you, the readers, can enjoy the factual retelling of the story down to its finer details.

I clearly remember that when movies and documentaries about Operation Entebbe were first released, while most viewers enjoyed the heroism portrayed on screen and were lapping up the details presented, I found myself smiling at my then girlfriend as a sweetener so as not to spoil her enjoyment of the movie. On the way home from one particular Entebbe based movie, I told her about my small part in the operation and revealed to her that not all the details in the films were accurate. Later on, as the number of years since the operation grew greater, whenever I listened to talks, panels, radio programs on the topic, I realized that most of the public was and still is unaware of the real details of the operation, and especially the way its commander, Yoni Netanyahu, was killed. I'm thankful I have the knowledge and opportunity to reveal them here for you in this book.

Late on Saturday afternoon, the decision was made to proceed with the operation. The Israeli planes took off, heading south across Africa to Uganda.

The old terminal in Entebbe where the hostages were held was squalid and dirty. Insects, including huge mosquitoes and flies, sucked at people's skin and drew blood, a further torment for the hostages who were already exhausted by the heat and the tension they had been under since their capture. Some had begun to lose hope as they felt helpless in front of the armed terrorists whose guns were continuously pointed at them. Every minute seemed like an hour and every day like a week. They felt like prisoners but unable to see the end of their imprisonment. The intense African heat of July added to the suffering of being held captive under the threat of being killed. They were even forbidden to talk, let alone laugh or tell jokes to each other to help lift the spirits.

Their sleeping conditions were difficult as the captives did not have even minimal privacy. Although the mattresses that had been provided were new, they were very uncomfortable as they were thin and made of cheap material. Some people snored during their sleep and woke others who could not then go back to sleep because the noise of the snoring increased as the hours drew on. There were those among them who smoked cigarettes, so the entire hall was soon filled with smoke. The adults did not take long to realize they were actually in a captivity with an unpredictable end. They were aware that their lives were under constant threat by armed fanatics who would not hesitate to shoot them with a blink of an eye.

Among the hostages was a 74-year-old British-Israeli widow named Dora Bloch. During one of the mealtimes at Entebbe, a piece of tough meat became stuck in Mrs. Bloch's throat. Her captors agreed she could be transferred to a hospital in the Ugandan capital of Kampala to have it removed. Tragically, after the hostage rescue operation, Mrs. Bloch was dragged screaming from her hospital bed by soldiers acting on the direct orders of President Idi Amin, who had been frustrated and humiliated by the successful Israeli operation. It was only after the fall of Amin's regime in 1979 that Dora Bloch's fate became known. An Israeli delegation to Uganda managed to locate the remains of Dora Bloch's body buried in a forest outside Kampala.

Late on the evening of Saturday, 3 July, the first Hercules plane, carrying Lt. Col. Yoni Netanyahu's commando force, landed successfully at Entebbe. Its wheels touched down at precisely the estimated time of 11:50 p.m. The combatants on board, whose mission was to storm the old terminal and release the hostages, began to take up their pre-planned positions ready for disembarkation. Headed by Yoni Netanyahu and his deputy Muki Betzer, nine of them slipped into the black Mercedes. The remaining 18 combatants sat waiting in two Land Rovers. Everything was ready for the disembarkation of the aircraft.

The paratroopers under Lt. Col. Matan Vilnai's command had already jumped off the plane while it was slowly taxiing towards the end of the runway. After it had stopped, they split into two small squads to perform the tasks assigned to them. One squad was charged with taking control of the watchtower and immobilizing it. The other squad had to place battery powered lights along the runway to keep it illuminated. While the two paratrooper squads were busy taking over the watchtower and illuminating the runway, Yoni Netanyahu's fighting force descended from the aircraft inside the vehicles that would ferry them towards their target, the old terminal.

In addition to the black Mercedes deception, all Netanyahu's fighters were wearing animal print army uniforms, just like those worn by Ugandan soldiers. The operation planners assumed that if the Israeli commando fighters looked like Ugandan soldiers, it would contribute to strengthening the surprise factor that was the key to the success of the entire operation and ultimate victory.

In order to avoid any dangerous confusion that could cause the Israeli commando fighters to accidentally shoot at each other, the Israeli soldiers wore white cotton hats (somewhat like those worn for protection against the sun). This would make it much easier for the fighters to identify their colleagues.

After the runway was illuminated by the paratroopers' squad, the rest of the planes now began to land, leaving a space of seven minutes between each. As soon as they stopped, the remaining forces were dropped off to make their way quickly to their positions, ready to start the storming of the terminal.

Major Shaul Mofaz's force landed on the second plane. Their task was to paralyze the watchtower to protect Netanyahu's assault force, and to serve as a reserve force for them if needed. Using the four BTR

The Mercedes car used by the Israeli fighters to deceive the Ugandans.

armored personnel carriers, they quickly made their way towards the old terminal area, following the car of their commander Netanyahu, who sat in the front seat of the Mercedes. He kept turning his head to make sure that the armored personnel carriers were keeping a short distance behind, and that all their lights were off. Around 200 yards from the terminal, Mofaz ordered his force to split into three squads according to plan: one, to eliminate the watch tower by the terminal; the second, to secure the east side of the terminal; and the third, to destroy the line of MiG-17 and MiG-21 fighter jets that were parked there, so that the Ugandan Air Force could not use them to shoot down the returning Hercules planes carrying the hostages and the commando fighters.

On the drive to the terminal, Yoni Netanyahu and his deputy Muki Betzer found themselves faced with an unexpected complication, a situation that caused a momentary disagreement between them, but nonetheless a disagreement that over the years was to become a nationally debated issue, which still resonates to this day.

When the Mercedes carrying the nine soldiers was just 300 yards from the old terminal, they encountered a checkpoint, which was actually the security gate for the terminal. Standing by the checkpoint, on either side of the road, were two armed Ugandan sentries. When they raised their guns and pointed them towards the Mercedes, Yoni became concerned and prepared his gun to shoot them. His deputy Betzer tried to dissuade him from this, explaining that it was a custom among Ugandan army soldiers to welcome you with their rifles raised, and reminded Yoni that he had already explained this fact during the training process and planning of the operation.

Betzer had been one of the Israeli officers training the Ugandan army in 1972 at the request of Idi Amin. While there he had learned about this unusual custom, in which whenever a presidential entourage or a vehicle of a senior commander arrives at the entrance to any military base or airport, the soldiers or sentries would aim their rifles at the vehicles. This was not to threaten them, but to let them know that they could proceed and that they would be secured by them. But Yoni thought otherwise. He believed it would be unwise to leave an armed sentry alive who could fire at the force once he realized that the Mercedes passengers were not Ugandan soldiers, and that President Idi Amin was not in fact with them. He was worried that the noise of the sentries firing back may remove the element of surprise and cause a devastating consequence. Yoni had to make a split-second decision. He gave the order for Giora Zussman, who was sitting behind him, to shoot the sentries with his silencer pistol. Zussman shot the first sentry who fell to the ground, but he did not die instantly and managed to fire back at the Mercedes. Yoni then shot him from close range and killed him. At this point the second sentry then fled. At that moment, everyone among the force knew that they had lost the element of surprise. The race against time had begun.

Yoni decided to continue as planned but the pace would be speeded up. According to the original plan, the idea was to have driven slowly and quietly so as not to arouse suspicion, and to make it look like this was the innocent arrival of Ugandan soldiers accompanying their president to the airport for a visit. However, circumstances had now changed. The unwritten rule of any combatant is simple, if circumstances change, or if you lose the element of surprise, you must act as fast as you can even if this means you have to make changes to your original plan. Yoni instructed the Mercedes driver to press his foot down hard on the accelerator and increase to the maximum speed. As they neared the terminal, a round of firing was suddenly heard coming from the watchtower. Yoni and his team felt like sitting ducks and knew they had to get to the terminal as quickly as possible. The powerful firing towards them from the tower continued, but that did not stop them from continuing their mission. Mofaz's force, whose task was to eliminate the watchtower, started intensively shooting towards it, giving Yoni and his team some cover for their final push towards the terminal.

Meanwhile, inside the terminal, everyone, hijackers and hostages, had begun to wake up. One of the terrorists peered outside into the darkness to see what was happening and who was shooting. Seeing the shooters dressed in animal print uniform just like the Ugandan army, he ordered the hostages to lie on the floor so they would not get hurt. He told the hostages and his colleagues that the drama outside appeared to be a conflict between Ugandan soldiers who had started shooting at each other, something that was not an unusual occurrence in Uganda.

Mofaz's force continued their heavy firing on the watchtower to allow Yoni and his team to reach the terminal. Yoni ordered the Mercedes driver to enter the square in front of the tower next to the terminal, thinking it would be a perfect spot from where he could successfully monitor and manage the onslaught on the terminal. Upon arrival, Yoni shouted to all the fighters to get out of the vehicles and start running as fast as possible towards the terminal. The first to leave their vehicles were the nine fighters in the Mercedes, led by Yoni Netanyahu and Muki Betzer, followed by the other fighters from the two Land Rovers. Upon Yoni's order, his team split into two squads. One ran to the right-hand corner of the terminal building, while the squad headed by deputy commander Muki Betzer began to move toward the main entrance. Yoni was to remain outside the terminal and monitor the onslaught. But the planned dividing up of Yoni's force turned out to be confusing. The rigorously trained commando soldiers found themselves in a mess due to the loss of the element of surprise that caused a change in the onslaught. Anyone who has participated in a battle knows that any spontaneous splitting up of forces under fire, contrary to the original plan, can be catastrophic and bring confusion between the groups, delay in the attack, and put the fighters' lives at great risk.

During the split, some of the fighters had become separated from their own squad members, resulting in chaos. The soldiers who lost contact with their squad for a few seconds also lost track of the other commando groups in those vital seconds before the storming of the terminal. These were critical moments that would determine the success or failure of the entire operation, prompting the fear that the terrorists would recover from their shock and open fire on the helpless hostages. All the forces, those on the ground and those who were monitoring the action from the two planes, now realized the importance of not delaying the onslaught for one more second.

Confusion had been created, but these well-trained commandos understood how to get out of this mess. The squad of nine fighters, whose mission was to break into the terminal, raced towards the building while spraying its windows with their gunfire. Yoni Netanyahu positioned himself in front of the building and continued to conduct the onslaught from outside. Unfortunately, someone noticed him and realized that this was a man with an important role in this battle. It was a Ugandan sentry who was stationed up in the watchtower. He began firing directly at Yoni who was an easy target to hit, completely exposed and with his full attention on conducting the onslaught. In fact, he was the only one of his team left outside the terminal as his fighters had already reached the building.

Yoni fell to the ground grimacing in pain. Fighters from Mofaz's force fired up at the watchtower and eliminated the Ugandan soldier who had shot their commander.

Within seconds of Yoni being hit, Muki Betzer took over command of the operation.

The commandos ran inside the terminal and started shooting. As they stormed into the hall where the hostages were held, they shouted to the captives in Hebrew and English, "Stay down! Stay down! We are Israeli soldiers; we are here to take you home." Most of the hostages lay completely still on the floor, with the exception of one, 19-year-old Jean-Jacques Maimoni. On seeing his Israeli saviors, Jean-Jacques jumped up in excitement, sealing his fate to die from the bullets of those who had come to rescue him. As he rose up, the Israeli fighters mistakenly thought he was one of the terrorists, possibly because of his young age and dark colored haired.

The fighters purged the hall with continuous and accurate gunfire, eliminating all the terrorists. Then they proceeded to the upper floor where they encountered armed Ugandan soldiers. Some of the Ugandans were able to get away, and some of them were killed in the exchange of fire.

Finally, the Israeli commandos began scouring the terminal rooms to see if there were any more terrorists or Ugandan soldiers.

The entire onslaught on the terminal lasted only one minute and forty seconds. During this short amount of time, all the terrorists who were the immediate threat to the lives of the hostages, along with 20 Ugandan soldiers, were killed by the Israeli commandos. Amazingly, none of the Israeli commandos who fought inside the terminal was killed. However, one, Sorin Hershko, a member of the Paratroopers Brigade, was critically wounded. He was shot directly in his neck and chest from close range by a Ugandan security guard. The bullet that penetrated Hershko's neck lodged in his spine, causing him severe damage. It left him paralyzed, and to this day he has spent his life in a wheelchair.

The mission was now completed. The Israeli forces quickly surrounded the airport and began to clear the entire area. Only when the area was deemed safe and effectively cleared, did the evacuation of the passengers begin. Golani soldiers, under the command of Lieutenant Colonel Uri Sagi, slowly escorted the group of hostages to the Hercules plane waiting for them near the terminal.

There was a sense of victory in the air. It was relief mixed with that of triumph. However, outside the terminal, the feeling was bleak. The 30-year-old commander Yonatan Netanyahu took his last breaths as he lay on a stretcher surrounded by his friends and five doctors who were desperately trying to revive him. Yoni had no chance of surviving the eight bullets fired at him, hitting him in his left arm and chest. The bullet that entered his chest came out through his back and on its millisecond course through his body had caused irreversible damage to his heart, lungs and respiratory system. Yoni was still alive but was losing blood at an alarming rate. He was driven at speed by one of the Land Rovers to the evacuation plane, which was already full with commandos seated on the plane's noisy and uncomfortable metal floor. A group of doctors tried to revive him, but their prolonged and determined efforts were of no avail. Just before the plane took off, Yoni passed away.

Sadly, apart from young Jean-Jacques Maimoni, shot by an Israeli rescuer in the belief he was one of the terrorists, there were two more fatalities among the hostages during the exchange of fire. Fifty-six-year-old Ida Borovitch, who had been lying near an inner door, was shot in cold blood by one of the terrorists when he realized that the shooting outside the building was not a dispute between Ugandan soldiers. The other was 52-year-old Pasco Cohen, accidentally shot by Israeli fighters when, like Jean-Jacques Maimoni, he stood up during the exchange of fire and started running with joy shouting "Israel has come to rescue us."

On the early morning of 4 July, all the returning planes carrying the fighters, the hostages, the bodies of the three dead

Lieutenant Colonel Yonatan "Yoni" Netanyahu.

hostages and of Yoni Netanyahu touched down in Israel. Prime Minister Rabin and Defense Minister Peres were there to greet them.

Two days later, the burial of Yonatan "Yoni" Netanyahu took place on Mount Herzl in Jerusalem. Thousands attended the funeral. Defense Minister Peres delivered the eulogy. Yoni's name became famous overnight across the country. His death was felt with great anguish, instilling a lasting note of grief about Entebbe's great achievement.

When the fighters returned, they all gathered for a post-combat debriefing to report the details of the operation. We, who served as a backup force, and were left waiting on the Sinai sands, were also invited. From the debriefing, I learned all the stages of the operation first hand, including the circumstances of the death of commander Netanyahu.

After attending the debriefing, the deep impression it left on me was astounding. However, when the fighters and the commanders began to discuss the circumstances that led to the death of such a brave and experienced commander, whose bright future in the Israeli army had been assured, the glowing picture began to fade a little. There was a feeling of frustration, with tongues being bitten. It turned out that Yoni had faltered in his judgment in two decisive instances. Firstly, when he ordered Giora Zussman to shoot the Ugandan sentry, and secondly, when he failed to neutralize the watchtower right at the beginning, when they were first exposed to it.

We all sadly shook our heads and asked ourselves how these errors could have been made by such an experienced commando as Netanyahu, who had survived dozens of more dangerous and complex operations than that of Entebbe; a national hero who had previously taken part in many daring espionage operations deep inside Syria and Lebanon. Most of these have never been disclosed, and never will be. Sadly, most of the participants in the operation held the view that Yoni was wrong in his judgment. These views were consolidated by IDF Chief of Staff Motta Gur, when, as part of the post operation investigation, he called into his office some of the fighters who took part in the takeover of the terminal. At the end of that meeting, Gur was very angry and told them, "Yoni Netanyahu was responsible for his own death. He knew that the watchtower was the immediate threat and had to be eliminated first. During the training, I told him to be extra aware of that watchtower and deal with it instantly, but he didn't. If he had, he wouldn't have been shot from that tower." Later on, Gur said he felt a moral obligation to tell the truth to Yoni's family, which he did, knowing that the truth would not please them.

This fierce and intense debate on Yoni Netanyahu's culpability will probably never subside. Dan Shomron, Motta Gur, Shimon Peres,

Yitzhak Rabin, and some of the other Cabinet members of the time have already died. The main character in the story who can answer questions and remove the fog, is the man killed in that battle and who will be forever silent.

I have voiced my opinion and personal view on this matter dozens of times, and have never changed it. I cannot determine, and would find it hard to agree, that Yoni made a mistake.

As a fighter who has been in difficult situations, where a decision is required in a split second, and in that split second to think ahead and see the whole picture and outcome, I tend to agree with his decision to shoot the sentry. I too would be concerned about leaving alive an armed enemy who could shoot me if he had the opportunity. In my eyes, Yoni was a hero, he was a special person, quiet, humble and a leader of great intelligence. I found no point in throwing accusations at a dead person. I would rather preserve the honor of a legendary warrior who died in a battle to save others.

The success of Operation Entebbe led Palestinian terrorist organizations to think twice before planning attacks on Israel, and changed their perception that they could eliminate our tiny country. The Entebbe operation improved Israel's image in the world and within itself. This stunning and audacious operation is considered a huge success and became a byword for military daring, and the subject of three blockbuster movies. It continues to be studied by armies and taught at military colleges around the world.

Epilogue

My own years of combat service has garnered praise and admiration, and undoubtedly helped me to gain self-confidence and a strong personality. Nonetheless it left me with bitter taste in my mouth and with a scar in my soul. I experienced horrific sights that will never leave my memory. I saw burnt bodies and the agony of my fellow soldiers who were writhing in flames. I lost 17 friends and three members of my family on the battlefields.

As an Israeli, I understand that the existence of a strong and secure democratic state is essential, when hearing about incidents where extreme right-wing Jew haters persecute and hurt Jewish people around the world—even in the USA, the model of democracy. If I am doomed to live by the sword because of this, then I accept this reality. After all, we, the Israelis, built a country under fire and still live under fire. War has become part of our lives. We were born in violence and we live in violence. I grew up in wars, in shelters and under bombings. Even when playing outside with other children, I could not really enjoy our games, because we would all be anticipating the terrifying wail of the siren that would direct us to the bomb shelter for a few hours, perhaps even for several nights.

I loved this amazing period of combat military service, serving in the best army in the world. It gave me the opportunity to do the impossible, to do in real life what James Bond does in the movies. But I felt I had been forced into taking part in a war I did not choose and did not want to be part of. Feelings of repulsion flooded over me whenever I remembered the horrific and irrational sights of a killing field, where civilized people were shooting at each other. The rationale of war appeared to me absurd, inconceivable, primitive. When eradicating a terrorist, these feelings vanished, but after a few days, a wave of disgusting scenes would swim in front of your eyes, as if teasing your consciousness and letting the depths of your mind transcend the emotion. Once, I came across an army friend shooting an already dead terrorist over and over again, as though the body lying motionless still presented a threat. I was very angry with my comrade as I felt he was displaying symptoms of a warped mentality. But then, it became clear to me the unifying reality in which we were all existing. My friend's unnecessary shooting at the dead terrorist was not intended to kill, it was an act of revenge. In the moments before we eliminated the terrorist, he had fired a round of bullets from his Kalashnikov at my friend who had not previously spotted him. In firing at his already dead adversary, my friend was allowing himself to feel he had honored the principle of being the first and quicker in killing whoever tried to kill you. The war for survival. We all felt like animals in the jungle and adopted the jungle imperative where only the stronger and faster will prevail. Animals, but with the ability to speak and think strategically.

It would only be natural to kill someone who came to kill me, but the more I saw of the enemy with whom I came into combat contact, the more the hatred for him diminished. The closer I was, sometimes at zero range where I could see the color of the enemy's eyes, I would feel a pang of compassion for him; I saw in front of me a living human being even though I could end his life. My finger would freeze on the trigger. Such situations put me in danger of death many times during an assault or a chase through Gaza. In some of these incidents, my underlying human feelings would not automatically activate my defensive combatant need to kill. This moral dilemma put me in mortal danger several times. A dilemma that wounded my soul and left scars on it, and these are scars that will probably never heal, as long as my memory is still able to function. Recollections keep taunting me with the names and faces of my dead friends, in particular one of our commanders who literally sacrificed his life to save us during one of the battles in the blazing fields of Lebanon. He was just one of our bold and inspirational commanders, who led us in battles during which I saw the impossible become possible, and certain death turned to survival. I have been witness to the highest degree of professionalism shown by fighters who were ready to sacrifice themselves if needed and to die for their friends on the battlefield. I have been in situations where I realized how powerful the personal skills of the warrior were, more so than the weapon he held in his hand; personal skills and qualities that may well have helped me survive the terrifying inferno of war.

But nonetheless, at the same time, I hated the damn war. The feeling of superiority and omnipotence dissipated whenever the horrific memories of scorched bodies reappeared in my mind, and of homeless refugees fleeing into the unknown with bags on their backs.

On a shift in 1977 defending our base in south Lebanon as part of our defensive operational activity.

Humanity has been engaged in wars since the dawn of its development. There has never been any interruption in this world suffering war in some of its regions. For thousands of years man has been searching for a reason for conflict and finding it easily. In the pre-historic era, wars were over land, however only for controlling food and water sources, not for annexation of territory. Today's wars are over land and power, taking over another country's wealth and valuable commodities such as oil, gold and precious metals. There are wars of nationalism, when one country wishes to prove superiority by invasion and violent subjugation, and this can arise from racist ideology as we saw in the Nazis' idealizing the "purity of the white race." Wars of imperialism, when leaders believe that by conquering other countries, they will bring glory and esteem to their nation. Wars of revolution, when people rise up against corrupt or despotic leadership, such as the French Revolution (1789–1799), and the Portuguese Revolution (1640–1668). Civil wars, such the Lebanese Civil War (1975–1990), American Civil War (1861–1865), Russian Civil War (1917–1923), Spanish Civil War (1936–1939), Yugoslav Wars (1991–1995) and Korean War (1950–1953). But above all, wars are executed over religion.

Religious conflicts often have very deep roots, adding fuel to the fiery battles and being the leading motive. Religion, if misinterpreted, results in brainwashing, extremism and loss of human compassion. Poisoned believers can bring themselves to easily murder in the name of religion, something we have been witnessing over recent decades, when extremist Muslims have blown up office towers, buses, trains, planes, restaurants, killing secular people or those of religions who, according to their warped view, are carrying out an act of apostasy of Muhammad and Islam. The objects of their hatred also include non-fanatical members of their own Muslim religion. Religious conflict can lead to an endless chain of retaliatory wars being set in motion which are very difficult to end. Not only different religions will fight against each other, conflict over religion can also arise between different branches within a religion. Protestant and Catholic Christians in Ireland, Sunni and Shiite Muslims in Lebanon, and so on.

One of the most notable conflicts was the Crusades, under the leadership of Pope Urban II, when a long and bloody campaign was instigated to try to regain control over the Holy Land. Religious conflict is continuing in many parts of the world and will continue as long as religion exists. In the Middle East, where various religious groups compete for territory and influence, the situation is worsening from year to year, and will do as long as the sects and groups in conflict are motivated by religion. Religion is a powerful force in the world, so it's not surprising it has resulted in tremendous conflict throughout history.

Leaders and politicians are the ones who wage wars. Their populations prefer to engage in trade, culture, art and the paths of peace that will connect them with other countries and cultures. A leader takes his country into war to justify his position of power and ability to lead his nation to prosperity and security, as his populace expect from him a daring deed of patriotism.

A leader who does not go to war will be considered weak and hapless. On August 5, 1945, twenty-four hours before America dropped the atomic bomb on Hiroshima, the Japanese decided to surrender and even sent a message to the Americans. From this we understand that it was no longer necessary to drop the deadly bomb, because the Japanese were no longer a fighting entity. But the American president at the time, Harry S.

The morning after returning from a dangerous patrol on Mount Har Dov on the Lebanese border in 1976, part of our defensive operational activity.

Truman, wanted to prove his power and leadership, having been under pressure from the American people who demanded an end to the conflict with Japan, and the return of their sons sent to fight in the Far East.

The war I took part in between Israel and the Palestinians is not Israel's war against the Palestinians, but on Palestinian terrorist organizations only. The terrorist groups did not start their war on Israel because of blockades on Gaza, or for the liberation of Palestinian lands. Their war started over a sacred place called Jerusalem. For them, Jerusalem was, and still is, a city consecrated only to Muslims, due to their belief that this is from where Muhammad ascended to heaven. The Al-Aqsa Mosque was first built on that site in the year 705 CE and is a place of pilgrimage. I base this fact on the initial statements of the terrorist organizations since their inception in the late 1960s, when they declared war on Israel after the Six Day War of 1967 to liberate holy Jerusalem from the Israelis. Up to 1967, there was never any blockade on Gaza, nor any checkpoints. There were no restrictions on movement and no killing of wanted terrorists; on the contrary, most Palestinians in both the West Bank and the Gaza Strip enjoyed the job opportunities offered in Israel. Conversely Jews from Israel visited Gaza to eat, buy groceries, fruits and vegetables and have their vehicles repaired. Despite Egypt and Israel officially still being at war, and the dangerous Fedayeen insurgents who would infiltrate Israel to kill its citizens, it was essentially a harmonious period between the Jews and Arabs living either side of the Gaza-Israel border. At that time, the Palestinian terrorist organizations had one goal and that was the destruction of Israel in order to liberate the holy city of Jerusalem. The reason for the conflict was purely religious.

In my heart I sympathize with the situation of the Palestinians. They live in poverty and without hope, only because they are constantly

Minutes before starting the operation in Damour, south of Beirut 1976 (my first baptism of fire).

in fear of their Hamas leaders, who forced the Palestinians to vote them into power. It is the corrupt leaders of Hamas who used the many millions of dollars they have received in international aid to continue the war with its indestructible neighbor Israel. Instead of building universities, schools, hospitals, infrastructure, and most importantly, investing in education, Hamas used this money to build tunnels and purchase weapons. They do not encourage their children to choose academic studies and better their lives. Instead, they are poisoning their minds with false promises of defeating Israel in a war with impossible odds. Many countries, including the United States, that have realized this, stopped their financial aid that was flowing into Gaza for many years. Even Saudi Arabia, at one time Gaza's main supporter, has lately stipulated that its funds sent into Gaza could not be used for armaments. The majority of Palestinians want to live peacefully alongside Israel, who throughout the years of occupation provided them with work and services such as electricity and water, and free urgent medical treatment.

I felt I had to do something to help. I felt a moral obligation to try to help the Palestinians break free from the extremists' shackles that have sentenced them to a life of poverty and misery. I learnt Arabic and studied the Qur'an to help me communicate more easily with locals, to better understand the conflict between the Israelis and Palestinians and decide where blame should be laid. In the eyes of my family and close friends, I was schizophrenic. To them it was surreal, because on the one hand I was a pro–Palestinian left-wing Israeli journalist, who developed close contacts and conversed with them, but on the other, I fought them as an Israeli soldier during the 28 years of my compulsory IDF reserve service. However, what bothered me in those years was not what my family and close friends thought of me, but the search for the truth. I couldn't rely on the media reports on the miserable status of the Palestinians as it was unbalanced, most of the times exaggerated and misleading just to gain global attention and empathy. I discovered this when a Palestinian freelance journalist from Hebron whom I was friendly with confessed to me that some of the media reports in Arab countries, in the Palestinian Authority and in some countries of Northern Europe, are written in a non-objective and biased way and without any pretense of accuracy.

Hamas is to blame for the sad and desperate life in the Gaza Strip, not Israel. Hamas chose violence and the destruction of Israel, instead of choosing to live side by side and wisely exploit its help and support, as the residents of the West Bank chose to do and who are now benefiting greatly from Israel. The Palestinians in the West Bank enjoy a life of prosperity in business and commerce with Israel, as well as low unemployment rates, good academic institutions and profitable tourism.

Half a million Palestinians in the West Bank make a living from working in Israel in agriculture, restaurants, industrial plants and food. Most of them are satisfied and live well.

When I am asked during my lectures or in media interviews what will be the eventual solution to the constant conflict between Israel and the terrorist organizations, I answer that it will come about only when this generation of leaders will die. A new and younger generation will be connected to the world via the internet, where those trapped in the cage of poverty and terrorism will discover the existence of another world. A world that offers opportunities to make money and develop a career, instead of sacrificing a young life for a piece of land. The younger generation will come to understand that Western countries, including Israel, provide the model for an ideal life. They will realize the viability of cooperating with these countries, and will begin the process with neighboring Israel, who will be happy to help them.

When that happens, it may well lead to long lasting peace between the two sides.

Index